AN INTRODUCTION TO MODERN LITERARY ARABIC

AN INTRODUCTION TO MODERN LITERARY ARABIC

BY

DAVID COWAN

CAMBRIDGE
UNIVERSITY PRESS

Published by the Press Syndicate of the University of Cambridge
The Pitt Building, Trumpington Street, Cambridge CB2 1RP
40 West 20th Street, New York, NY 10011–4211, USA
10 Stamford Road, Oakleigh, Melbourne 3166, Australia

First published 1958
Reprinted 1968, 1970, 1973, 1975 (twice), 1976,
1978, 1980, 1982, 1983, 1984, 1986, 1988, 1990, 1993, 1995, 1998

ISBN 0 521 09240 X paperback

Transferred to digital printing 2000

PREFACE

The purpose of this little work is to explain to the student, in as concise a manner as possible, the grammatical structure of the modern Arabic literary language as it is found to-day in newspapers, magazines, books, the radio and public speaking. In it I have endeavoured to restrict the material to the bare minimum which may serve as a stepping-stone to a deeper study of Arabic. I am far from claiming that it contains everything that a scholar should know but certainly he should know everything it contains. As the fundamental grammar of written Arabic has hardly changed at all during the last thirteen centuries this book may well serve as an introduction to the classical language also. Having once mastered its contents the student should have a sound grasp of Arabic grammar and can then direct his studies towards modern literature or classical according to his needs and inclinations.

As regards the method he should follow, it is, of course, better if he can find an Arab or scholar of Arabic to direct him; but, failing this, I suggest that he adopt the following plan. Firstly, the Introduction on the writing of Arabic should be thoroughly assimilated before the actual lessons are tackled. Then each lesson should be worked through carefully and the student should not proceed from one lesson to the following before he is quite convinced that he has mastered the material in the first one. Although a full transcription has been given of all Arabic words and sentences in the first ten lessons this is a help which should be dispensed with as early as possible. The student should obtain from the outset two alphabetically indexed note books, one of which can be easily adapted for Arabic, and enter into these each new word he comes across. In another note book he should write out the paradigms of the verbs which are scattered thoughout the book. These three note books should be his constant companions and referred to whenever he has a free moment. His exercises he must make for himself using the material he has worked with. All exercises and examples should be rewritten *without* the vowel marks so that the student becomes accustomed to reading Arabic without the vowels as it generally appears in print or in manuscript. If the above-mentioned plan of study is followed the student should acquire a sound knowledge of Arabic grammar in about six months.

But that is only the beginning! Arabic is an extremely rich language and requires years of study to master. However, if this book is worked through conscientiously the student should have, as it were, the foundation and steel framework of his house which he can then proceed to build brick by brick with the aid of a dictionary and intercourse with Arabic speakers. For a thorough study of Arabic, Wright's *Grammar of the Arabic Language* (2 vols., Cambridge University Press, reprinted 1955) is indispensable. When later on some ease in reading has been acquired, the radio is an aid by which the ear may be attuned to the sound of the language and it goes without saying that a stay in an Arabic-speaking country would be of inestimable value.

If the student of my little work one day becomes a master of Arabic it will have been through his own efforts and all I shall be able to claim is that I put him on the right road towards his goal.

CONTENTS

Lesson V

Lesson VI

Lesson VII

Lesson VIII

Lesson IX

Lesson X

LESSON XI

LESSON XII

LESSON XIII

LESSON XIV

LESSON XV

LESSON XVI

LESSON XVII

وَمَا تَوْفِيقِي إِلَّا بِٱللّٰهِ

INTRODUCTION

1. The Arabic Alphabet

The Arabic alphabet consists of 29 letters, all of which, with the exception of the first, are consonants. They are written from right to left. Most of these letters vary slightly according to whether they (i) stand alone, (ii) are joined to the preceding letter only, (iii) are joined to the preceding and following letters, (iv) are joined to the following letter only. There are no capital letters.

The following table shows the different forms of the letters of the alphabet:

		joined to:			
Arabic name	standing alone	preceding letter	preceding and following letters	following letter only	trans-literation
1. أَلِفٌ *'alif*	ا	ـا	—	—	*see note* 1
2. بَاءٌ *Bā'*	ب	ـب	ـبـ	بـ	*b*
3. تَاءٌ *Tā'*	ت	ـت	ـتـ	تـ	*t*
4. ثَاءٌ *Thā'*	ث	ـث	ـثـ	ثـ	*th*
5. جِيمٌ *Jīm*	ج	ـج ـج	ـجـ ـجـ	جـ	*j*
6. حَاءٌ *Ḥā'*	ح	ـح ـح	ـحـ ـحـ	حـ	*ḥ*
7. خَاءٌ *Khā'*	خ	ـخ ـخ	ـخـ ـخـ	خـ	*kh*
8. دَالٌ *Dāl*	د	ـد	—	—	*d*
9. ذَالٌ *Dhāl*	ذ	ـذ	—	—	*dh*
10. رَاءٌ *Rā'*	ر	ـر	—	—	*r*
11. زَايٌ *Zāy*	ز	ـز	—	—	*z*
12. سِينٌ *Sīn*	س	ـس	ـسـ	سـ	*s*
13. شِينٌ *Shīn*	ش	ـش	ـشـ	شـ	*sh*

	Arabic name	standing alone	joined to: preceding letter	preceding and following letters	following letter only	trans-literation
14.	صَادٌ *Ṣād*	ص	ـص	ـصـ	صـ	*ṣ*
15.	ضَادٌ *Ḍād*	ض	ـض	ـضـ	ضـ	*ḍ*
16.	طَاءٌ *Ṭā'*	ط	ـط	ـطـ	طـ	*ṭ*
17.	ظَاءٌ *Ẓā'*	ظ	ـظ	ـظـ	ظـ	*ẓ*
18.	عَيْنٌ *ʿayn*	ع	ـع	ـعـ	عـ	ʿ
19.	غَيْنٌ *Ghayn*	غ	ـغ	ـغـ	غـ	*gh*
20.	فَاءٌ *Fā'*	ف	ـف	ـفـ	فـ	*f*
21.	قَافٌ *Qāf*	ق	ـق	ـقـ	قـ	*q*
22.	كَافٌ *Kāf*	ك	ـك	ـكـ	كـ	*k*
23.	لَامٌ *Lām*	ل	ـل	ـلـ	لـ	*l*
24.	مِيمٌ *Mīm*	م	ـم	ـمـ	مـ	*m*
25.	نُونٌ *Nūn*	ن	ـن	ـنـ	نـ	*n*
26.	هَاءٌ *Hā'*	ه	ـه	ـهـ	هـ	*h*
27.	وَاوٌ *Wāw*	و	ـو	—	—	*w*
28.	يَاءٌ *Yā'*	ى ي	ـى ـي	ـيـ	يـ	*y*
29.	هَمْزَةٌ *Hamza*	ء	—	—	—	'

As a simplification it can be said that most letters are joined to a preceding one simply by a small connecting stroke. In conjunction with a following letter those which can be joined (see note 3) merely lose their tails if they have such. In this case those letters which are provided with dots move these above, or below, the main part of the letter which remains. The letters to be especially noted and mastered are ع, غ, ك, ه and ى. Where two alternatives are given the one on the right hand side is the usual one in modern printing and that on the left the form for manuscript. ل followed by ا is written لا *not* لـا.

Note 1. أَلِفٌ *'alif* has two uses. Firstly it indicates a long *ā* (see § 3) and secondly it acts as the bearer of هَمْزَة *Hamza* (see § 6).

Note 2. When the letter *hā'* (ه) denotes the feminine ending of nouns and adjectives it is written with two dots above (ة) and pronounced '*t*'. This is known as تَاءٌ مَرْبُوطَة *Tā' Marbūṭa* (tied *t*) for, when linked with a following genitive, it must *always* be pronounced '*t*'. *Tā' Marbūṭa* and its following vowel (case ending) are not pronounced at the end of a sentence or complete clause. In modern spoken Arabic it only has the '*t*' value when it is immediately followed by a noun or pronoun in the genitive.

Note 3. The six letters ا, د, ذ, ر, ز and و cannot be joined to the *following* letters.

Note 4. The letters ت, ث, د, ذ, ر, ز, س, ش, ص, ض, ط, ظ, ل and ن are known as 'sun letters' (حُرُوف شَمْسِيَّة *ḥurūf shamsīya*) and assimilate the '*l*' of the definite article أَلْ (*al*) as will be shown in Lesson I.

The letters و and ى are called 'weak letters' (حُرُوف ٱلْعِلَّة *ḥurūf-al-ع illa*) for they occasionally become ا or disappear altogether when they are radical consonants.

2. Pronunciation of the Consonants

The following letters are pronounced more or less as in English:

ب = *b*, ت = *t*, ث = *th* as in 'think', ج = *j* (in Lower Egypt as *g* in 'get'), د = *d*, ذ = *dh* as *th* in 'that', ر = *r* (strongly rolled), ز = *z*, س = *s* as in 'so', ش = *sh*, ف = *f*, ك = *k*, ل = *l*, م = *m*, ن = *n*, ه = *h*, و = *w*, ي = *y* as in 'yet'. (N.B. In Egypt ى = *y* standing alone or joined to a preceding letter is generally written without the two dots.)

A special word has to be said about the following consonants:

ح is an emphatic '*h*' pronounced with a strong and sustained expulsion of the breath.

خ is like '*ch*' in the Scots 'Loch' or the German 'Ach' but with a more rasping, guttural sound.

ص is an emphatic '*s*' pronounced with the teeth slightly apart, pressing the tip of the tongue against the lower teeth and raising the tongue to press also against the upper teeth and palate.

ض is an emphatic '*d*', or in certain countries (e.g. Iraq) '*th*' as in 'that', pronounced with the tongue pressing hard against the edge of the upper teeth with the tip protruding. The tongue and upper teeth part company rather violently to allow a following vowel sound to come through or another consonant to be articulated.

ط is an emphatic '*t*' pronounced with tongue and teeth in the same position as for ض.

ظ is an emphatic '*z*' or voiced '*th*' pronounced with tongue and teeth in the same position as for ص. It is often confused with ض.

ع is a guttural stop pronounced with constriction of the larynx. Orientalists are accustomed to transliterate this letter by an inverted comma but as this may encourage the student to neglect it it has been retained here in the transliteration.

غ is exactly the sound one makes while gargling.

ق is a guttural '*k*' pronounced from the back of the throat. Colloquially, with the exception of Lower Egypt and some parts of Syria and Palestine where it generally becomes a glottal stop, it is almost universally pronounced as '*g*' in 'go'.

ء (*Hamza*) is the glottal stop (see § 6).

These consonants which are very difficult for English-speaking people to pronounce should preferably be learnt from Arabs.

3. Vowels

In Arabic there are three vowel marks which are written directly above or below the consonants they *follow*.

These are: ـَ = *a* (as in the English 'pat'), ـُ = *u* (as in 'put') and ـِ = *i* (as in 'pit'); e.g. بَ *ba*, بُ *bu*, بِ *bi*. These three vowels are *short* but may be lengthened by a following unmarked ا, و and ى, e.g. بَا *bā*, بُو *bū*, بِي *bī*.

In certain common words a long *ā* is expressed by a small *'alif* written above the consonant, e.g. ذٰلِكَ *dhālika*, that, اَللّٰهُ *Allāhu*, God, لٰكِنْ *lākin*, but, etc.

In Arabic phonetics the sound groups '*awu*' and '*ayu*', which only occur at the end of a word, are contracted to '*ā*' and in the latter case written ـَى..., e.g. تَقْوَى *taqwā*, piety. Note that the ى is vowelless and does not have the two dots. As the accent is never on the last syllable of the *written* word this '*ā*' tends to be pronounced short and *must* be pronounced short before هَمْزَةُ ٱلْوَصْلِ *hamzat-al-waṣl* (see § 6), hence its Arabic name أَلِفٌ مَقْصُورَةٌ *'alif maqṣūra* or shortened *'alif*.

The sign that a consonant is *not followed* by a vowel is ـْـ, e.g. بِبْ *bib*. This sign is called سُكُونْ *sukūn* or 'resting'.

With this sign and the weak consonants و and ي we can thus make two diphthongs composed of a *short* '*a*' followed by a vowelless و or ي which in pronunciation *must be given full consonantal value*, e.g. بَوْ *baw* and بَيْ *bay*. Thus '*aw*' and '*ay*' are almost identical with 'ough' in 'bough' and 'igh' in 'bight'.

The vowel marks and other orthographic signs explained in this introduction (with the exception of مَدَّةٌ *madda* (§ 7) and هَمْزَةُ ٱلْقَطْعِ *hamzat-al-qaṭ*ع (§ 6)) are generally omitted in manuscript and in printed books from which it will be seen that Arabic writing is a form of shorthand. They are always written in editions of the *Qur'ān*, generally in older collections of poetry, in school books and in cases of difficulty or obscurity in well-edited books. They do not represent all the vowels in Arabic phonetics but change more or less according to their proximity to different consonants.

In this work I have not attempted to give more than a transliteration of the Arabic in the first few lessons and have not tried to give exact phonetic equivalents of the vowel values. But if the proper vowel lengths are borne in mind and if the consonants are properly pronounced which the student should endeavour to do right from the beginning of his studies the consonants will force the true pronunciation of the vowels.

4. Doubled Consonants

If two identical consonants come together and are not separated by a vowel only one is written with the mark ـّـ above it. This mark is called شَدَّةٌ *shadda* or 'strengthening'. Thus we have عَلَّمَ ع*allama* (for عَلْلَمَ), he taught. It is *important* for the student to pronounce such doubling of a consonant clearly as the meaning might otherwise be quite different.

Vowelless dental consonants are generally assimilated to a following ت *t*, the first being written without any sign and the second receiving '*shadda*', e.g. قُدتُّ *quttu* for قُدْتُ *qudtu*, I led. The latter is not considered incorrect but in any case the correct pronunciation of the consonants would bring about this assimilation.

A vowelless ن *n* assimilates to a following ل *l* either in pronunciation or actually in writing as in the conjunctions أَلَّا *'allā* for أَنْ لَا *'an. lā* (that not) and إِلَّا *'illā* for إِنْ لَا *'in lā* (if not, otherwise).

See Lesson I for the assimilation of the '*l*' of the definite article to the 'sun letters'.

5. '*Tanwīn*' or Nūnation

When the three vowel marks are written double at the end of a word, e.g. ـٌ, ـً and ـٍ they represent the three case endings, nominative, accusative and genitive, of a fully declined, *indefinite* noun or adjective (see Lesson V). The second vowel is pronounced '*n*'! Thus we have كَلْبٌ *kalbun*, a dog (nom.), كَلْبًا *kalban*, a dog (acc.) and كَلْبٍ *kalbin*, a dog (gen.). This process of doubling the final vowel is called تَنْوِين *tanwīn* or, by orientalists, nūnation, or 'n'ing', from the Arabic name for the letter *n*. Note that the accusative ending اً... is also followed by an *'alif*, exceptions to this rule being the endings ةً and ىً... (*'alif maqṣūra*) contracted from '*ayan*'), and after هَمْزَةُ ٱلْقَطْعِ *hamzat-al-qaṭ‘* preceded by a long *ā*, e.g. كَلْبَةً *kalbatan*, a bitch (acc.), هُدًى *hudan*, guidance (all three cases), جَزَاءً *jazā'an*, a recompense (acc.). At the end of a sentence or complete clause اً... may be pronounced as a long *ā* and the other case endings not pronounced at all.

6. *Hamza*

There are two kinds of *hamza*, هَمْزَةُ ٱلْقَطْعِ *hamzat-al-qaṭ‘* 'the cutting hamza' and هَمْزَةُ ٱلْوَصْلِ *hamzat-al-waṣl* 'the joining hamza'.

The first of these is a pure glottal stop with full consonantal value and in well-edited books and periodicals is generally written. At the beginning of a word it is always written on *'alif*, e.g. أَكَلَ *'akala*, he ate, أُكِلَ *'ukila*, it was eaten, إِنْسَانٌ *'insānun*, a human being. In the middle or at the end of a word it is written on ا, و or ى (without the dots) or standing alone on the line of writing as determined by the vowels coming before and after, e.g. سَأَلَ *sa'ala*, he asked, سُئِلَ *su'ila*, he was asked, قَرَأَ *qara'a*, he read, قُرِئَ *quri'a*, it was read, بَؤُسَ *ba'usa*, he was wretched, جَرُؤَ *jaru'a*, he was bold, جُزْءٌ *juz'un*, a part.

Through reading the student will acquire a feeling about the proper bearer for *hamzat-al-qaṭʿ*. If a systematic tabulation of the ways of writing it is preferred, I refer him to Wright's *Arabic Grammar*, vol. I, pp. 16–18.

Hamzat-al-waṣl always occurs at the beginning of a word and its vowel is written above or below *'alif.* If any word precedes it *hamzat-al-waṣl* and its vowel *must be elided.* It is not actually written although we sometimes find it written as ـٔـ. Modern opinion, however, does not approve of this use of ـٔـ which is reserved for *hamzat-al-qaṭʿ*. The sign of the elision is ـٱـ which I transliterate by ⌒.

The *hamza* is *hamzat-al-waṣl* in the following cases:

(i) In the definite article اَلْ *al*, e.g. اَلْبَيْتُ *al-baytu*, the house, *but* بَابُ ٱلْبَيْتِ *bābu ⌒l-bayti*, the door of the house.

(ii) In the relative pronouns اَلَّذِي *alladhī*, who, which, etc. (see Lesson X, § 39).

(iii) In the imperative of the Ist form of the verb (see Lesson XIV), e.g. اِذْهَبْ *idhhab* go, *but* قُلْتُ ٱذْهَبْ *qultu ⌒dhhab*, I said: go!

(iv) In the perfect, imperative and verbal noun of the VII, VIII, IX and X forms of the verb (see Lessons XXI and XXII), e.g. اِنْطَلَقَ *inṭalaqa*, he went off, *but* وَٱنْطَلَقَ *wa⌒nṭalaqa, and* he went off.

(v) In the following common words:

اِبْنٌ	*ibnun*, a son.	اِبْنَةٌ	*ibnatun*, a daughter.
اِمْرُؤٌ	*imru'un*, a man.	اِمْرَأَةٌ	*imra'atun*, a woman.
اِثْنَانِ	*ithnāni*, two (masc.).	اِثْنَتَانِ	*ithnatāni*, two (fem.).
اِسْمٌ	*ismun*, a name.		

Long vowels followed by *hamzat-al-waṣl must be pronounced short*, although they may remain written long, since it is a general rule in Arabic that two vowelless consonants or a long vowel and a vowelless consonant cannot come together, e.g. أَبُو ٱلْوَلَدِ *'abu⌒l-waladi, not 'abū⌒l-waladi*, the boy's father, فِي ٱلْبَيْتِ *fi⌒l-bayti, not fī⌒l-bayti*, in the house.

If the word preceding *hamzat-al-waṣl* ends with a vowelless consonant a vowel must be inserted to facilitate the liaison. In most cases this is '*i*', e.g. قَدْ ذَهَبَ *qad dhahaba*, he has gone, *but* قَدِ ٱنْطَلَقَ *qadi͡nṭalaqa*, he has gone off.

The preposition مِنْ *min*, from, takes '*a*' *before the definite article* becoming مِنَ *mina*.

The personal pronouns هُمْ *hum*, they, أَنْتُمْ *'antum*, you, كُمْ *kum*, you (acc. and gen.) and the 2nd pers. masc. plural ending of the perfect تُمْ *tum*, become, هُمُ *humu*, أَنْتُمُ *'antumu*, كُمُ *kumu* and تُمُ *tumu* when followed by *hamzat-al-waṣl*, e.g. هُمُ ٱلْمُلُوكُ *humu͡l-mulūku*, they (are) the kings.

N.B. بِسْمِ ٱللّٰهِ *Bismi͡llāhi*, In the name of God, where the *'alif* of إِسْمٌ *ismun*, a name, is elided as well as *hamzat-al-waṣl*.

7. *Madda*

When *hamzat-al-qaṭ*ع written on *'alif* is followed by a long *ā* the second *'alif* is written horizontally over the first and the *hamza* and vowel mark omitted, e.g. آكِلٌ *'ākilun*, eating, اَلْقُرْآنُ *al-qur'ānu*, the Qur'ān. So the group آ = *'ā*. This sign is called مَدَّةٌ *madda* or 'lengthening'. As a general rule when the form of the word demands that two *'alifs* come together they are written آ, no matter which of them is the bearer of *hamzat-al-qaṭ*ع, e.g. آلَفَ *'ālafa* is written for both أَالَفَ *'ālafa*, he frequented s.o. and أَأْلَفَ *'a'lafa*, he reconciled.

8. Accent

The accent or stress is as important in Arabic as it is in English. If you divide the word into syllables you can determine where the accent will fall. Arabic words can be divided into short or long syllables. A short or open syllable consists of consonant+vowel, a long or closed syllable of consonant+long vowel or consonant+vowel+vowelless consonant. Thus كَتَبَ *kataba*, he wrote, is ⏑⏑⏑, مُقَاتِلٌ *muqātilun*, a fighter, is ⏑–⏑–, مَكْتُوبٌ *maktūbun*, a letter, is – – –; and مَدْرَسَةٌ *madrasatun*, a school, is –⏑⏑–. The accent is *never* on the last syllable of a word (including case and verb endings) but falls on the nearest long or closed syllable to the last, e.g. *muqấtilun*, *maktū́bun*, *mádrasatun*. If there is no long syllable before the last the accent falls on the first syllable, e.g. *kátaba*. Prefixed *hamzat-al-waṣl* is ignored, e.g. إِنْطَلَقَ *inṭálaqa*, he went off. Note especially مَتَى *mátā*, when? and such short disyllabic words.

Colloquial Arabic has its own rules for the accent which do not always agree with those for written Arabic.

9. Punctuation

The following punctuation marks are commonly used in Modern Arabic:

. ، : ؛ ! ؟ « »

Note. In this introduction I have transliterated the few technical terms of grammar given according to the usage of spoken Arabic in omitting the case endings. Thus I write *madda* (مَدَّةٌ) for *maddatun* and *sukūn* (سُكُونٌ) for *sukūnun*. The transliteration of the examples in the early lessons is given in full with all case and verb endings.

LESSON I

10. The Article

There is no indefinite article in Arabic.

The definite article for all cases, numbers and genders is أَلْ *al*, which is written prefixed to the word it defines. The defined noun or adjective loses its 'nūnation' (Introduction, § 5), e.g.

كِتَابٌ *kitābun*, a book.	اَلْكِتَابُ *al-kitābu*, *the* book.
قَلَمٌ *qalamun*, a pen.	اَلْقَلَمُ *al-qalamu*, *the* pen.

The *hamza* of the definite article is *hamzat-al-waṣl* (Introduction, § 6) so that the '*a*' must be elided if preceded by any word, e.g. اَلْكِتَابُ وَٱلْقَلَمُ *al-kitābu wa͡l-qalamu*, the book *and* the pen.

When the noun or adjective defined by أَلْ *al* begins with one of the 'sun' letters (Introduction, § 1, note 4) the '*l*' of the definite article is assimilated to the 'sun' letter which is written with <u>sh</u>*adda* (Introduction, § 4) the '*l*' of the article losing its *sukūn* (Introduction § 3), e.g.

رَجُلٌ *rajulun*, a man.	اَلرَّجُلُ *ar-rajulu*, *the* man.
سَفَرٌ *safarun*, a journey.	اَلسَّفَرُ *as-safaru*, *the* journey.

As the '*l*' of the article remains written in Arabic although losing its force most modern Arabists prefer to write it in transliteration, e.g. *al-rajulu, al-safaru.* But of course since these words begin with 'sun' letters the '*l*' must be assimilated in pronunciation as indicated above. *Special attention should be paid to the 'sun' letters as the above practice will be followed in this work.*

11. Gender

There are two grammatical genders in Arabic, masculine and feminine. All the words in this lesson are of masculine gender.

12. Nominal Sentences

In simple nominal sentences consisting of subject and predicate the copulae 'is' and 'are' are not expressed. Adjectives or nouns used as predicates of a preceding definite noun remain indefinite, e.g.

اَلرَّجُلُ حَاضِرٌ *al-rajulu ḥāḍirun,* the man is present.

اَلْبَيْتُ كَبِيرٌ *al-baytu kabīrun,* the house is big.

اَلْكِتَابُ صَغِيرٌ *al-kitābu ṣaghīrun,* the book is small.

Any adjective may be used as a noun, e.g.

اَلْفَقِيرُ غَائِبٌ *al-faqīru ghā'ibun,* the poor (man) is absent.

اَلْعَالِمُ فَقِيرٌ *al-ɛālimu faqīrun,* the learned (man) is poor.

Adjectives follow the nouns they qualify. If the noun is definite the adjective must receive the definite article, e.g.

وَلَدٌ صَغِيرٌ *waladun ṣaghīrun,* a small boy.

اَلْوَلَدُ ٱلصَّغِيرُ *al-waladu‿l-ṣaghīru,* the small boy.

رَجُلٌ ثَرِيٌّ *rajulun tharīyun,* a wealthy man.

اَلرَّجُلُ ٱلثَّرِيُّ *al-rajulu‿l-tharīyu,* the wealthy man.

13. Singular Personal Pronouns

أَنَا	*'ánā*, I.	هُوَ	*húwa*, he, it.
أَنْتَ	*'ánta*, thou (masc.).	هِيَ	*híya*, she, it.
أَنْتِ	*'ánti*, thou (fem.).		

The second person singular pronouns are used in ordinary address e.g. أَنْتَ عَالِمٌ *'anta ʿālimun*, you are learned. Apart from such honorific modes of address as 'Your Excellency', 'Your Lordship', etc., the plural is occasionally used for the singular to denote respect.

Note where the accent falls in these pronouns.

14. Interrogative Particles

The interrogative of simple sentences such as those given above is made by prefixing the particles هَلْ *hal* or أَ *'a* (spoken question marks) or merely by the tone of the voice. هَلْ *hal* becomes هَلِ *hali* before *hamzat-al-waṣl*, e.g.

هَلْ هُوَ غَنِيٌّ؟ *hal huwa ghanīyun?* Is he rich?

هَلِ ٱلْوَلَدُ غَائِبٌ؟ *hali ‿l-waladu ghā'ibun?* Is the boy absent?

Of these two spoken question marks هَلْ *hal* is much more common than أَ *'a*, the latter asking the question about the word following.

If أَ *'a* is followed by *hamzat-al-waṣl* the two classically form *madda* (Introduction, § 7), e.g.

آلسَّفَرُ طَوِيلٌ؟ *'āl-safaru ṭawīlun?* Is the journey long?

Supplementary Vocabulary

عَرَبِيٌّ *ʿarabīyun*, Arabic, an Arab.

فَرَنْسِيٌّ *faransīyun*, French.

جَدِيدٌ *jadīdun*, new.

جَاهِلٌ *jāhilun*, ignorant.

أَيْنَ؟ *'ayna?* where?

نَعَمْ *naعam*, yes. جِدًّا *jiddan*, very (adverbial accusative).

إِنْكِلِيزِيٌّ *'inkilīẓīyun*, English. اَلْيَوْمَ *al-yawma*, to-day (adverbial accusative).

قَصِيرٌ *qaṣīrun*, short. لَا *lā*, no.

قَدِيمٌ *qadīmun*, old (of things).

Exercise I

اَلْوَلَدُ ٱلصَّغِيرُ حَاضِرٌ. هَلِ ٱلْبَيْتُ كَبِيرٌ؟ لَا، هُوَ صَغِيرٌ جِدًّا. اَلْكِتَابُ صَغِيرٌ وَٱلْقَلَمُ قَصِيرٌ. هَلْ هُوَ عَالِمٌ كَبِيرٌ؟ لَا، هُوَ رَجُلٌ جَاهِلٌ. اَلْبَيْتُ قَدِيمٌ جِدًّا. أَأَنْتَ رَجُلٌ غَنِيٌّ؟ نَعَمْ، أَنَا ثَرِيٌّ جِدًّا. هَلْ هُوَ كِتَابٌ فَرَنْسِيٌّ؟ لَا، هُوَ كِتَابٌ إِنْكِلِيزِيٌّ. هُوَ عَرَبِيٌّ فَقِيرٌ. أَيْنَ ٱلرَّجُلُ ٱلْعَالِمُ؟ هُوَ غَائِبٌ ٱلْيَوْمَ. هُوَ وَلَدٌ قَصِيرٌ جِدًّا. اَلْقَلَمُ جَدِيدٌ وَٱلْكِتَابُ قَدِيمٌ. هَلِ ٱلسَّفَرُ طَوِيلٌ؟ لَا، هُوَ قَصِيرٌ. اَلْبَيْتُ ٱلْكَبِيرُ قَدِيمٌ. هَلِ ٱلْكِتَابُ كَبِيرٌ؟ لَا، هُوَ صَغِيرٌ. اَلرَّجُلُ ٱلْعَالِمُ فَقِيرٌ وَٱلرَّجُلُ ٱلْجَاهِلُ غَنِيٌّ.

Transliteration

al-waladu ⌒l-ṣaghīru ḥāḍirun. hali ⌒l-baytu kabīrun? lā, huwa ṣaghīrun jiddan. al-kitābu ṣaghīrun wa⌒l-qalamu qaṣīrun. hal huwa عālimun kabīrun? lā, huwa rajulun jāhilun. al-baytu qadīmun jiddan. 'a'anta rajulun ghanīyun? naعam, 'anā tharīyun jiddan. hal huwa kitābun faransīyun? la, huwa kitābun 'inkilīẓīyun. huwa عarabīyun faqīrun. 'ayna ⌒l-rajulu⌒l-عālimu? huwa ghā'ibun⌒l-yawma. huwa waladun qaṣīrun jiddan. al-qalamu jadīdun wa⌒l-kitābu qadīmun. hali ⌒l-safaru ṭawīlun? lā, huwa qaṣīrun. al-baytu ⌒l-kabīru qadīmun. hali ⌒l-kitābu kabīrun? lā, huwa ṣaghīrun. al-rajulu ⌒l-عālimu faqīrun wa⌒l-rajulu ⌒l-jāhilu ghanīyun.

Translation

The small boy is present. Is the house big? No, it is very small. The book is small and the pen is short. Is he a great scholar? No, he is an ignorant man. The house is very old. Are you a rich man? Yes, I am very wealthy. Is it a French book? No, it is an English book. He is a poor Arab. Where is the learned man? He is absent to-day. He is a very short boy. The pen is new and the book is old. Is the journey long? No, it is short. The big house is old. Is the book big? No, it is small. The learned man is poor and the ignorant man is rich.

LESSON II

15. The Feminine

In general the feminine is formed from the masculine (participles or nouns indicating professions) by suffixing ةٌ... *atun* (Introduction, § 1, note 2), e.g.

هُوَ كَاتِبٌ *huwa kātibun*, he is a writer.

هِيَ كَاتِبَةٌ *hiya kātibatun*, she is a writer.

هُوَ مُدَرِّسٌ *huwa mudarrisun*, he is a teacher.

هِيَ مُدَرِّسَةٌ *hiya mudarrisatun*, she is a teacher.

هُوَ طَبَّاخٌ *huwa ṭabbākhun*, he is a cook.

هِيَ طَبَّاخَةٌ *hiya ṭabbākhatun*, she is a cook.

The feminine ending ةٌ... *atun* occurs in many words which have no masculine form, e.g.

مَدِينَةٌ *madīnatun*, a city.

جُنَيْنَةٌ *junaynatun*, a garden (diminutive of جَنَّةٌ *jannatun*, اَلْجَنَّةُ *al-Jannatu*, Paradise).

مَحْكَمَةٌ *maḥkamatun*, a law-court.

It is occasionally, although rarely, found in words *which are masculine*, e.g.

خَلِيفَةٌ *khalīfatun*, a successor, Caliph.

عَلَّامَةٌ *ʿallāmatun*, a savant.

رَحَّالَةٌ *raḥḥālatun*, a great traveller, globe-trotter.

These two latter are intensive forms of the active participle.

Other feminine endings are ـَى... *ā* (Introduction, §3) and ـَاءُ... *ā'u* (when singular) suffixed to the *last* radical of the word. Both of these are without 'nūnation', e.g.

ذِكْرَى *dhikrā*, remembrance, souvenir.

صَحْرَاءُ *ṣaḥrā'u*, a desert.

The following classes of words are feminine without requiring the distinctive feminine ending:

(i) All words and proper names which are by their nature feminine, e.g.

أُمٌّ *'ummun*, a mother. عَرُوسٌ *ɛarūsun*, a bride.

أُخْتٌ *'ukhtun*, a sister. عَجُوزٌ *ɛajūzun*, an old woman.

Participles which with a special meaning can only be applied to females such as حَامِلٌ *ḥāmilun* pregnant, مُرْضِعٌ *murḍiɛun* suckling (adj.).

(ii) Most (though not all) names of countries and cities, e.g.

مِصْرُ *Miṣru*, Egypt, Cairo. فَرَنْسَا *Faránsā*, France.

اَلْهِنْدُ *Al-Hindu*, India. لَنْدَنُ *Landanu*, London.

Note that such proper names which have no definite article have also no 'nūnation' (see Lesson V).

(iii) Most (though not all) parts of the body which occur in pairs, e.g.

عَيْنٌ *ɛaynun*, an eye. يَدٌ *yadun*, a hand.

أُذْنٌ *'udh(u)nun*, an ear. رِجْلٌ *rijlun*, a foot.

(iv) A number of words which are feminine by usage, e.g.

رِيحٌ *rīḥun*, a wind. حَرْبٌ *ḥarbun*, a war.

دَارٌ *dārun*, a house (note that بَيْتٌ *baytun* is masc.).

نَارٌ *nārun*, a fire. أَرْضٌ *'arḍun*, earth, ground.

اَلشَّمْسُ *al-shamsu*, the sun.

A number of words are of common gender and may be masculine or feminine, e.g.

حَالٌ *ḥālun* (also حَالَةٌ *ḥālatun*), a state, condition.

طَرِيقٌ *ṭarīqun*, a road.

سُوقٌ *sūqun*, a market (usually fem.).

سِكِّينٌ *sikkīnun*, a knife (usually fem.).

For reference full lists of these last two classes of nouns will be found in Wright's *Arabic Grammar*, vol. I, pp. 180–3.

The feminine ending ـَةٌ... *atun* is used to form the singular from collective nouns, e.g.

عِنَبٌ	*ʿinabun*, grapes.	عِنَبَةٌ	*ʿinabatun*, a grape.
تُفَّاحٌ	*tuffāḥun*, apples.	تُفَّاحَةٌ	*tuffāḥatun*, an apple.
تِينٌ	*tīnun*, figs.	تِينَةٌ	*tīnatun*, a fig.
دَجَاجٌ	*dajājun*, poultry.	دَجَاجَةٌ	*dajājatun*, a hen.

Lastly note that *all plurals which do not refer to rational beings are* **grammatically feminine singular** (see Lesson IV, p. 27).

The following are a few simple examples illustrating the foregoing rules:

أَنْتِ طَبَّاخَةٌ مَاهِرَةٌ *'anti ṭabbākhatun māhiratun*, you (fem.) are a clever cook.

اَلسَّيِّدَةُ ٱلْغَنِيَّةُ حَاضِرَةٌ *al-sayyidatu ʾl-ghanīyatu ḥādiratun*, the rich lady is present.

اَلْمُدَرِّسُ عَلَّامَةٌ شَهِيرٌ *al-mudarrisu ʿallāmatun shahīrun*, the teacher is a famous savant.

هِيَ عَرُوسٌ جَمِيلَةٌ *hiya ʿarūsun jamīlatun*, she is a beautiful bride.

اَلْجُنَيْنَةُ صَغِيرَةٌ *al-junaynatu ṣaghīratun*, the garden is small.

اَلْجُنَيْنَةُ ٱلْكَبِيرَةُ جَمِيلَةٌ *al-junaynatu ʾl-kabīratu jamīlatun*, the big garden is beautiful.

لَنْدَنُ مَدِينَةٌ عَظِيمَةٌ *Landanu madīnatun ʿaẓīmatun*, London is a mighty city.

يَدٌ قَوِيَّةٌ *yadun qawīyatun*, a strong hand.

اَلْمَحْكَمَةُ دَارٌ كَبِيرَةٌ *al-maḥkamatu dārun kabīratun*, the law-court is a large building (house).

اَلتُّفَّاحَةُ لَذِيذَةٌ *al-tuffāḥatu ladhīdhatun*, the apple is delicious.

دَجَاجَةٌ صَغِيرَةٌ *dajājatun ṣaghīratun*, a small hen.

Supplementary Vocabulary

مَشْهُورٌ *mashhūrun*, famous.

هَادِئٌ *hādi'un*, quiet, gentle, calm.

لَطِيفٌ *laṭīfun*, pleasant, charming.

مَوْضِعٌ *mawḍiʿun*, a place.

ضَعِيفٌ *ḍaʿīfun*, weak.

خَيَّاطٌ *khayyāṭun*, a tailor.

مَلِكٌ *malikun*, a king.

بِلَادٌ *bilādun* (fem.), a country.

إِمْرَأَةٌ *imra'atun*, a woman.

Exercise II

هِيَ سَيِّدَةٌ فَرَنْسِيَّةٌ مَشْهُورَةٌ جِدًّا. هَلْ أَنْتِ غَنِيَّةٌ؟ لَا، أَنَا فَقِيرَةٌ جِدًّا. أَيْنَ ٱلْخَيَّاطَةُ ٱلْإِنْكِلِيزِيَّةُ؟ هِيَ غَائِبَةٌ ٱلْيَوْمَ. هَلِ ٱلرِّيحُ شَدِيدَةٌ ٱلْيَوْمَ؟ لَا، هِيَ هَادِئَةٌ. اَلْمَلِكَةُ ٱلْغَنِيَّةُ مَشْهُورَةٌ. هَلِ ٱلتُّفَّاحَةُ نَظِيفَةٌ؟ نَعَمْ، وَهِيَ لَذِيذَةٌ جِدًّا. اَلدَّارُ ٱلْقَدِيمَةُ صَغِيرَةٌ (اَلْبَيْتُ ٱلْقَدِيمُ صَغِيرٌ). اَلْعَرُوسُ ٱلْجَمِيلَةُ لَطِيفَةٌ. اَلْهِنْدُ بِلَادٌ غَنِيَّةٌ. هَلِ ٱلسُّوقُ صَغِيرَةٌ؟ لَا، هِيَ كَبِيرَةٌ جِدًّا. هَلِ ٱلْجُنَيْنَةُ مَوْضِعٌ جَمِيلٌ؟ نَعَمْ، هِيَ مَوْضِعٌ لَطِيفٌ جِدًّا. اَلِٱمْرَأَةُ ٱلْفَقِيرَةُ ضَعِيفَةٌ. هَلْ أَنْتِ ضَعِيفَةٌ؟ لَا، أَنَا قَوِيَّةٌ.

Transliteration

hiya sayyidatun faransīyatun mashūratun jiddan. hal 'anti ghanīyatun? lā, 'anā faqīratun jiddan. 'ayna l-khayyāṭatu ‿l-'inkilīzīyatu? hiya ghā'ibatuni ‿l-yawma. hali ‿l-rīḥu shadīdatuni ‿l-yawma? lā, hiya hādi'atun.

al-malikatu ⌒l-ghanīyatu mashhūratun. hali ⌒l-tuffāḥatu naẓīfatun? naʿam, wahiya ladhīdhatun jiddan. al-dāru ⌒l-qadīmatu ṣaghīratun (al-baytu ⌒l-qadīmu ṣaghīrun). al-ʿarūsu ⌒l-jamīlatu laṭīfatun. al-Hindu bilādun ghanīyatun. hali ⌒l-sūqu ṣaghīratun? lā, hiya kabīratun jiddan. hali ⌒l-junaynatu mawḍiʿun jamīlun? naʿam, hiya mawḍiʿun laṭīfun jiddan. ali⌒mraʾatu ⌒l-faqīratu ḍaʿīfatun. hal ʾanti ḍaʿīfatun? lā, ʾanā qawīyatun.

Translation

She is a very famous French lady. Are you (fem.) rich? No, I am very poor. Where is the English dressmaker (tailoress)? She is absent to-day. Is the wind strong to-day? No, it is gentle. The rich queen is famous. Is the apple clean? Yes, and it is very delicious. The old house is small. The beautiful bride is charming. India is a rich country. Is the market small? No, it is very big. Is the garden a beautiful place? Yes, it is a very pleasant place. The poor woman is weak. Are you (fem.) weak? No, I am strong.

LESSON III

16. The Dual

In Arabic there are three numbers, singular with which we have already dealt shortly, dual and plural. In colloquial Arabic the dual is almost confined to periods of time and the dual parts of the body but in written Arabic it must be used to express two things of a kind.

The nominative dual ending is انِ... *āni* and the accusative *and* genitive ending يْنِ... *ayni* added to the singular of the word after removal of the case ending (Introduction, § 5), e.g.

كِتَابَانِ *kitābāni*, two books (nom).

كِتَابَيْنِ *kitābayni*, two books (acc. *and* gen.).

Before the dual ending the suffix ة becomes an ordinary ت *t* and the *hamza* in the feminine ending اءُ... *āʾu* changes into و *w*, e.g.

سَيِّدَةٌ *sayyidatun*, a lady.

سَيِّدَتَانِ *sayyidatāni*, two ladies (nom.).

سَيِّدَتَيْنِ *sayyidatayni*, two ladies (acc. and gen.).

تُفَّاحَتَانِ *tuffāḥatāni*, two apples (nom.).

صَحْرَاوَانِ *ṣaḥrāwāni*, two deserts (nom).

صَحْرَاوَيْنِ *ṣaḥrāwayni*, two deserts (acc. and gen.).

Adjectives agree in number with the nouns they qualify and in the dual they invariably have the same endings, e.g.

سَيِّدَانِ كَبِيرَانِ *sayyidāni kabīrāni*, two old (great) gentlemen (nom.).

تُفَّاحَتَانِ لَذِيذَتَانِ *tuffāḥatāni ladhīdhatāni*, two delicious apples.

عَيْنَانِ كَبِيرَتَانِ *ʿaynāni kabīratāni*, two large eyes.

اَلْمَدِينَتَانِ عَظِيمَتَانِ *al-madīnatāni ʿaẓīmatāni*, the two cities are great.

اَلْمُدَرِّسَانِ عَالِمَانِ *al-mudarrisāni ʿālimāni*, the two teachers are learned.

17. The Sound Masculine Plural

There are two kinds of plural in Arabic. Firstly we have the sound plural the use of which is practically confined (at least in the masculine) to participles and nouns indicating the profession or habitual action. Secondly there is the so-called broken plural which is made according to many patterns by altering the vowels within or outside the framework of the radical consonants. We shall come to the broken plural in the next lesson.

The masculine endings of the sound plural are ...ُونَ *ūna* (nom.) and ...ِينَ *īna* (acc. and gen.), e.g.

مُدَرِّسُونَ *mudarrisūna*, teachers (nom.).

مُدَرِّسِينَ *mudarrisīna*, teachers (acc. and gen.).

فَلَّاحُونَ *fallāḥūna*, peasants (nom.).

فَلَّاحِينَ *fallāḥīna*, peasants (acc. and gen.).

طَبَّاخُونَ فَرَنْسِيُّونَ *ṭabbākhūna faransīyūna*, French cooks (nom.).

18. The Sound Feminine Plural

In the feminine sound plural the ending ـَةٌ ... *atun* becomes ـَاتٌ ... *ātun* in the nominative and ـَاتٍ ... *ātin* in the *accusative and genitive*, e.g.

مُدَرِّسَةٌ *mudárrisatun*, a female teacher.

مُدَرِّسَاتٌ *mudarrisátun*, female teachers (nom.).

مُدَرِّسَاتٍ *mudarrisātin*, female teachers (acc. and gen.).

سَيِّدَاتٌ *sayyidātun*, ladies (nom.).

سَيِّدَاتٍ *sayyidātin*, ladies (acc. and gen.).

اَلْغَسَّالَاتُ مَشْغُولَاتٌ *al-ghassālātu mashghūlātun*, the washerwomen *are busy.*

Many nouns, especially foreign words, and most masculine diminutives (see Lesson XI) take the sound feminine plural ending, e.g.

حَيَوَانٌ	*ḥayawānun*, an animal,	pl.	حَيَوَانَاتٌ	*ḥayawānātun.*
نَبَاتٌ	*nabātun*, a plant,	pl.	نَبَاتَاتٌ	*nabātātun.*
جُنَيْهٌ	*junayhun*, a pound (£),	pl.	جُنَيْهَاتٌ	*junayhātun.*
تِلِفُونٌ	*tilifōnun*, a telephone,	pl.	تِلِفُونَاتٌ	*tilifōnātun.*
كُلَيْبٌ	*kulaybun*, a small dog,	pl.	كُلَيْبَاتٌ	*kulaybātun.*

Note especially the following sound plurals:

إِبْنٌ *ibnun*, a son, pl. بَنُونَ *banūna*

(also أَبْنَاءٌ *'abnā'un*, 1st form of the broken plural. See next lesson).

بِنْتٌ *bintun*, a daughter, girl, pl. بَنَاتٌ *banātun.*

أُمٌّ *'ummun*, a mother, pl. أُمَّهَاتٌ *'ummahātun.*

أُخْتٌ *'ukhtun*, a sister, pl. أَخَوَاتٌ *'akhawātun.*

In the word سَنَةٌ *sanatun*, a year, the third radical consonant و *w* has disappeared but turns up again in the plural, viz. سَنَوَاتٌ *sanawātun*. An alternative plural of سَنَةٌ *sanatun* is سِنُونَ *sinūna* (masc. sound pl.!).

19. Dual and Plural Personal Pronouns

These are:

نَحْنُ *náḥnu*, we.

أَنْتُمْ *'ántum*, you (masc.).

أَنْتُنَّ *'antúnna*, you (fem.).

أَنْتُمَا *'ántumā*, you (masc. and fem. dual).

هُمْ *hum*, they (masc.).

هُنَّ *húnna*, they (fem.).

هُمَا *húmā*, they (masc. and fem. dual).

Examples of the dual and sound plural:

هُمَا رَجُلَانِ شَهِيرَانِ *humā rajulāni shahīrāni*, they are two famous men.

سَيِّدَتَانِ شَهِيرَتَانِ *sayyidatāni shahīratāni*, two famous ladies.

صَحْرَاوَانِ عَظِيمَتَانِ *ṣaḥrāwāni ʿaẓīmatāni*, two great deserts.

اَلْأُخْتَانِ غَنِيَّتَانِ *al-'ukhtāni ghanīyatāni*, the two sisters are rich.

اَلْكِتَابَانِ ٱلْكَبِيرَانِ *al-kitābāni ◠l-kabīrāni*, the two big books.

اَلْفَلَّاحَانِ ٱلْفَقِيرَانِ حَاضِرَانِ *al-fallāḥāni ◠l-faqīrāni ḥāḍirāni*, the two poor peasants are present.

اَلسَّيِّدَاتُ غَائِبَاتٌ *al-sayyidātu ghā'ibātun*, the ladies are absent.

اَلْأَخَوَاتُ فَقِيرَاتٌ *al-'akhawātu faqīrātun*, the sisters are poor.

اَلسَّنَوَاتُ (اَلسِّنُونَ) طَوِيلَةٌ *al-sanawātu (al-sinūna) ṭawīlatun*, the years are long.

(N.B. Abstract plurals are grammatically *feminine singular*.)

هُمْ مُدَرِّسُونَ عَالِمُونَ	*hum mudarrisūna ʿālimūna*, they are learned teachers.
أَنْتُمَا غَنِيَّانِ	*'antumā ghanīyāni*, you (two) are rich.
نَحْنُ نَجَّارُونَ	*naḥnu najjārūna*, we are carpenters.
هُنَّ خَيَّاطَاتٌ مَاهِرَاتٌ	*hunna khayyāṭātun māhirātun*, they are clever dressmakers (tailoresses).

Supplementary Vocabulary

سَعِيدٌ	*saʿīdun*, happy.	حَزِينٌ	*ḥazīnun*, sad.
عَامِلٌ	*ʿāmilun*, a workman.	قُطْرٌ	*quṭrun* (masc.), a country.
اَلنِّيلُ	*al-Nīlu*, the Nile.	اَلْفُرَاتُ	*al-Furātu*, the Euphrates.
نَهْرٌ	*nahrun*, a river.	لِمَ ؟	*lima?*, why?

Exercise III

اَلْمَلِكَانِ غَنِيَّانِ. اَلْخَيَّاطَتَانِ مَاهِرَتَانِ. هُمَا فَلَّاحَانِ فَقِيرَانِ. هَلِ ٱلرَّجُلَانِ
سَعِيدَانِ؟ لَا، هُمَا حَزِينَانِ. اَلطَّبَّاخُونَ ٱلْفَرَنْسِيُّونَ مَشْهُورُونَ. اَلْأُمَّهَاتُ
سَعِيدَاتٌ. نَحْنُ عَامِلَانِ فَقِيرَانِ. هُمْ فَلَّاحُونَ. مِصْرُ وَٱلْهِنْدُ قُطْرَانِ عَظِيمَانِ.
هَلْ هُنَّ غَنِيَّاتٌ؟ نَعَمْ، هُنَّ غَنِيَّاتٌ جِدًّا. اَلْأُمَّهَاتُ وَٱلْأَخَوَاتُ حَزِينَاتٌ.
اَلنِّيلُ وَٱلْفُرَاتُ نَهْرَانِ طَوِيلَانِ. أَيْنَ ٱلْمُدَرِّسُونَ ٱلْفَرَنْسِيُّونَ؟ هُمْ حَاضِرُونَ.
اَلْمَلِكَتَانِ جَمِيلَتَانِ. اَلْمَلِكَتَانِ ٱلْجَمِيلَتَانِ جَاهِلَتَانِ. اَلسَّنَوَاتُ سَعِيدَةٌ. لِمَ أَنْتُنَّ
حَزِينَاتٌ؟

Transliteration

al-malikāni ghanīyāni. al-khayyāṭatāni māhiratāni. humā fallāḥāni faqīrāni. hali ‿l-rajulāni saʿīdāni? lā, humā ḥazīnāni. al-ṭabbākhūna ‿l-faransīyūna mashhūrūna. al-'ummahātu saʿīdātun. naḥnu ʿāmilāni faqīrāni. hum fallāḥūna. Miṣru wa‿l-Hindu quṭrāni ʿaẓīmāni. hal hunna ghanīyātun? naʿam, hunna ghanīyātun jiddan. al-'ummahātu wa‿l-

'akhawātu ḥazīnātun. al-Nīlu wa⁀l-Furātu nahrāni ṭawīlāni. 'ayna ⁀l-mudarrisūna ⁀l-faransīyūna? hum ḥāḍirūna. al-malikatāni jamīlatāni. al-malikatāni ⁀l-jamīlatāni jāhilatāni. al-sanawātu saعīdatun. lima 'antunna ḥazīnātun?

Translation

The two kings are rich. The two dressmakers are clever. They are two poor peasants. Are the two men happy? No, they are sad. (The) French cooks are famous. The mothers are happy. We are (two) poor workman. They are peasants. Egypt and India are great countries. Are they (fem.) rich? Yes, they are very rich. The mothers and sisters are sad. The Nile and the Euphrates are long rivers. Where are the French teachers? They are present. The two queens are beautiful. The two beautiful queens are ignorant. The years are happy. Why are you (fem. pl.) sad?

LESSON IV

20. The Broken Plural

Note. The vast majority of words in the Arabic vocabulary can be traced back to a triliteral verbal root, the third person masculine singular of the perfect of the simple verb. Thus from كَتَبَ *kataba*, he wrote, a host of derivatives exist such as كِتَابٌ *kitābun*, a book, كِتَابَةٌ *kitābatun*, writing (verbal noun), كَاتِبٌ *kātibun*, writing (active participle), a clerk, مَكْتُوبٌ *maktūbun*, written, a letter, مَكْتَبٌ *maktabun*, a school, office, etc. As there is no infinitive of an Arabic verb it is under the third person masculine singular of the perfect of the simple verb that an idea *and* its derivatives are to be looked for in the dictionary. There is a large number of nouns and particles which are not traceable back to a verbal root but these are arranged in the dictionary as if verbal roots existed for them. Further a large number of four-radical verbal roots exists but they are far outnumbered by the three-radical verbal roots.

When an Arab sees the three letters, *k*, *t* and *b*, the idea of writing is immediately engendered in his mind, but it is only when the radicals are, as it were, clothed with vowels and perhaps adjunct consonants that they acquire a definite meaning. The adjunct consonants which are used to form certain derivatives of the root idea and which, of course, may also be radicals are contained in the mnemonic word سَأَلْتُمُونِيهَا *sa'altumūnīhā*, meaning 'You asked me for them!' If any of the remaining 19 letters of the alphabet occurs in a word it must be a radical.

When the Arabs began to study their language after the Islamic expansion in the seventh century they took the simplest word in their language فَعَلَ *faع ala*, he did, and used its three radicals ف *f*, ع and ل *l*, quite independently of any idea of doing to depict the various patterns of words which they found existed. In this way they say that كَتَبَ *kataba*, he wrote, is of the pattern فَعَلَ *faع ala*, كُتِبَ *kutiba*, it was written, of the pattern فُعِلَ *fuع ila*, كِتَابٌ *kitābun*, a book, of the pattern فِعَالٌ *fiع ālun*, مَكْتُوبٌ *maktūbun*, a letter, of the pattern مَفْعُولٌ *mafع ūlun*, مَكْتَبٌ *maktabun*, a school, of the pattern مَفْعَلٌ *mafع alun* and so on.

There are very many such word patterns in Arabic with the most important of which it is hoped to make the student familiar in this book. When the student can see a word at a glance as a pattern of فَعَلَ *faع ala* he can consider that he has unlocked the door leading, after much hard work and diligent study, to a mastery of the Arabic language.

The most common patterns of the broken plural of nouns and adjectives are the following:

From three-radical words:

(i) أَفْعَالٌ *'afع ālun*, e.g.

أَقْلَامٌ *'aqlāmun*, pl. of قَلَمٌ *qalamun*, a pen.

أَسْوَاقٌ *'aswāqun*, pl. of سُوقٌ *sūqun*, a market.

أَوْلَادٌ *'awlādun*, pl. of وَلَدٌ *waladun*, a boy.

أَبْنَاءٌ *'abnā'un*, pl. of إِبْنٌ *ibnun* (3rd radical و *w* omitted), a son.

آبَاءٌ *'ābā'un*, pl. of أَبٌ *'abun* (3rd radical و *w* omitted), a father. (In these last two note the change of the 3rd radical و *w* into ء after long *ā*.)

Note that شَيْءٌ *shay'un*, a thing, has the irregular broken plural أَشْيَاءُ *'ashyā'u without 'nūnation'* (see next lesson).

(ii) فُعُولٌ *fuʿūlun*, e.g.

سُيُوفٌ *suyūfun*, pl. of سَيْفٌ *sayfun*, a sword.

بُيُوتٌ *buyūtun*, pl. of بَيْتٌ *baytun*, a house.

(N.B. بَيْتٌ *baytun* a verse of poetry, has as its plural أَبْيَاتٌ *'abyātun.*)

قُلُوبٌ *qulūbun*, pl. of قَلْبٌ *qalbun*, a heart.

حُدُودٌ *ḥudūdun*, pl. of حَدٌّ *ḥaddun*, a limit, frontier.

جُيُوشٌ *juyūshun*, pl. of جَيْشٌ *jayshun*, an army.

(iii) فُعُلٌ *fuʿulun*, e.g.

كُتُبٌ *kutubun*, pl. of كِتَابٌ *kitābun*, a book.

رُسُلٌ *rusulun*, pl. of رَسُولٌ *rasūlun*, a messenger.

مُدُنٌ *mudunun*, pl. of مَدِينَةٌ *madīnatun*, a city.

طُرُقٌ *ṭuruqun*, pl. of طَرِيقٌ *ṭarīqun*, a road.

دُورٌ *dūrun* (for دُوُرٌ *duwurun*), pl. of دَارٌ *dārun* (for دَوَرٌ *dawarun*), a house.

(iv) فِعَالٌ *fiʿālun*, e.g.

رِجَالٌ *rijālun*, pl. of رَجُلٌ *rajulun*, a man.

بِحَارٌ *biḥārun*, pl. of بَحْرٌ *baḥrun*, a sea.

رِيَاحٌ *riyāḥun*, pl. of رِيحٌ *rīḥun*, a wind.

طِوَالٌ *ṭiwālun*, pl. of طَوِيلٌ *ṭawīlun*, long.

جِبَالٌ *jibālun*, pl. of جَبَلٌ *jabalun*, a mountain.

(v) أَفْعُلٌ *'afʿulun*, e.g.

أَعْيُنٌ *'aʿyunun*, pl. of عَيْنٌ *ʿaynun*, an eye.

أَرْجُلٌ *'arjulun*, pl. of رِجْلٌ *rijlun*, a foot.

أَنْهُرٌ *'anhurun*, pl. of نَهْرٌ *nahrun*, a river.

أَشْهُرٌ 'ashhurun, pl. of شَهْرٌ shahrun, a month.

أَسْهُمٌ 'as-humun, pl. of سَهْمٌ sahmun, a share (in a company).

(N.B. سَهْمٌ *sahmun* an arrow, has as its plural سِهَامٌ *sihāmun*.)

(vi) فُعَلَاءُ *fuعalā'u* (*no* '*nūnation*'), e.g.

خُلَفَاءُ *khulafā'u*, pl. of خَلِيفَةٌ *khalīfatun*, a successor, Caliph.

سُفَرَاءُ *sufarā'u*, pl. of سَفِيرٌ *safīrun*, an ambassador.

أُمَرَاءُ *'umarā'u*, pl. of أَمِيرٌ *'amīrun*, an emir, prince, commander.

بُخَلَاءُ *bukhalā'u*, pl. of بَخِيلٌ *bakhīlun*, miserly, a miser.

فُقَرَاءُ *fuqarā'u*, pl. of فَقِيرٌ *faqīrun*, poor.

(vii) أَفْعِلَاءُ *'afعilā'u* (*no* '*nūnation*'), e.g.

أَقْرِبَاءُ *'aqribā'u*, pl. of قَرِيبٌ *qarībun*, near, a relative.

أَصْدِقَاءُ *'aṣdiqā'u*, pl. of صَدِيقٌ *ṣadīqun*, a friend.

أَغْنِيَاءُ *'aghniyā'u*, pl. of غَنِيٌّ *ghanīyun*, rich.

أَقْوِيَاءُ *'aqwiyā'u*, pl. of قَوِيٌّ *qawīyun*, strong.

أَطِبَّاءُ *'aṭibbā'u*, pl. of طَبِيبٌ *ṭabībun*, a physician.

(N.B. أَطِبَّاءُ *'aṭibbā'u* is for أَطْبِبَاءُ *'aṭbibā'u*, see Lesson XV, § 56.)

(viii) فُعْلَانٌ *fuعlānun*, e.g.

بُلْدَانٌ *buldānun*, pl. of بِلَادٌ *bilādun* (fem.), a country.

فُرْسَانٌ *fursānun*, pl. of فَارِسٌ *fārisun*, a horseman.

قُضْبَانٌ *quḍbānun*, pl. of قَضِيبٌ *qaḍībun*, a rod, rail.

شُبَّانٌ *shubbānun*, pl. of شَابٌّ *shābbun*, a youth.

شُجْعَانٌ *shujعānun*, pl. of شُجَاعٌ *shujāعun*, brave.

From four-radical words (or many words of three radicals plus an adjunct letter):

(ix) فَعَالِلُ *faعālilu* (*no* '*nūnation*'), e.g.

مَكَاتِبُ *makātibu*, pl. of مَكْتَبٌ *maktabun*, an office.

جَدَاوِلُ *jadāwilu*, pl. of جَدْوَلٌ *jadwalun*, a list, stream.

تَجَارِبُ *tajāribu*, pl. of تَجْرِبَةٌ *tajribatun*, a trial, experiment.

مَدَارِسُ *madārisu*, pl. of مَدْرَسَةٌ *madrasatun*, a school.

مَرَاكِبُ *marākibu*, pl. of مَرْكَبٌ *markabun*, a ship.

In addition to this pattern we have فَعَالِلَةٌ *faعālilatun* (*with* '*nūnation*') from persons of four radicals, e.g.

تَلَامِذَةٌ *talāmid͟hatun*, pl. of تِلْمِيذٌ *tilmīd͟hun*, a pupil.

أَسَاتِذَةٌ *'asātid͟hatun*, pl. of أُسْتَاذٌ *'ustād͟hun*, a professor.

دَكَاتِرَةٌ *dakātiratun*, pl. of دُكْتُورٌ *doktōrun*, a doctor.

(x) فَعَالِيلُ *faعālīlu* (*no* '*nūnation*'), e.g.

صَنَادِيقُ *ṣanādīqu*, pl. of صُنْدُوقٌ *ṣundūqun*, a box, chest.

مَجَانِينُ *majānīnu*, pl. of مَجْنُونٌ *majnūnun*, mad.

مَفَاتِيحُ *mafātīḥu*, pl. of مِفْتَاحٌ *miftāḥun*, a key.

فَوَانِيسُ *fawānīsu*, pl. of فَانُوسٌ *fānūsun*, a lamp.

كَرَاسِيُّ *karāsīyu*, pl. of كُرْسِيٌّ *kursīyun*, a chair.

If in the four-radical word the vowel between the third and fourth radicals is short the broken plural is of the ninth pattern. If it is long the plural is of the tenth pattern.

A complete list of the patterns of the broken plural will be found as an appendix to this book. For a full treatment of the subject reference should be made to Wright's *Arabic Grammar*, vol. I, pp. 199–233.

However, the student should, as he learns a new word, find out its plural, or singular, and learn the two together without unduly worrying himself about its pattern. Many words have more than one form of the broken plural but by reading the student will become familiar with the form most commonly used.

The following important plurals should be noted:

نَاسٌ *nāsun* (rarely أُنَاسٌ *'unāsun*), people, pl. of إِنْسَانٌ *'insānun*, a man, human being.

نِسَاءٌ *nisā'un* and نِسْوَةٌ *niswatun*, women, pl. of اِمْرَأَةٌ *imra'atun*, a woman. [اَلْمَرْأَةُ *al-mar'atu*, the woman, in which the initial *hamzat-al-waṣl* falls out, is applied to 'woman' in general as in the phrase اَلْمَرْأَةُ اَلْمِصْرِيَّةُ ذَكِيَّةٌ *al-mar'atu ͡l-miṣrīyatu dhakīyatun*, the Egyptian woman is intelligent.]

إِخْوَانٌ *'ikhwānun* and إِخْوَةٌ *'ikhwatun*, pls. of أَخٌ *'akhun* (3rd radical و *w* omitted), a brother.

[N.B. إِخْوَانٌ *'ikhwānun* is generally used for 'brothers' or 'brethren' in a political or religious movement, etc. إِخْوَةٌ *'ikhwatun* is used for brothers by blood relationship.]

Lastly the student's attention is once more drawn to the fact that all Arabic plurals which do not refer to rational beings are grammatically feminine singular so that all adjectives qualifying plurals of inanimate objects or abstract ideas and all pronouns replacing such must be in the feminine singular. There are occasional exceptions to the above rule, especially in older Arabic, but the student is advised to follow it in his own composition.

Examples of the broken plural:

أَوْلَادٌ صِغَارٌ *'awlādun ṣighārun*, little boys.

اَلْأَسْوَاقُ كَبِيرَةٌ *al-'aswāqu kabīratun*, the markets are big.

سُيُوفٌ حَادَّةٌ *suyūfun ḥāddatun*, sharp swords.

اَلْبُيُوتُ كَثِيرَةٌ *al-buyūtu kathīratun*, the houses are many.

كُتُبٌ عَرَبِيَّةٌ *kutubun ʿarabīyatun*, Arabic books.

اَلْمُدُنُ غَنِيَّةٌ *al-mudunu ghanīyatun*, the cities are rich.

اَلرِّجَالُ فُقَرَاءُ *al-rijālu fuqarā'u*, the men are poor.

جِبَالٌ عَظِيمَةٌ *jibālun عaẓīmatun*, mighty mountains.

سُفَرَاءُ مِصْرِيُّونَ *sufarā'u miṣrīyūna*, Egyptian ambassadors.

اَلْبُخَلَاءُ أَغْنِيَاءُ *al-bukhalā'u 'aghniyā'u*, (the) misers are rich.

رِجَالٌ أَقْوِيَاءُ *rijālun 'aqwiyā'u*, strong men.

اَلشُّبَّانُ شُجْعَانٌ *al-shubbānu shujعānun*, the youths are brave.

أَطِبَّاءُ مَهَرَةٌ (pl. of مَاهِرٌ) *'aṭibbā'u maharatun*, clever physicians.

اَلْمَدَارِسُ قَلِيلَةٌ *al-madārisu qalīlatun*, the schools are few.

عَرَائِسُ جَمِيلَاتٌ (pl. of عَرُوسٌ) *عarā'isu jamīlātun*, beautiful brides.

اَلْأَسَاتِذَةُ غَائِبُونَ *al-'asātidhatu ghā'ibūna*, the professors are absent.

اَلتَّلَامِذَةُ حَاضِرُونَ *al-talāmidhatu ḥāḍirūna*, the pupils are present.

مَفَاتِيحُ ثَقِيلَةٌ *mafātīḥu thaqīlatun*, heavy keys.

اَلْمَجَانِينُ سُعَدَاءُ (pl. of سَعِيدٌ) *al-majānīnu suعadā'u*, madmen are happy.

Supplementary Vocabulary

دَائِمًا *dā'iman* (adv. acc.), always.

خَفِيفٌ *khafīfun*, light.

رَدِيءٌ *radī'un*, bad.

قَصِيرٌ *qaṣīrun*, short.

Exercise IV

اَلْآبَاءُ وَٱلْأُمَّهَاتُ مَشْغُولُونَ. هَلِ ٱلْأَوْلَادُ وَٱلْبَنَاتُ سُعَدَاءُ؟ نَعَمْ، هُمْ سُعَدَاءُ دَائِمًا. اَلرِّجَالُ أَغْنِيَاءُ وَٱلنِّسَاءُ جَمِيلَاتٌ. اَلْأَغْنِيَاءُ سُعَدَاءُ. هَلِ ٱلْأَسَاتِذَةُ حَاضِرُونَ؟ لَا، هُمْ غَائِبُونَ. اَلْمَفَاتِيحُ خَفِيفَةٌ. اَلْمَفَاتِيحُ ٱلْخَفِيفَةُ صَغِيرَةٌ.

اَلْإِخْوَةُ وَٱلْأَخَوَاتُ حِزَانٌ. اَلْكُتُبُ ٱلصَّغِيرَةُ خَفِيفَةٌ. اَلشُّبَّانُ أَقْوِيَاءُ وَٱلشَّابَّاتُ
جَمِيلَاتٌ. اَلْمَكَاتِبُ كَبِيرَةٌ. اَلصَّنَادِيقُ ثَقِيلَةٌ. اَلْأَطِبَّاءُ ٱلْمَهَرَةُ مَشْهُورُونَ.
اَلْفَارِسُ ٱلْعَرَبِيُّ شُجَاعٌ. اَلْمَدِينَةُ كَبِيرَةٌ وَٱلدُّورُ كَثِيرَةٌ. اَلْحُدُودُ طَوِيلَةٌ وَٱلطُّرُقُ
رَدِيئَةٌ. اَلْبَحْرُ هَادِئٌ. اَلْقُضْبَانُ قَصِيرَةٌ.

Transliteration

al-’ābā’u wa‿l-’ummahātu mashghūlūna. hali ‿l-’awlādu wa‿l-banātu suʿadā’u? naʿam, hum suʿadā’u dā’iman. al-rijālu ’aghniyā’u wa‿l-nisā’u jamīlātun. al-’aghniyā’u suʿadā’u. hali ‿l-’asātidhatu ḥāḍirūna? lā, hum ghā’ibūna. al-mafātīḥu khafīfatun. al-mafātīḥu ‿l-khafīfatu ṣaghīratun. al-’ikhwatu wa‿l-’akhawātu ḥizānun. al-kutubu ‿l-ṣaghīratu khafīfatun. al-shubbānu ’aqwiyā’u wa‿l-shābbātu jamīlātun. al-makātibu kabīratun. al-ṣanādīqu thaqīlatun. al-’aṭibbā’u ‿l-maharatu mashhūrūna. al-fārisu ‿l-ʿarabīyu shujāʿun. al-madīnatu kabīratun wa‿l-dūru kathīratun. al-ḥudūdu ṭawīlatun wa‿l-ṭuruqu radī’atun. al-baḥru hādi’un. al-quḍbānu qaṣīratun.

Translation

The fathers and mothers are busy. Are the boys and girls happy? Yes, they are always happy. The men are rich and the women are beautiful. The rich men are happy. Are the professors present? No, they are absent. The keys are light. The light keys are small. The brothers and sisters are sad. The small books are light. The youths are strong and the young women are beautiful. The offices are large. The boxes are heavy. The clever physicians are famous. The Arab horseman is brave. The town is big and the houses are many. The frontiers are long and the roads are bad. The sea is calm. The rails are short.

LESSON V

21. Declension

There are three declensions in Arabic.

(i) The *1st Declension* to which the vast majority of nouns and adjectives, singulars and broken plurals, belong has three cases, nominative, accusative and genitive. Three case endings have already been referred to in the Introduction, § 5.

Thus we have:

nom.	رَجُلٌ	*rajulun*, a man.	اَلرَّجُلُ	*al-rajulu*, the man.
acc.	رَجُلًا	*rajulan*, a man.	اَلرَّجُلَ	*al-rajula*, the man.
gen.	رَجُلٍ	*rajulin*, (of) a man.	اَلرَّجُلِ	*al-rajuli*, (of) the man.
nom.	رِجَالٌ	*rijālun*, men.	اَلرِّجَالُ	*al-rijālu*, the men.
acc.	رِجَالًا	*rijālan*, men.	اَلرِّجَالَ	*al-rijāla*, the men.
gen.	رِجَالٍ	*rijālin*, (of) men.	اَلرِّجَالِ	*al-rijāli*, (of) the men.
nom.	مَلِكَةٌ	*malikatun*, a queen.	اَلْمَلِكَةُ	*al-malikatu*, the queen.
acc.	مَلِكَةً	*malikatan*, a queen.	اَلْمَلِكَةَ	*al-malikata*, the queen.
gen.	مَلِكَةٍ	*malikatin*, (of) a queen.	اَلْمَلِكَةِ	*al-malikati*, (of) the queen.

The case endings of the sound plural and the dual have already been given in Lesson III, which should be once more referred to.

Note that the *indefinite* accusative, *with the exception of* the feminine ending ةً... *atan*, has an extra *'alif* which is, however, omitted after *hamzat-al-qaṭ*ع preceded by long *ā*, e.g.

جَزَاءً *jazā'an*, a reward, punishment (acc.).

(ii) The *2nd Declension* to which belong most proper names and certain adjectival and broken plural forms has no 'nūnation'. In this declension the genitive is the same as the accusative in most proper names and in indefinite nouns and adjectives.

Thus we have:

nom.	عُمَرُ	ع*umaru*, Omar.
acc. *and* gen.	عُمَرَ	ع*umara*, Omar.
nom.	مِصْرُ	*Miṣru*, Egypt.
acc. *and* gen.	مِصْرَ	*Miṣra*, Egypt.
nom.	سُفَرَاءُ	*sufarā'u*, ambassadors.

acc. *and* gen. سُفَرَاءَ *sufarā'a*, ambassadors.

nom. تَعْبَانُ *taعbānu*, tired.

(N.B. Neo-Arabic and colloquial. The classical form is تَعِبٌ *taعibun.*)

acc. *and* gen. تَعْبَانَ *taعbāna*, tired.

When a noun or adjective of this declension becomes definite by the addition of the definite article or a following genitive of a noun or a pronoun then it has *all three case endings* as in the 1st declension, e.g.

nom. اَلسُّفَرَاءُ *al-sufarā'u*, the ambassadors.

acc. اَلسُّفَرَاءَ *al-sufarā'a*, the ambassadors.

gen. اَلسُّفَرَاءِ *al-sufarā'i*, (of) ambassadors.

nom. سُفَرَاءُ مِصْرَ *sufarā'u Miṣra*, the ambassadors of Egypt.

acc. سُفَرَاءَ مِصْرَ *sufarā'a Miṣra*, the ambassadors of Egypt.

gen. سُفَرَاءِ مِصْرَ *sufarā'i Miṣra*, (of) ambassadors of Egypt.

Many well-known proper names, mostly participles or adjectives, belong to the 1st declension, e.g.

nom. مُحَمَّدٌ *Muḥammadun*, Mohammed.

acc. مُحَمَّدًا *Muḥammadan*, Mohammed.

gen. مُحَمَّدٍ *Muḥammadin*, (of) Mohammed.

nom. عَلِيٌّ *عalīyun*, Ali.

acc. عَلِيًّا *عalīyan*, Ali.

gen. عَلِيٍّ *عalīyin*, (of) Ali.

By practice in reading well-edited books the student will learn to which declension a proper name belongs.

Note the extra و *w* in the following proper name:

عَمْرٌو *عamrun* (nom.), Amr. عَمْرًا *عamran* (acc.), Amr.

عَمْرٍو *عamrin* (gen.), (of) Amr.

(iii) The *3rd Declension* has only one ending for all three cases. All nouns and adjectives in this class end in أَلِفٌ مَقْصُورَةٌ *'alif maqṣūra* or shortened *'alif* (see Introduction, § 3) which is ىَ... *ā* (contracted from the three case endings يٌ... *ayu, aya, ayi*) or ا... *ā* (contracted from the three case endings وٌ... *awu, awa, awi*). Both these ways of writing shortened *'alif* may have 'nūnation'.

Thus we have:

هُدًى *húdan*, guidance (all three cases).

اَلْهُدَى *al-húdā*, the guidance (all three cases).

عَصًا *ʿáṣan* (fem.), a stick, cane (all three cases).

اَلْعَصَا *al-ʿáṣā*, the stick (all three cases).

To this declension belong words with the feminine ending ىَ... *ā* suffixed to the last radical, e.g.

ذِكْرَى *dhikrā*, remembrance (all three cases).

Roughly speaking the three cases are used in the same way as in most European languages with some important exceptions to be noted later.

22. The Genitive

If a noun or adjective used as a noun is governed by a genitive it is thereby defined and cannot take the definite article. Thus in a genitive construction like 'the key of the door of the house' only the last noun can have the definite article, viz.

مِفْتَاحُ بَابِ ٱلْبَيْتِ *miftāḥu* (nom.) *bābi ◠l-bayti.*

If one wants to say something like 'the key of *a* door of the house' then the phrase has to be turned to 'the key of a door from the doors of the house', viz.

مِفْتَاحُ بَابٍ مِنْ أَبْوَابِ ٱلْبَيْتِ *miftāḥu bābin min 'abwābi ◠l-bayti,*

even though this appears somewhat clumsy to the European mind.

A word cannot be separated from a following genitive, the Arabs considering a phrase such as كِتَابُ ٱلْوَلَدِ *kitābu ˷l-waladi*, the boy's book, to be grammatically one word. Thus any adjective qualifying 'book' must follow the genitive and receive the definite article, viz.

كِتَابُ ٱلْوَلَدِ ٱلْكَبِيرُ *kitābu ˷l-waladi ˷l-kabīru*, the boy's big book.

As can be seen it is sometimes not at all clear to which noun of a possessive construction a following adjective refers, especially when the text is not vowel-pointed.

When two or more nouns are governed by the same genitive then according to the strict rules of classical Arabic the genitive must follow the first noun. Thus a phrase like 'the pupil's pen and book' has to be rendered 'the pen of the pupil and *his* book', viz.

قَلَمُ ٱلتِّلْمِيذِ وَكِتَابُهُ *qalamu ˷l-tilmīdhi wakitābuhu*.

The genitive of the personal pronouns will be dealt with in Lesson VII.

However, if two words governed by the same genitive have a close logical connection they may both precede the genitive as in the phrase

إِسْمُ وَعُنْوَانُ ٱلرَّجُلِ *ismu waعunwānu ˷l-rajuli*, the man's name and address.

Masculine sound plurals and masculine and feminine duals lose their final ن *n* when governed by a genitive, e.g.

فَلَّاحُو مِصْرَ *fallāḥū Miṣra*, the peasants (nom.) of Egypt.

فَلَّاحِي مِصْرَ *fallāḥī Miṣra*, the peasants (acc. and gen.) of Egypt.

مُدَرِّسُو ٱلْمَدْرَسَةِ *mudarrisū ˷l-madrasati*, the teachers (nom.) of the school.

نَجَّارِي ٱلْمَدِينَةِ *najjārī ˷l-madīnati*, the carpenters (acc. and gen.) of the town.

عَيْنَا ٱلْبِنْتِ *عaynā ˷l-binti*, the girl's two eyes (nom.).

بِنْتَا ٱلرَّئِيسِ *bintā ˷l-ra'īsi*, the President's two daughters (nom.).

Note again that a long vowel before *hamzat-al-waṣl*, even though written long, is pronounced short.

رِجْلَيِ ٱلْوَلَدِ *rijlayi ◠l-waladi*, the boy's two feet (acc. and gen.).

مُدَرِّسَتَيِ ٱلْبَنَاتِ *mudarrisatayi ◠l-banāti*, the girls' two teachers (acc. and gen.).

Note the vowel '*i*' added to the vowelless '*y*' of the diphthong ending of the accusative and genitive of the dual to facilitate the elision of the following *hamzat-al-waṣl*.

The words أَبٌ *'abun*, a father, أَخٌ *'akhun*, a brother and حَمٌ *ḥamun*, a father-in-law (otherwise regular in all cases), have the following forms when followed by a genitive:

أَبُو مَحْمُودٍ *'abū Maḥmūdin*, Mahmud's father (nom.).

أَبَا مَحْمُودٍ *'abā Maḥmūdin*, Mahmud's father (acc.).

أَبِي مَحْمُودٍ *'abī Maḥmūdin*, Mahmud's father (gen.).

أَخُو مُحَمَّدٍ *'akhū Muḥammadin*, Mohammed's brother (nom.).

أَخَا مُحَمَّدٍ *'akhā Muḥammadin*, Mohammed's brother (acc.).

أَخِي مُحَمَّدٍ *'akhī Muḥammadin*, Mohammed's brother (gen.).

حَمُو فَاطِمَةَ *ḥamū Fāṭimata*, Fatima's father-in-law (nom.).

حَمَا فَاطِمَةَ *ḥamā Faṭimata*, Fatima's father-in-law (acc.).

حَمِي فَاطِمَةَ *ḥamī Fāṭimata*, Fatima's father-in-law (gen.).

(N.B. حَمَاةٌ *ḥamātun*, a mother-in-law, is quite regular.)

Note that the word فَمٌ *famun*, a mouth (otherwise regular in all cases) when followed by a genitive may become فُو *fū*, فَا *fā*, فِي *fī*, viz.

فُو مُحَمَّدٍ *fū Muḥammadin*, Mohammed's mouth (nom.).

فَا مُحَمَّدٍ *fā Muḥammadin*, Mohammed's mouth (acc.).

فِي مُحَمَّدٍ *fī Muḥammadin*, Mohammed's mouth (gen.).

(This construction is, however, archaic and modern usage prefers to treat فَمٌ *famun*, a mouth, regularly.)

The noun ذُو *dhū*, owner or possessor, is always followed by a genitive and is used to form adjectives (see next lesson), e.g.

ذُو عِلْمٍ *dhū ʿilmin*, the master of learning, learned (nom.).

ذَا عِلْمٍ *dhā ʿilmin*, the master of learning, learned (acc.).

ذِي عِلْمٍ *dhī ʿilmin*, the master of learning, learned (gen.).

Lastly the indefinite genitive is used to denote the material from which or for which a thing is made, e.g.

قِطْعَةُ لَحْمٍ *qiṭʿatu laḥmin*, a piece of meat.

سَاعَةُ ذَهَبٍ *sāʿatu dhahabin*, a gold watch.

مِلْعَقَةُ فِضَّةٍ *milʿaqatu fiḍḍatin*, a silver spoon.

ثَوْبُ حَرِيرٍ *thawbu ḥarīrin*, a silk garment.

فِنْجَانُ قَهْوَةٍ *finjānu qahwatin*, a cup of coffee or a coffee-cup.

بَرَّادُ شَايٍ *barrādu shāyin*, a pot of tea or a tea-pot.

Note that such nouns, although governed by a genitive, are indefinite contrary to the rule given at the beginning of this section.

23. Prepositions

In Arabic prepositions govern the genitive, e.g.

مِنْ بَيْتِ ٱلْمُدَرِّسِ *min bayti ᵕl-mudarrisi*, from the teacher's house.

مِنَ ٱلْمَدْرَسَةِ *mina ᵕl-madrasati*, from the school.

عَلَى صُنْدُوقٍ *ʿalā ṣundūqin*, on a box.

عَلَى ٱلْجَبَلِ *ʿalā ᵕl-jabali*, on the mountain.

فِي قَصْرِ ٱلْأَمِيرِ *fī qaṣri ᵕl-'amīri*, in the prince's palace.

فِي ٱلْمَحْكَمَةِ *fī ᵕl-maḥkamati*, in the law-court.

حَتَّى ٱلصَّبَاحِ *ḥattā ᵕl-ṣabāḥi*, until the morning.

Note that the long vowel with which some prepositions end must be shortened in pronunciation before *hamzat-al-waṣl.*

The two prepositions بِ *bi*, at, in, and لِ *li*, to, for, are written connected to the words they govern, e.g.

بِٱلْقَاهِرَةِ *bi⁀l-Qāhirati*, in Cairo.

لِمُحَمَّدٍ *li Muḥammadin*, to, for Mohammed.

Note بِسْمِ ٱللّٰهِ *Bismi⁀llāhi*, In the name of God, where the *'alif* as well as the *hamzat-al-waṣl* of إِسْمٌ *ismun*, a name, is elided.

If a word begins with the definite article the *'alif* is elided after the preposition لِ *li*, to, for, e.g.

لِلرَّجُلِ *li⁀l-rajuli*, to, for, the man,

and if the word itself begins with the letter ل *l* then the whole of the definite article is elided, e.g.

لِلَّيْلِ *li⁀l-layli*, to the night.

لِلُّغَةِ *li⁀l-lughati*, to the language.

There is a type of preposition which is really a noun in the accusative, the construction being an accusative of place or time, e.g.

عِنْدَ ٱلْوَزِيرِ *ʿinda ⁀l-wazīri*, with the minister, 'chez le ministre'.

تَحْتَ ٱلْكُرْسِيِّ *taḥta ⁀l-kursīyi*, under the chair.

فَوْقَ ٱلْأَرْضِ *fawqa ⁀l-'arḍi*, above the ground.

بَعْدَ ٱلْحَفْلَةِ *baʿda ⁀l-ḥaflati*, after the party.

قَبْلَ ٱلظُّهْرِ *qabla ⁀l-ẓuhri*, before noon.

Examples:

وَعْدُ ٱلرَّجُلِ ٱلشَّرِيفِ مُحْتَرَمٌ

waʿdu ⁀l-rajuli ⁀l-sharīfi muḥtaramun,
The promise of a (lit. the) noble man is honoured.

جَزَاءُ ٱلْخَيْرِ بِالشَّرِّ عَمَلٌ قَبِيحٌ

jazāʾu ⌢l-khayri bi⌢l-sharri ʿamalun qabīḥun,
The rewarding of good with evil is a disgraceful deed.

ثَوْبُ أَبِي مُحَمَّدٍ قَدِيمٌ

thawbu ʾabī Muḥammadin qadīmun,
Mohammed's father's garment is old.

شَعْرُ أُخْتِ ٱلْوَلَدِ جَمِيلٌ

shaʿru ʾukhti ⌢l-waladi jamīlun,
The boy's sister's hair is beautiful.

رِجْلَا ٱلْعَرُوسِ صَغِيرَتَانِ

rijlā ⌢l-ʿarūsi ṣaghīratāni,
The bride's (two) feet are small.

شُغْلُ مُوَظَّفِي ٱلْحُكُومَةِ مُتْعِبٌ

shughlu muwaẓẓafī ⌢l-ḥukūmati mutʿibun,
The work of (the) government officials is tiring.

كَرَمُ ٱلْعَرَبِ ٱلْمَعْرُوفُ

karamu ⌢l-ʿarabi ⌢l-maʿrūfu,
The Arabs' well-known generosity.

لَعِبُ ٱلْأَطْفَالِ ٱلصِّغَارِ لَطِيفٌ

laʿibu ⌢l-ʾaṭfāli ⌢l-ṣighāri laṭīfun,
(The) small children's play is delightful.

اَلْقَلَمُ ٱلْجَدِيدُ عَلَى مَكْتَبِ ٱلْمُدَرِّسِ

al-qalamu ⌢l-jadīdu ʿalā maktabi ⌢l-mudarrisi,
The new pen is on the teacher's desk.

اَلْجَارُ قَبْلَ ٱلدَّارِ وَٱلرَّفِيقُ قَبْلَ ٱلطَّرِيقِ

al-jāru qabla ⌢l-dāri wa⌢l-rafīqu qabla ⌢l-ṭarīqi,
The neighbour (should be chosen) before the house, the companion before the way.

Supplementary Vocabulary

جَذَّابٌ	*ja<u>dh</u><u>dh</u>ābun*, attractive.	اَلصِّينُ	*al-Ṣīnu*, China.
سَارٌّ	*sārrun*, pleasing.	ذَكِيٌّ	*<u>dh</u>akīyun*, clever.
مَا (مَاذَا)؟	*mā* (*mā<u>dh</u>ā*)? what?	قَبِيحٌ	*qabīḥun*, ugly, wicked.
مَطْبَخٌ	*maṭba<u>kh</u>un*, a kitchen.	هَدِيَّةٌ	*hadīyatun*, a present.

Exercise V

أَيْنَ ٱلسُّفَرَاءُ؟ هُمْ فِي قَصْرِ ٱلْمَلِكِ. أَخُو مُحَمَّدٍ فِي ٱلْجُنَيْنَةِ ٱلصَّغِيرَةِ. عَيْنَا ٱلْبِنْتِ جَذَّابَتَانِ. هَلِ ٱلْقَاهِرَةُ فِي فَرَنْسَا؟ لَا، هِيَ فِي مِصْرَ. اَلسَّفَرُ إِلَى ٱلصِّينِ طَوِيلٌ. سَاعَةُ ٱلذَّهَبِ ثَقِيلَةٌ. فِنْجَانُ قَهْوَةٍ فِي ٱلصَّبَاحِ شَيْءٌ سَارٌّ. أَبُو ٱلْبِنْتِ رَجُلٌ مَشْهُورٌ. اِبْنُ ٱلْمُدَرِّسَةِ وَلَدٌ ذَكِيٌّ. مَا ٱسْمُ ٱلْوَلَدِ؟ اِسْمُ ٱلْوَلَدِ عَلِيٌّ. هَلْ بِنْتَا ٱلْمَلِكِ جَمِيلَتَانِ؟ لَا، هُمَا قَبِيحَتَانِ جِدًّا. أَيْنَ ٱلطَّبَّاخَةُ؟ هِيَ فِي ٱلْمَطْبَخِ. هَلِ ٱلْمُدَرِّسُونَ فِي ٱلْمَدْرَسَةِ؟ لَا، هُمْ فِي ٱلسُّوقِ. هِيَ هَدِيَّةٌ لِلسَّيِّدَةِ مِنِ ٱبْنِ ٱلْوَزِيرِ.

Transliteration

'ayna ⌒l-sufarā'u? hum fī qaṣri ⌒l-maliki. 'a<u>kh</u>ū Muḥammadin fī ⌒l-junaynati ⌒l-ṣa<u>gh</u>īrati. ʿaynā ⌒l-binti ja<u>dh</u><u>dh</u>ābatāni. hali ⌒l-Qāhiratu fī Faransā? lā, hiya fī Miṣra. al-safaru 'ilā ⌒l-Ṣīni ṭawīlun. sāʿatu ⌒l-<u>dh</u>ahabi <u>th</u>aqīlatun. finjānu qahwatin fī ⌒l-ṣabāḥi <u>sh</u>ay'un sārrun. 'abū ⌒l-binti rajulun ma<u>sh</u>hūrun. ibnu ⌒l-mudarrisati waladun <u>dh</u>akīyun. mā ⌒smu ⌒l-waladi? ismu ⌒l-waladi ʿalīyun. hal bintā ⌒l-maliki jamīlatāni? lā, humā qabīḥatāni jiddan. 'ayna ⌒l-ṭabbā<u>kh</u>atu? hiya fī ⌒l-maṭba<u>kh</u>i. hali ⌒l-mudarrisūna fī ⌒l-madrasati? lā, hum fī ⌒l-sūqi. hiya hadīyatun li⌒l-sayyidati mini ⌒bni ⌒l-wazīri.

Translation

Where are the ambassadors? They are in the king's palace. Mohammed's brother is in the small garden. The girl's eyes are attractive. Is Cairo in France? No, it is in Egypt. The journey to China is long. *The* gold watch is heavy. *A* cup of coffee in the morning is a pleasing thing. The girl's father is a famous man. The (fem.) teacher's son is a clever boy. What is the boy's name? The boy's name is Ali. Are the king's two daughters beautiful? No, they are very ugly. Where is the cock? She is in the kitchen. Are the teachers in the school? No, they are in the market. It is a present for the lady from the minister's son.

LESSON VI

24. Adjectives

As has already been noted the Arab makes no grammatical distinction between noun and adjective and any adjective may be used as a noun. Adjectival patterns, like nominal patterns, make their plurals either according to the pattern for the sound plural or according to the many broken plural patterns. This can only be determined through practice in reading or reference to a good dictionary.

There exist numerous adjectival patterns the most important of which are the following:

(i) فَاعِلٌ *fāعilun*, actually the active participle of the simple verb, e.g.

جَاهِلٌ *jāhilun*, ignorant, pl. جُهَّالٌ *juhhālun*.

تَاجِرٌ *tājirun*, trading, a merchant, pl. تُجَّارٌ *tujjārun*.

كَاتِبٌ *kātibun*, writing, a clerk, pl. كُتَّابٌ *kuttābun*.

عَالِمٌ *عālimun*, learned, a savant, pl. عُلَمَاءُ *عulamā'u*.

(ii) فَعِيلٌ *faعīlun* (more commonly adjectival than nominal), e.g.

سَعِيدٌ *saعīdun*, happy, fortunate, pl. سُعَدَاءُ *suعadā'u*.

كَرِيمٌ *karīmun*, generous, pl. كُرَمَاءُ *kuramā'u*.

شَرِيفٌ *sharīfun*, noble, pl. أَشْرَافٌ *'ashrāfun*.

غَبِيٌّ *ghabīyun*, stupid, pl. أَغْبِيَاءُ *'aghbiyā'u*.

(iii) فَعْلَانُ *faɛlānu* (2nd declension) from simple verbs of the pattern فَعِلَ *faɛila* denoting temporary state, e.g.

كَسْلَانُ *kaslānu*, lazy, pl. كَسَالَى *kasālā*, fem. sing. كَسْلَى *kaslā*.

عَطْشَانُ *ɛaṭshānu*, thirsty, pl. عَطَاشَى *ɛaṭāshā*, fem. sing. عَطْشَى *ɛaṭshā*.

نَعْسَانُ *naɛsānu*, sleepy, pl. نَعَاسَى *naɛāsā*, fem. sing. نَعْسَى *naɛsā*.

N.B. In Modern Arabic the pattern فَعْلَانُ *faɛlānu* usually takes the sound endings in the feminine and plural, e.g. تَعْبَانُ *taɛbānu*, tired, pl. تَعْبَانُونَ *taɛbānūna*, fem. sing. تَعْبَانَةٌ *taɛbānatun*.

(iv) فَعُولٌ *faɛūlun* is an intensive form of patterns (i) and (iii), e.g.

جَهُولٌ *jahūlun*, very ignorant.

كَسُولٌ *kasūlun*, very lazy.

(v) فَعَّالٌ *faɛɛālun* denoting habitual action or profession, e.g.

أَكَّالٌ *'akkālun*, always eating, gluttonous.

عَدَّاءٌ *ɛaddā'un*, always running, a runner.

Patterns (iv) and (v) take the regular feminine and sound plural endings.

(vi) مَفْعُولٌ *mafɛūlun* actually the passive participle of simple verbs, e.g.

مَسْرُورٌ *masrūrun*, pleased, overjoyed.

مَشْغُولٌ *mashghūlun*, occupied, busy.

This pattern takes the sound plural endings when it refers to rational beings, otherwise broken plural (see Lesson IV, pattern (x)), or the sound feminine plural ending, e.g.

مَرْسُومٌ *marsūmun*, a decree, pl. مَرَاسِيمُ *marāsīmu*.

مَوْضُوعٌ *mawḍūɛun*, a subject, topic, pl. مَوْضُوعَاتٌ *mawḍūɛātun*.

(vii) The pattern أَفْعَلُ *'afعalu*, fem. sing. فَعْلَاءُ *faعlā'u*, masc. and fem. pl. فُعْلٌ *fuعlun* is confined to adjectives denoting colours or defects of the body, e.g.

أَسْوَدُ *'aswadu*, black, fem. sing. سَوْدَاءُ *sawdā'u*, pl. سُودٌ *sūdun*.

أَحْمَرُ *'aḥmaru*, red, fem. sing. حَمْرَاءُ *ḥamrā'u*, pl. حُمْرٌ *ḥumrun*.

أَصْفَرُ *'aṣfaru*, yellow, fem. sing. صَفْرَاءُ *ṣafrā'u*, pl. صُفْرٌ *ṣufrun*.

أَخْضَرُ *'akhḍaru*, green, fem. sing. خَضْرَاءُ *khaḍrā'u*, pl. خُضْرٌ *khuḍrun*.

أَبْيَضُ *'abyaḍu*, white, fem. sing. بَيْضَاءُ *bayḍā'u*, pl. بِيضٌ *bīḍun*.

N.B. The sound group '*uy*' being repugnant to Arab ears '*u*' changes into '*i*' the vowel cognate to the following consonant.

أَبْكَمُ *'abkamu*, dumb, fem. sing. بَكْمَاءُ *bakmā'u*, pl. بُكْمٌ *bukmun*.

أَطْرَشُ *'aṭrashu*, deaf, fem. sing. طَرْشَاءُ *ṭarshā'u*, pl. طُرْشٌ *ṭurshun*.

أَعْمَى *'aعmā* (for أَعْمَيُ *'aعmayu*, see Introduction § 3), blind, fem. sing. عَمْيَاءُ *عamyā'u*, pl. عُمْيٌ *عumyun*.

The dual of this pattern, as of the preceding ones, is regular except that here the هَمْزَةُ ٱلْقَطْعِ *hamzat-al-qaṭع* in the feminine changes into و *w*, e.g.

أَسْوَدَانِ *'aswadāni*, two black men.

سَوْدَاوَانِ *sawdāwāni*, two black women.

25. Comparative and Superlative

The pattern أَفْعَلُ *'afعalu* is also used to form the comparative and superlative of patterns (i), (ii) and (iii) above and in the comparative it is the same for masculine, feminine, dual and plural. In a comparison 'than' is expressed by the preposition مِنْ *min*, e.g.

ٱلْوَلَدُ أَكْبَرُ مِنَ ٱلْبِنْتِ *al-waladu 'akbaru mina ◡l-binti*, the boy is bigger (older) than the girl.

اَلْوَلَدَانِ أَكْبَرُ مِنَ ٱلْبِنْتَيْنِ *al-waladāni 'akbaru mina⌒l-bintayni*, the (two) boys are older than the (two) girls.

اَلْمَدْرَسَةُ أَصْغَرُ مِنَ ٱلْمَحْكَمَةِ *al-madrasatu 'aṣgharu mina ⌒l-maḥkamati*, the school is smaller than the law-court.

اَلرِّجَالُ أَقْوَى مِنَ ٱلنِّسَاءِ *al-rijālu 'aqwā mina ⌒l-nisā'i*, men are stronger than women.

اَلتَّاجِرُ أَسْعَدُ حَالًا مِنَ ٱلْفَلَّاحِ *al-tājiru 'asعadu ḥālan mina ⌒l-fallāḥi*, the merchant is better off (happier as regards state) than the peasant.

If the second and third radicals of an adjective are the same in the pattern أَفْعَلُ *'afعalu* they are run together and the vowel of the second radical thrown back on the first, e.g.

أَصَمُّ *'aṣammu* (for أَصْمَمُ *'aṣmamu*), deaf.

شَدِيدٌ *shadīdun*, strong, violent.

أَشَدُّ *'ashaddu*, stronger, more violent.

جَدِيدٌ *jadīdun*, new,

أَجَدُّ *'ajaddu*, newer.

If an adjective is of pattern (vii) or a passive participle or a participle of a derived verb (to be dealt with later) then it cannot form its comparative as above. The phrase has to be turned as follows:

أَشَدُّ سَوَادًا *'ashaddu sawādan*, stronger as regards blackness, blacker.

أَكْثَرُ سُرُورًا *'aktharu surūran*, more as regards joy, more pleased.

مُجْتَهِدٌ *mujtahidun*, industrious (active participle of a derived verb).

أَكْثَرُ ٱجْتِهَادًا *'aktharu ⌒jtihādan*, more as regards industry, more industrious.

N.B. أَقَلُّ لَذَّةً *'aqallu ladhdhatan*, less as regards deliciousness, less delicious.

Note the use of the substantives خَيْرٌ *khayrun*, good, and شَرٌّ *sharrun*, evil, in the comparison:

اَلصَّلَاةُ خَيْرٌ مِنَ ٱلنَّوْمِ   *al-ṣalātu khayrun mina ∩l-nawmi*, prayer is better than sleep.

اَلْقَتْلُ شَرٌّ مِنَ ٱلسَّرِقَةِ   *al-qatlu sharrun mina ∩l-sariqati*, murder is worse than theft.

If the comparative form أَفْعَلُ *'afɛalu* becomes definite by the prefixing of the definite article or the addition of a following genitive then it becomes *superlative* in meaning, e.g.

اَلْأَكْبَرُ   *al-'akbaru*, the greatest one.

أَعْلَمُ ٱلنَّاسِ   *'aɛlamu ∩l-nāsi*, the most learned of men.

أَصْغَرُهُمْ   *'aṣgharuhum*, the smallest of them.

The superlative has a feminine form فُعْلَى *fuɛlā*, e.g.

اَلْحَرْبُ ٱلْكُبْرَى   *al-ḥarbu ∩l-kubrā*, the Great(est) War.

مِصْرُ ٱلْعُلْيَا   *Miṣru ∩l-ɛulyā*, Upper (Highest) Egypt.

Note that ...ى ...ā (أَلِفٌ مَقْصُورَةٌ *'alif maqṣūra*) following a 'y' is generally written ا..., as it always is when followed by a suffix.

أَفْعَلُ *'afɛalu*, when superlative, either takes the sound plural ending or, more usually, forms a broken plural, e.g.

أَكَابِرُ ٱلْقَوْمِ   *'akābiru ∩l-qawmi*, the greatest (men) of the nation.

حُسْنَيَاتُ ٱلسَّيِّدَاتِ   *ḥusnayātu ∩l-sayyidāti*, the most beautiful (of the) ladies.

Note especially the very common superlative construction:

أَكْرَمُ رَجُلٍ   *'akramu rajulin*, <u>the</u> most generous man.

أَذْكَى وَلَدٍ   *'adhkā waladin*, <u>the</u> most intelligent boy (comp. adj. from ذَكِيٌّ *dhakīyun* intelligent).

هُوَ مِنْ أَغْنَى ٱلنَّاسِ   *huwa min 'aghnā ∩l-nāsi*, he is one of the richest men.

26. Compound Adjectives

The Arabic language is very rich in compound adjectives, examples of which are the following:

قَلِيلُ ٱلْعَقْلِ *qalīlu ᵔl-ʿaqli*, little of intelligence, stupid.

كَثِيرُ ٱلْمَالِ *kathīru ᵔl-māli*, much of wealth, rich.

طَوِيلُ ٱللِّسَانِ *ṭawīlu ᵔl-lisāni*, long of the tongue, impertinent.

Such adjectives are indefinite and when qualifying a definite noun must have the article, e.g.

اَلرَّجُلُ ٱلْكَثِيرُ ٱلْمَالِ *al-rajulu ᵔl-kathīru ᵔl-māli*, the rich man.

اَلْإِمْرَأَةُ ٱلطَّوِيلَةُ ٱللِّسَانِ *aliᵔmra'atu ᵔl-ṭawīlatu ᵔl-lisāni*, the impertinent woman.

The nouns صَاحِبٌ *ṣāḥibun*, a companion, master, إِبْنٌ *ibnun*, a son, أَبٌ *'abun*, a father, أُمٌّ *'ummun*, a mother, أَخٌ *'akhun*, a brother and ...ذُو *dhū*... the possessor of... plus nouns denoting qualities or properties are very frequently used to form compound adjectives, e.g.

صَاحِبُ عِلْمٍ *ṣāḥibu ʿilmin*, master of learning, learned.

إِبْنُ حَرَامٍ *ibnu ḥarāmin*, the son of what is forbidden, a bastard.

أَبُو لِحْيَةٍ *'abū liḥyatin*, the father of a beard, bearded.

أَخُو ثِقَةٍ *'akhū thiqatin*, the brother of trust, trustworthy.

ذُو لُبٍّ *dhū lubbin*, the possessor of a heart (i.e. of intelligence, the heart being, according to the ancient Arabs, the seat of the intellect), intelligent.

The word ...ذُو *dhū*... (acc. ...ذَا *dhā*..., gen. ...ذِي *dhī*...) has as its feminine ذَاتٌ *dhātun* which also has an independent existence with the meaning of self or person.

Their duals are:

masc. ...ذَوَا *dhawā*... (nom.),

...ذَوَيْ *dhaway*... (acc. and gen.).

fem. ذَوَاتَا... *dhawatātā*... (nom.)

ذَوَاتَيْ... *dhawātay*... (acc. and gen.)

Their plurals are:

masc. ذَوُو... *dhawū*... (nom.),

ذَوِي... *dhawī*... (acc. and gen.).

fem. ذَوَاتُ... *dhawātu*... (nom.),

ذَوَاتِ... *dhawāti*... (acc. and gen.).

Lastly the opposite of simple adjectives may be formed by prefixing the pronoun غَيْرٌ *ghayrun*, someone other, something other, e.g.

غَيْرُ شَرِيفٍ *ghayru sharīfin*, other than noble, ignoble.

غَيْرُ مُمْكِنٍ *ghayru mumkinin*, other than possible, impossible.

Examples:

أُخْتُ ٱلتَّاجِرِ جَالِسَةٌ عَلَى كُرْسِيٍّ خَشَبٍ

'ukhtu ⌒l-tājiri jālisatun ع alā kursīyi khashabin,
The merchant's sister is sitting on a wooden chair.

أَخُو عُمَرَ أَجْهَلُ وَلَدٍ فِي ٱلْمَدْرَسَةِ

'akhū ع umara 'ajhalu waladin fi ⌒l-madrasati,
Omar's brother is the most ignorant boy in the school.

اَلرَّجُلُ ٱلْكَسْلَانُ ذُو هُمُومٍ كَثِيرَةٍ

al-rajulu ⌒l-kaslānu dhū humūmin (sing. هَمٌّ *hammun*) *kathīratin,*
The lazy man is the possessor of (has) many cares.

هَلِ ٱلْكِتَابُ ٱلْأَحْمَرُ عَلَى ٱلْمَائِدَةِ ٱلْخَضْرَاءِ؟

hali ⌒l-kitābu ⌒l-'aḥmaru ع alā ⌒l-mā'idati ⌒l-khaḍrā'i?
Is the red book on the green table?

لَا، هُوَ فِي ٱلدُّرْجِ ٱلْأَكْبَرِ تَحْتَ كُتُبِ فَاطِمَةَ

lā, huwa fi ⌒l-durji ⌒l-'akbari taḥta kutubi Fāṭimata,
No, it is in the largest drawer under Fatima's books.

هِيَ ذَاتُ عَيْنَيْنِ زَرْقَاوَيْنِ جَمِيلَتَيْنِ

hiya dhātu ʿaynayni ȥarqāwayni jamīlatayni,
She is the possessor of (has) two beautiful blue eyes.

قَلَمُ ٱلْمُدَرِّسِ أَطْوَلُ مِنْ قَلَمِ ٱلتِّلْمِيذِ

qalamu ⁀l-mudarrisi ʾaṭwalu min qalami ⁀l-tilmīdhi,
The teacher's pen is longer than the pupil's.

اَلتَّلَامِذَةُ ٱلْكِبَارُ قَاعِدُونَ عَلَى ٱلْأَرْضِ أَمَامَ ٱلشَّيْخِ

al-talāmidhatu ⁀l-kibāru qāʿidūna ʿalā ⁀l-ʾarḍi ʾamāma ⁀l-shaykhi,
The big pupils are sitting on the ground before the shaykh.

اَلسَّفَرُ وَقْتَ ٱلْحَرْبِ غَيْرُ مُمْكِنٍ

al-safaru waqta ⁀l-ḥarbi (acc. of time) *ghayru mumkinin,*
Travel in time of war is impossible.

اَلتُّفَّاحُ أَلَذُّ مِنَ ٱلْبُرْتُقَالِ

al-tuffāḥu ʾaladhdhu mina ⁀l-burtuqāli,
Apples are more delicious than oranges.

اَلْوَلَدُ ٱلطَّوِيلُ ٱللِّسَانِ غَيْرُ مَحْبُوبٍ

al-waladu ⁀l-ṭawīlu ⁀l-lisāni ghayru maḥbūbin,
The impertinent boy is not liked.

Supplementary Vocabulary

غُرْفَةٌ *ghurfatun*, a room.

جَامِعَةٌ *jāmiʿatun*, an university.

صَوَابٌ *ṣawābun* (noun), what is right.

أَمْرِيكَا (أَمِيرِكَا) *ʾAmrīkā* (*ʾAmērikā*), America.

مَعَ *maʿa*, with.

زَوْجٌ *ȥawjun*, a spouse.

Exercise VI

أَبْنَاءُ ٱلتُّجَّارِ أَكَّالُونَ. اَلْأَوْلَادُ ٱلْأَغْبِيَاءُ غَيْرُ مَحْبُوبِينَ. اَلْأَمِيرَةُ مَسْرُورَةٌ بِهَدِيَّةِ ٱلْوَزِيرِ. مَرَاسِيمُ ٱلْمَلِكِ مُحْتَرَمَةٌ. حَمُو عَلِيٍّ رَجُلٌ كَسْلَانُ. تَلَامِذَةُ ٱلْمَدْرَسَةِ مُجْتَهِدُونَ. اَلسَّفَرُ إِلَى أَمْرِيكَا غَيْرُ مُمْكِنٍ. أَيْنَ ٱلْمَائِدَةُ ٱلْحَمْرَاءُ؟ هِيَ فِي غُرْفَةِ ٱلنَّوْمِ. اَلشَّيْخُ أَعْلَمُ مِنَ ٱلْكَاتِبِ. اَلْبَنَاتُ أَجْمَلُ مِنَ ٱلْأَوْلَادِ. اَلتُّجَّارُ ٱلْأَغْنِيَاءُ أَسْعَدُ مِنَ ٱلْفَلَّاحِينَ ٱلْفُقَرَاءِ. هُوَ أَعْلَمُ أُسْتَاذٍ فِي ٱلْجَامِعَةِ. أَسْيُوطُ مَدِينَةٌ فِي مِصْرَ ٱلْعُلْيَا. اَللّٰهُ أَعْلَمُ بِٱلصَّوَابِ. هُوَ ذُو عَيْنَيْنِ سَوْدَاوَيْنِ. أَيْنَ زَوْجَةُ ٱلْأُسْتَاذِ؟ هِيَ فِي ٱلْمَطْبَخِ مَعَ ٱلطَّبَّاخَةِ ٱلسَّوْدَاءِ. أَنْتُمْ طِوَالُ ٱللِّسَانِ. زَوْجُ ٱلْأَمِيرَةِ ٱلْمَشْهُورَةِ أَغْنَى رَجُلٍ فِي ٱلْبِلَادِ.

Transliteration

'abnā'u ⌢l-tujjāri 'akkālūna. al-'awlādu ⌢l-aghbiyā'u ghayru maḥbūbīna. al-'amīratu masrūratun bihadīyati ⌢l-wazīri. marāsīmu ⌢l-maliki muḥtaramatun. ḥamū عalīyin rajulun kaslānu. talāmidhatu ⌢l-madrasati mujtahidūna. al-safaru 'ilā 'Amrīkā ghayru mumkinin. 'ayna ⌢l-mā'idatu ⌢l-ḥamrā'u? hiya fī ghurfati ⌢l-nawmi. al-shaykhu 'aعlamu mina ⌢l-kātibi. al-banātu 'ajmalu mina ⌢l-'awlādi. al-tujjāru ⌢l-'aghniyā'u 'asعadu mina ⌢l-fallāḥīna ⌢l-fuqarā'i. huwa 'aعlamu 'ustādhin fī ⌢l-jāmiعati. 'Asyūṭu madīnatun fī Miṣra ⌢l-عulyā. Allāhu 'aعlamu bi⌢l-ṣawābi. huwa dhū عaynayni sawdāwayni. 'ayna zawjatu ⌢l-'ustādhi? hiya fī ⌢l-maṭbakhi maعa ⌢l-ṭabbākhati ⌢l-sawdā'i. 'antum ṭiwālu ⌢l-lisāni. zawju ⌢l-'amīrati ⌢l-mashhūrati 'aghnā rajulin fī ⌢l-bilādi.

Translation

The merchants' sons are gluttons. (The) stupid boys are not loved. The princess is pleased with the minister's present. The decrees of the king are respected. Ali's father-in-law is a lazy man. The pupils of the school are industrious. The journey to America is not possible (i.e. it is not possible to journey to America). Where is the red table? It is in the bed-room (lit. the room of sleep). The shaykh is more learned than the clerk. The girls are more beautiful than the boys. The rich merchants are happier than the poor peasants. He is the most learned professor in the university. Asyut is a town in Upper Egypt. God is the best knower of what is right. He has black eyes. Where is the professor's wife? She is in the kitchen with the negro cook. You (pl.) are impertinent. The husband of the famous princess is the richest man in the country.

LESSON VII

27. Pronominal Suffixes

Having noted the nominative of the personal pronouns in Lessons I and III we now come to their oblique cases, accusative and genitive. These are suffixes added to the verb in the case of the accusative and to a noun or preposition in the case of the genitive. They are identical in both cases with the exception of the 1st person singular. They are:

1st person sing. acc. نِي *nī*, gen. ـِي... *ī* (usually ـِيَ... *iya*, before هَمْزَةُ ٱلْوَصْلِ *hamzat-al-waṣl*).

2nd person sing. masc. acc. and gen. كَ *ka*.

2nd person sing. fem. acc. and gen. كِ *ki*.

3rd person sing. masc. acc. and gen. هُ *hu*.

3rd person sing. fem. acc. and gen. هَا *hā*.

1st person plur. acc. and gen. نَا *nā*.

2nd person plur. masc. acc. and gen. كُمْ *kum*.

2nd person plur. fem. acc. and gen. كُنَّ *kunna*.

2nd person dual masc. and fem. acc. and gen. كُمَا *kumā*.

3rd person plur. masc. acc. and gen. هُمْ *hum*.

3rd person plur. fem. acc. and gen. هُنَّ *hunna*.

3rd person dual masc. and fem. acc. and gen. هُمَا *humā*.

If we add these pronominal suffixes to the simple verb ضَرَبَ *ḍaraba*, he struck, we have:

ضَرَبَنِي *ḍárabanī*, he struck me.

ضَرَبَكَ *ḍárąbaka*, he struck you (masc. sing.).

ضَرَبَكِ *ḍárabaki*, he struck you (fem. sing.).

ضَرَبَهُ *ḍárabahu*, he struck him (it).

ضَرَبَهَا *ḍárabahā*, he struck her (it).

ضَرَبَنَا *ḍárabanā*, he struck us.

ضَرَبَكُمْ *ḍárabakum*, he struck you (masc. pl.).

ضَرَبَكُنَّ *ḍarabakúnna*, he struck you (fem. pl.)

ضَرَبَكُمَا *ḍárabakumā*, he struck you (masc. and fem. dual).

ضَرَبَهُمْ *ḍárabahum*, he struck them (masc. pl.).

ضَرَبَهُنَّ *ḍarabahúnna*, he struck them (fem. pl.).

ضَرَبَهُمَا *ḍárabahumā*, he struck them (masc. and fem. dual).

Note the shift of the accent as the pronominal suffixes are considered an integral part of the word (see Introduction § 8).

If we add the pronominal suffixes to a noun we have:

كِتَابِي *kitábī* (all three cases), my book (the book of me!).

كِتَابُكَ *kitábuka*, (nom.) your book.

كِتَابُكِ *kitábuki*, (nom.) your book.

كِتَابُهُ *kitábuhu*, (nom.) his book.

كِتَابُهَا *kitábuhā*, (nom.) her book.

كِتَابُنَا *kitábunā*, (nom.) our book.

كِتَابُكُمْ *kitábukum*, (nom.) your book.

كِتَابُكُنَّ *kitābukúnna*, (nom.) your book.

كِتَابُكُمَا *kitábukumā*, (nom.) your book.

كِتَابُهُمْ *kitábuhum*, (nom.) their book.

كِتَابُهُنَّ *kitābuhúnna*, (nom.) their book.

كِتَابُهُمَا *kitábuhumā*, (nom.) their book.

The suffixes هُ *hu*, هُمْ *hum*, هُنَّ *hunna* and هُمَا *humā*, change their 'u' to 'i' if they are *immediately* preceded by 'i', 'ī' or the diphthong 'ay', e.g.

فِي كِتَابِهِ *fī kitābihi*, in his book.   فِيهِمْ *fīhim*, in them.

فِي بُيُوتِهِنَّ *fī buyūtihinna*, in their houses.

فِي قَصْرَيْهِمَا *fī qaṣrayhimā*, in their two palaces.

But note مِنْهُ *minhu*, from him, as هُ *hu* is not immediately preceded by 'i'.

The ending ةٌ... *atun* changes into an ordinary ت *t* when followed by one of the pronominal suffixes, e.g.

لِمُدَرِّسَتِهِ *limudarrisatihi*, to his (fem.) teacher.

The nouns أَبٌ *'abun*, a father, أَخٌ *'akhun*, a brother and حَمٌ *ḥamun*, a father-in-law, take their lengthened forms noted in Lesson V when followed by a pronominal suffix with the exception of the 1st person singular, e.g.

أَبُوهُ *'abūhu*, his father (nom.).

أَخَاكَ *'akhāka*, your brother (acc.).

حَمِيهَا *ḥamīhā*, (of) her father-in-law (gen.).

but أَبِي *'abī*, my father, أَخِي *'akhī*, my brother and حَمِي *ḥamī*, my father-in-law (all three cases).

If the 1st person singular pronominal suffix ـِي... *ī* is preceded by a long vowel or the diphthong ـَيْ... *ay* it becomes يَ *ya* and *not* ـِي... *ī*, e.g.

يَدَايَ *yadāya*, my (two) hands (nom.).

بَيْنَ يَدَيَّ *bayna yadayya*, between my hands = in front of me.

Note especially مُعَلِّمِيَّ *muɛallimīya*, my teachers (all three cases). Contrary to what one would expect the nominative is not مُعَلِّمُويَ *muɛallimūya* owing to the Arabs' dislike of the combination of '*u*' and '*y*'.

Those prepositions which end with ـَى... *ā* (أَلِفٌ مَقْصُورَةٌ *'alif maqṣūra*) change it to the diphthong ـَيْ... *ay* when followed by a pronominal suffix, e.g.

عَلَيَّ *ɛalayya*, on me.

إِلَيْنَا *'ilaynā*, to(wards) us.

لَدَيْهِمْ *ladayhim*, with them (chez eux).

It is also important to note that when a suffix is added to the preposition لِ *li*, to, for, it changes to لَ *la*, e.g.

لِي *lī*, to, for me

but لَكَ *laka*, to, for you.

لَهُ *lahu*, to, for him.

28. 'To have'

The Arabs have no exact equivalent of the English verb 'to have', the nearest approach to it being the verb مَلَكَ *malaka*, he possessed.

'To have' is, however, more commonly expressed by one of the prepositions لِ *li*, to, عِنْدَ *ɛinda* or لَدَى *ladā*, with (chez) or مَعَ *maɛa*, with, in the company of, followed by the pronominal suffixes, e.g.

لِي قَلَمٌ *lī qalamun*, I have a pen (mihi est calamus).

لَهُ ٱلْحَقُّ *lahu ͡l-ḥaqqu*, he has the right, is right.

عِنْدَنَا كُتُبٌ حَمْرَاءُ كَثِيرَةٌ *عindanā kutubun ḥamrāʾu ka<u>th</u>īratun*, we have many red books.

مَعَهَا سَاعَةُ ذَهَبٍ *maعahā sāعatu <u>dh</u>ahabin*, she has a gold watch (with her now).

Examples:

هَلْ هُمْ فِي بُيُوتِهِمْ؟

hal hum fī buyūtihim?

Are they in their houses?

نَعَمْ، وَأَصْحَابُهُمْ مَعَهُمْ

naعam, wa'aṣḥābuhum maعahum,

Yes, and their friends are with them.

اَلْبَنَاتُ لَهُنَّ شُغْلٌ كَثِيرٌ

al-banātu lahunna <u>sh</u>ug<u>h</u>lun ka<u>th</u>īrun,

The girls have much work.

هَلْ مَعَكَ كِبْرِيتٌ؟

hal maعaka kibrītun?

Have you matches (lit. sulphur)?

نَعَمْ، هُوَ فِي جَيْبِي

naعam, huwa fī jaybī,

Yes, they are (lit. it is) in my pocket.

أَبِي رَجُلٌ مُحْتَرَمٌ، هُوَ أَكْبَرُ مِنْ أَبِي مُحَمَّدٍ

'abī rajulun muḥtaramun. Huwa 'akbaru min 'abī Muḥammadin,

My father is an honoured man. He is older than Mohammed's father.

يَدَاهَا نَاعِمَتَانِ لِلْغَايَةِ

yadāhā nāعimatāni li‿l-<u>gh</u>āyati,

Her hands are exceedingly soft (lit. soft to the limit).

أَخُونَا رَئِيسُ مَكْتَبِهِ

'a<u>kh</u>ūnā ra'īsu maktabihi,

Our brother is the head of his office.

هَلْ أَنْتُمْ قَاعِدُونَ بِلَا شُغْلٍ؟

hal 'antum qāعidūna bilā shughlin?

Are you sitting idle (lit. without work)?

لَا، نَحْنُ مَشْغُولُونَ بِكِتَابَةِ دَرْسِنَا

lā, naḥnu mashghūlūna bikitābati darsinā,

No, we are busy writing our lesson (lit. occupied with the writing of our lesson).

Supplementary Vocabulary

عَمٌّ *عammun*, a (paternal) uncle.

وَاجِبٌ *wājibun*, a duty, incumbent.

اِعْتِنَاءٌ بِ *iعtinā'un*, (paying) attention, (taking) care.

دَرْسٌ *darsun* (pl. دُرُوسٌ *durūsun*), a lesson.

وَسِخٌ *wasikhun*, dirty.

Exercise VII

بَيْتِي أَكْبَرُ مِنْ بَيْتِكَ. لَهُ غُرْفَتَانِ فِي بَيْتِ عَمَّتِهِ. يَدَاهَا بَيْضَاوَانِ وَشَعْرُهَا
أَسْوَدُ. أَيْنَ مُحَمَّدٌ ٱلْيَوْمَ؟ هُوَ فِي ٱلْمَحْكَمَةِ مَعَ أَبِيهِ. مُعَلِّمِيَّ (مُدَرِّسِيَّ) عُلَمَاءُ
مَشْهُورُونَ. مَدْرَسَتُنَا أَجَدُّ مِنْ مَدْرَسَتِكُمْ. لِأَصْحَابِهِمْ بَيْتٌ كَبِيرٌ فِي مَدِينَةِ
ٱلْقَاهِرَةِ. أُخْتُهُ ٱلصَّغِيرَةُ نَعْسَى. اَلْاِعْتِنَاءُ بِدُرُوسِنَا وَاجِبٌ عَلَيْنَا. أَقْلَامُهُمْ زَرْقَاءُ
وَأَقْلَامُكُمْ خَضْرَاءُ. أَخِي تَاجِرٌ غَنِيٌّ فِي بَارِيسَ. لِأَمِيرِنَا قَصْرٌ جَمِيلٌ عَلَى جَبَلٍ.
ثَوْبُكَ أَوْسَخُ مِنْ ثَوْبِ أَبِيكَ. لِلنَّاسِ ٱلْفُقَرَاءِ بُيُوتٌ تَحْتَ ٱلْأَرْضِ.

Transliteration

baytī 'akbaru min baytika. lahu ghurfatāni fī bayti عammatihi. yadāhā bayḍāwāni washaعruhā 'aswadu. 'ayna Muḥammaduni ◠l-yawma? huwa fī ◠l-maḥkamati maعa 'abīhi. muعallimīya (mudarrisīya) عulamā'u mashhūrūna. madrasatunā 'ajaddu min madrasatikum. li'aṣḥābihim baytun kabīrun fī madīnati ˀl-Qāhirati. 'ukhtuhu ˀl-ṣaghīratu naʿsā. aliʿ tinā'u bidurūsinā wājibun ʿalaynā. 'aqlāmuhum zarqā'u wa'aqlāmukum khaḍrā'u. 'akhī tājirun ghanīyun fī Bārīsa. li'amīrinā qaṣrun jamīlun ʿalā jabalin. thawbuki 'awsakhu min thawbi 'abīki. liˀl-nāsi ˀl-fuqarā'i buyūtun taḥta ˀl-'arḍi.

Translation

My house is bigger than yours (your house). He has two rooms in his (paternal) aunt's house. Her hands are white and her hair is black. Where is Mohammed to-day? He is in the law-court with his father. My teachers are famous scholars. Our school is newer than your school. Their friends have a large house in the city of Cairo. His little sister is sleepy. It is our duty to pay attention to our lessons. Their pens are blue and yours are green. My brother is a rich merchant in Paris. Our prince has a beautiful palace on a mountain. Your (fem.) garment is dirtier than your father's. The poor people have houses underground.

LESSON VIII

29. The Perfect of a Simple Verb

As stated in the introductory note to Lesson IV in the Arabic language the root of an idea is nearly always a simple verb. There being no infinitive we find a root idea and its derivatives arranged in the dictionary under the heading of the 3rd person masculine singular of a simple verb.

This may consist of three or four radicals, their simple patterns being فَعَلَ *faʿala*, فَعُلَ *faʿula* or فَعِلَ *faʿila* and فَعْلَلَ *faʿlala*. The vast majority of Arabic verbs have three radicals.

It should be noted that a verb of the pattern فَعُلَ *faʿula always* indicates a permanent quality, e.g. قَبُحَ *qabuḥa*, he was ugly, wicked, and a verb of the pattern فَعِلَ *faʿila* a temporary or passing state or action.

There are two tenses only, the perfect, denoting an action which at the time indicated was complete and finished, and the imperfect, denoting an action which is or was incomplete at a stated or implied time.

The perfect of the simple verb is conjugated according to the following paradigm:

1st person sing.	فَعَلْتُ	*faʿá(u)(i)ltu.*
2nd person sing. masc.	فَعَلْتَ	*faʿálta.*

2nd person sing. fem.	فَعَلْتِ	*faعálti.*
3rd person sing. masc.	فَعَلَ	*fáعala.*
3rd person sing. fem.	فَعَلَتْ	*fáعalat.*
1st person plur.	فَعَلْنَا	*faعálnā.*
2nd person plur. masc.	فَعَلْتُمْ	*faعáltum.*
2nd person plur. fem.	فَعَلْتُنَّ	*faعaltúnna.*
2nd person dual masc. and fem.	فَعَلْتُمَا	*faعáltumā.*
3rd person plur. masc.	فَعَلُوا	*fáعalū.*
3rd person plur. fem.	فَعَلْنَ	*faعálna.*
3rd person dual masc.	فَعَلَا	*fáعalā,*
3rd person dual fem.	فَعَلَتَا	*fáعalatā.*

Note the extra *'alif* with which the 3rd person plur. masc. ends and that the 3rd person duals are formed by merely adding an *'alif* to the 3rd person sing. masc. and fem.

According to the above paradigm the simple verb ضَرَبَ *ḍaraba*, he struck, is conjugated as follows:

ضَرَبْتُ	*ḍarabtu*, I struck or have struck.
ضَرَبْتَ	*ḍarabta*, you (masc.) struck.
ضَرَبْتِ	*ḍarabti*, you (fem.) struck.
ضَرَبَ	*ḍaraba*, he struck.
ضَرَبَتْ	*ḍarabat*, she struck.
ضَرَبْنَا	*ḍarabnā*, we struck.
ضَرَبْتُمْ	*ḍarabtum*, you (masc.) struck.
ضَرَبْتُنَّ	*ḍarabtunna*, you (fem.) struck.

ضَرَبْتُمَا *ḍarabtumā*, you (masc. and fem. dual) struck.

ضَرَبُوا *ḍarabū*, they (masc.) struck.

ضَرَبْنَ *ḍarabna*, they (fem.) struck.

ضَرَبَا *ḍarabā*, they (masc. dual) struck.

ضَرَبَتَا *ḍarabatā*, they (fem. dual) struck.

A four-radical such as تَرْجَمَ *tarjama*, he translated, is conjugated in the perfect tense in exactly the same way, e.g.

تَرْجَمْتُ *tarjamtu*, I translated.

تَرْجَمْتَ *tarjamta*, you translated, etc.

If one wishes to emphasize that the action is complete one may prefix the particle قَدْ *qad* or لَقَدْ *laqad* to the perfect, e.g.

قَدْ كَتَبْتُ *qad katabtu*, I have written.

لَقَدْ ذَهَبُوا *laqad dhahabū*, They have gone.

The perfect is negated by prefixing مَا *mā*, e.g.

مَا كَتَبْنَا *mā katabnā*, We did not write.

مَا حَسُنَ فِعْلُهُ *mā ḥasuna fiعluhu*, His action was not good.

مَا سَمِعُوا *mā samiعū*, They did not hear.

The pronominal suffixes given in the previous lesson are suffixed to the verb as objects and when this happens the following small changes are to be noted:

(i) The 3rd person plur. masc. loses its *'alif*, e.g.

ضَرَبُونِي *ḍarabūnī*, They struck me.

سَمِعُوهَا *samiعūhā*, They heard her.

(ii) The 2nd person plur. masc. فَعَلْتُمْ *faɛaltum* becomes فَعَلْتُمُو *faɛaltumū*, e.g.

كَتَبْتُمُوهُ *katabtumūhu*, you (masc. pl.) wrote it.

تَرْجَمْتُمُوهَا *tarjamtumūhā*, you translated them.

(Note هَا *hā* (fem. sing.), since 'them' presumably refers to something inanimate or abstract.)

30. Word Order

The most approved word order in grammatical Arabic is verb+subject +object, e.g.

كَتَبَ ٱلْمُعَلِّمُ ٱلدَّرْسَ عَلَى ٱلسَّبُّورَةِ

kataba ⌒l-muɛallimu ⌒l-darsa ɛalā ⌒l-sabbūrati,

The teacher wrote the lesson on the blackboard,

but one very often finds the subject put first, e.g.

ٱلْخَبَّازُ خَبَزَ ٱلْخُبْزَ فِي ٱلْفُرْنِ

al-khabbāzu khabaza ⌒l-khubza fī ⌒l-furni,

The baker baked the bread in the oven.

Now, if the verb is placed first in the sentence it *must always be in the singular* even though the subject may be plural or dual, e.g.

سَرَقَ ٱللُّصُوصُ مَالَ ٱلتَّاجِرِ

saraqa ⌒l-luṣūṣu māla ⌒l-tājiri (sing. لِصٌّ *liṣṣun*),

The robbers stole the merchant's property.

ذَهَبَ ٱلرَّجُلَانِ إِلَى ٱلسُّوقِ

dhahaba ⌒l-rajulāni 'ilā ⌒l-sūqi,

The two men went to the market.

غَسَلَتِ ٱلْبَنَاتُ ثِيَابَهُنَّ

ghasalati ⌒l-banātu thiyābahunna (sing. ثَوْبٌ *thawbun*),

The girls washed their clothes.

سَمِعَتِ ٱلِٱمْرَأَتَانِ ٱلصَّدَى

samiᶜati ⁀li⁀mra'atāni ⁀l-ṣadā,
The two women heard the echo.

But if the subject *precedes* the verb then the verb *must agree in number* as well as in gender, e.g.

اَللُّصُوصُ سَرَقُوا مَالَ ٱلتَّاجِرِ

al-luṣūṣu saraqū māla ⁀l-tājiri.

اَلرَّجُلَانِ ذَهَبَا إِلَى ٱلسُّوقِ

al-rajulāni dhahabā 'ilā ⁀l-sūqi.

اَلْبَنَاتُ غَسَلْنَ ثِيَابَهُنَّ

al-banātu ghasalna thiyābahunna.

اَلِٱمْرَأَتَانِ سَمِعَتَا ٱلصَّدَى

ali⁀mra'atāni samiᶜatā ⁀l-ṣadā.

(Note that إِمْرَأَةٌ *imra'atun*, a women, begins with هَمْزَةُ ٱلْوَصْلِ *hamzat-al-waṣl.*)

If the subject is a collective the verb may be either masculine or feminine singular according to whether we think of the collective as a singular (i.e. a group) or as a plural of irrational beings, e.g.

نَزَلَ or نَزَلَتِ ٱلْحَمَامُ عَلَى ٱلسَّطْحِ

nazala (nazalati) ⁀l-ḥamāmu ᶜalā ⁀l-saṭḥi,
The pigeons alighted on the roof.

The masculine is, however, preferred by stylists.

31. The Passive of the Perfect

The passive of the perfect is formed according to the patterns فُعِلَ *fuᶜila* and فُعْلِلَ *fuᶜlila*, e.g.

كُتِبَ *kutiba*, It was written,
تُرْجِمَ *turjima*, It was translated,

and conjugated in exactly the same manner as the active given above.

If the agent is mentioned in the sentence one *cannot use the passive.* Therefore a sentence such as 'this book was written by Dickens' must be turned to read 'Dickens wrote this book'.

Examples:

رَجَعْتُ مِنَ ٱلصَّيْدِ بِلَا شَيْءٍ

rajaعtu mina ⌒l-ṣaydi bilā s͟hay'in,

I came back from the hunt empty-handed (lit. without a thing).

هَلْ ذَهَبْتَ مَعَ أَخِيكَ إِلَى ٱلْجِبَالِ؟

hal d͟hahabta maعa 'ak͟hīka 'ilā ⌒l-jibāli?

Did you go to the mountains with your brother?

لَا، بَعَثَ لَنَا أَبُونَا خِطَابًا بِقُدُومِهِ

lā, baعat͟ha lanā 'abūnā k͟hiṭāban biqudūmihi,

No, our father sent us a letter announcing (lit. with) his arrival.

شَرِبَتِ ٱلْبَنَاتُ ٱلشَّايَ ثُمَّ غَسَلْنَ ٱلْفَنَاجِينَ

s͟haribati ⌒l-banātu ⌒l-s͟hāya t͟humma g͟hasalna ⌒l-fanājīna,

The girls drank (the) tea then they washed the cups.

لَقَدْ سَمِعْنَا ذٰلِكَ عِدَّةَ مَرَّاتٍ

laqad samiعnā d͟hālika عiddata marrātin,

We have heard that a number of times.

هَلْ تُرْجِمَ ٱلْكِتَابُ إِلَى ٱللُّغَةِ ٱلْإِنْكِلِيزِيَّةِ؟

hal turjima ⌒l-kitābu 'ilā ⌒l-lug͟hati ⌒l-'ingilīzīyati?

Has the book been translated into the English language?

أَقَدِمْتُنَّ قَبْلَ ٱلظُّهْرِ؟

'aqadimtunna qabla ⌒l-ẓuhri?

Did you (fem.) arrive before noon?

لَا، مَا قَدِمْنَا إِلَّا بَعْدَ ٱلظُّهْرِ بِسَاعَتَيْنِ

lā, mā qadimnā 'illā baعda ⌒l-ẓuhri bisāعatayni,

No, we only arrived (by) two hours after noon.

(Note إِلَّا.....مَا *mā.....'illā,* not.....except, only. Cf. French ne.....que.)

SUPPLEMENTARY VOCABULARY

طَائِرَةٌ *ṭā'iratun* (pl. طَائِرَاتٌ *ṭā'irātun*), an aircraft.

سَرِيعٌ *sarīʿun*, swift.

هَوَاءٌ *hawā'un*, air.

قِطَارٌ *qiṭārun* (pl. قُطُرٌ *quṭurun*), a train.

مَتَى؟ *mátā?* when?

كَسَرَ *kasara*, he broke.

مَنْ؟ *man?* who?

قَمِيصٌ *qamīṣun* (pl. قُمْصَانٌ *qumṣānun*), a shirt.

كَلْبٌ *kalbun* (pl. كِلَابٌ *kilābun*), a dog.

أَيْضًا *'ayḍan*, also, too.

مَكْتَبَةٌ *maktabatun* (pl. مَكْتَبَاتٌ *maktabātun*), a library, bookshop.

EXERCISE VIII

نَزَلَتِ ٱلطَّائِرَةُ عَلَى ٱلْأَرْضِ بَعْدَ سَاعَةٍ فِي ٱلْهَوَاءِ. أَذَهَبَتِ ٱلْخَادِمَةُ إِلَى ٱلسُّوقِ؟ نَعَمْ، ذَهَبَتْ إِلَى ٱلسُّوقِ مَعَ صَدِيقَتِهَا. مَتَى رَجَعَتَا؟ رَجَعَتَا بَعْدَ ٱلظُّهْرِ. شَرِبَ ٱلرِّجَالُ قَهْوَتَهُمْ ثُمَّ ذَهَبُوا إِلَى ٱلصَّيْدِ. بَعَثَتْ أُمُّنَا خِطَابًا طَوِيلًا لِأَبِينَا فِي أَمْرِيكَا. مَنْ ضَرَبَ كَلْبِي؟ ضَرَبَهُ أَبُو ٱلْبِنْتِ. هَلْ ذَهَبْتُمَا إِلَى بَارِيسَ بِٱلطَّائِرَةِ؟ لَا، ذَهَبْنَا بِٱلْقِطَارِ. اَلطَّائِرَةُ أَسْرَعُ مِنَ ٱلْقِطَارِ. مَا سَمِعْنَا ذٰلِكَ أَكْثَرَ مِنْ مَرَّةٍ. مَنْ غَسَلَ قَمِيصِي؟ غَسَلَتْهُ ٱلْغَسَّالَةُ مَعَ قُمْصَانِ أَخِيكَ. مَتَى تُرْجِمَتِ ٱلْكُتُبُ إِلَى ٱللُّغَةِ ٱلْعَرَبِيَّةِ؟ تُرْجِمَتْ مِنْ (مُنْذُ) زَمَانٍ. بَعَثَتِ ٱلْمُدَرِّسَاتُ كُتُبَهُنَّ إِلَى مَكْتَبَةِ ٱلْجَامِعَةِ. هَلْ كَسَرَتِ ٱلْخَادِمَةُ ٱلسَّاعَةَ؟ نَعَمْ، وَسَرَقَتْ أَشْيَاءَ كَثِيرَةً أَيْضًا.

TRANSLITERATION

nazalati ⌒l-ṭā'iratu ʿalā ⌒l-'arḍi baʿda sāʿatin fī ⌒l-hawā'i. 'adhahabati ⌒l-khādimatu 'ilā ⌒l-sūqi? naʿam, dhahabat 'ilā ⌒l-sūqi maʿa ṣadīqatihā. mátā rajaʿatā? rajaʿatā baʿda ⌒l-ẓuhri. shariba ⌒l-rijālu qahwatahum thumma dhahabū 'ilā ⌒l-ṣaydi. baʿathat 'ummunā khiṭāban ṭawīlan li'abīnā fī 'Amrīkā. man ḍaraba kalbī? ḍarabahu 'abū ⌒l-binti. hal dhahabtumā 'ilā Bārīsa bi⌒l-ṭā'irati? lā, dhahabnā bi⌒l-qiṭāri. al-

ṭā'iratu 'asraʿu mina ʼl-qiṭāri. mā samiʿnā dh̲ālika 'akth̲ara (adv. acc.) *min marratin. man gh̲asala qamīṣī? gh̲asalat-hu ʼl-gh̲assālatu maʿa qumṣāni 'akh̲īka. matā turjimati ʼl-kutubu 'ilā ʼl-lugh̲ati ʼl-ʿarabīyati? turjimat min (mundh̲u) zamānin. baʿathati ʼl-mudarrisātu kutubahunna 'ilā maktabati ʼl-jāmiʿati. hal kasarati ʼl-kh̲ādimatu ʼl-sāʿata? naʿam, wasaraqat 'ash̲yā'a kath̲īratan 'ayḍan.*

Translation

The aircraft landed (lit. descended on the ground) after an hour in the air. Did the servant go to the market? Yes, she went to the market with her friend. When did they return? They returned in the afternoon. The men drank their coffee then went to the hunt. Our mother sent a long letter to our father in America. Who beat my dog? The girl's father beat him. Did you (two) go to Paris by air? No, we went by train. The aircraft is quicker than the train. We did not hear that more than once. Who washed my shirt? The washerwoman washed it along with your brother's shirts. When were the books translated into Arabic. They were translated a long time ago (lit. since a time). The (fem.) teachers sent their books to the university library. Did the servant break the clock? Yes, and she stole many things too.

LESSON IX

32. The Perfect of كَانَ *kāna*, he was

We noted in Lesson I that the copulae 'am', 'is' and 'are' are not expressed. However, 'was' and 'were' are expressed by the perfect of the verb 'to be', e.g.

كَانَ *kāna*, he was.

This verb, the only auxiliary one in Arabic, is a so-called hollow verb (to be dealt with later) the middle radical of which seems to have fallen out. It is a contraction of كَوَنَ *kawana*, the sound group ـَوَـ... *awa* (note both *a*'s short) generally contracting to ـَا... *ā* according to Arabic phonetics.

It is conjugated as follows:

كُنْتُ *kuntu*, I was.

كُنْتَ *kunta*, you (masc.) were.

كُنْتِ *kunti*, you (fem.) were.

كَانَ *kāna*, he was.

كَانَتْ *kānat*, she was.

كُنَّا *kunnā*, we were.

كُنْتُمْ *kuntum*, you (masc.) were.

كُنْتُنَّ *kuntunna*, you (fem.) were.

كُنْتُمَا *kuntumā*, you (masc. and fem. dual) were.

كَانُوا *kānū*, they (masc.) were.

كُنَّ *kunna*, they (fem.) were.

كَانَا *kānā*, they (masc. dual) were.

كَانَتَا *kānatā*, they (fem. dual) were.

Note the short *u* to which the middle radical و *w* shrinks in the 1st and 2nd persons and in the 3rd person plur. fem.

Any person of كَانَ *kāna* and the same person of the perfect of any other verb may be combined to form the plu. perfect of the latter. The finite particle قَدْ *qad* but *not* لَقَدْ *laqad* may be inserted before the second perfect, e.g.

كَانَ كَتَبَ لَهُمْ خِطَابًا طَوِيلًا *kāna kataba lahum khiṭāban ṭawīlan*, He had written them a long letter.

كُنْتُ قَدْ فَرِحْتُ بِنَجَاحِهِ *kuntu qad fariḥtu binajāḥihi*, I had rejoiced at his success.

كَانَتْ فَهِمَتْ مَعْنَاهُ *kānat fahimat maʿnāhu*, She had understood its meaning.

(Note the change of the أَلِفٌ مَقْصُورَةٌ *'alif maqṣūra* of مَعْنًى *maʿnan* (3rd declension) a meaning, idea, to ا... *ā* before the pronominal suffix),

كُنَّا شَرِبْنَا قَهْوَةً مَعَهَا *kunnā sharibnā qahwatan maʿahā*, We had drunk coffee with her.

كَانُوا ذَهَبُوا إِلَى ٱلْمَدِينَةِ *kānū dhahabū 'ilā ⌒l-madīnati*, They had gone to the city.

كُنَّ لَعِبْنَ مَعَ أَخَوَاتِهِنَّ *kunna laعibna maعa 'akhawāti-hinna*, They (fem.) had played with their sisters.

33. Predicate of كَانَ *kāna*

If the predicate of كَانَ *kāna* is a noun or adjective this *must be in the accusative*, e.g.

كَانَ مُحَمَّدٌ تَاجِرًا *kāna Muḥammadun tājiran*, Mohammed was a merchant.

كُنْتُ سَعِيدًا فِي شَبَابِي *kuntu saعīdan fī shabābī*, I was happy in my youth.

كُنْتَ تَعْبَانَ لَمَّا حَضَرْتُ لِزِيَارَتِكَ *kunta taعbāna lammā ḥaḍartu liziyāratika*, You were tired when I came to visit you (lit. for your visit).

كَانَتْ بِنْتًا لَطِيفَةً *kānat bintan laṭīfatan*, She was a charming girl.

كُنَّا جَالِسِينَ فِي ٱنْتِظَارِ ٱلْأُسْتَاذِ *kunnā jālisīna fi ⌒ntiẓāri ⌒l-'ustādhi*, We were sitting awaiting (lit. in expectation of) the professor.

كُنْتُمْ فُقَرَاءَ مُنْذُ سَنَةٍ *kuntum fuqarā'a mundhu sanatin*, You were poor a year ago.

كُنَّ مَشْغُولَاتٍ بِٱلْخِيَاطَةِ *kunna mashghūlātin bi ⌒l-khiyāṭati*, They (fem.) were occupied with sewing.

34. Adverbs

The Arabic language is exceedingly poor in adverbs, the common way of rendering an adverb being to use the corresponding adjective in the accusative, e.g.

رَكَضَ سَرِيعًا *rakaḍa sarīعan*, He ran swiftly.

قَدِمَ بَطِيئًا *qadima baṭī'an*, He approached slowly.

One may also use the verbal noun of the verb in question qualified by an adjective to form an absolute accusative, e.g.

رَكَضَ رَكْضًا سَرِيعًا *rakaḍa rakḍan sarīعan*, He ran a swift running (swiftly).

قَدِمَ قُدُومًا بَطِيئًا *qadima qudūman baṭī'an*, He approached slowly.

كَتَبَ كِتَابَةً جَمِيلَةً *kataba kitābatan jamīlatan*, He wrote beautifully.

There are many patterns for the verbal nouns of simple verbs but فَعْلٌ *faعlun* and فُعُولٌ *fuعūlun* are by far the most common. These are generally given in the better dictionaries side by side with their verbs. Verbs of the pattern فَعِلَ *faعila* denoting a temporary state generally make their verbal nouns according to the pattern فَعَلٌ *faعalun*, e.g.

عَطِشَ *عaṭi<u>sh</u>a*, he was (became) thirsty.

عَطَشٌ *عaṭa<u>sh</u>un*, thirst.

فَرِحَ *fariḥa*, he rejoiced.

فَرَحٌ *faraḥun*, rejoicing, joy.

35. Verbal and Nominal Sentences

As stated in the preceding lesson it is usual in Arabic for the verb of the sentence to come first, such a sentence being known as a verbal sentence. A nominal sentence is one which begins with a noun or a pronoun.

Nominal sentences we very often find introduced by the particle إِنَّ *'inna* after which the *subject is in the accusative and the predicate in the nominative*, e.g.

إِنَّ مُحَمَّدًا رَجُلٌ غَنِيٌّ *'inna Muḥammadan rajulun <u>gh</u>anīyun*, Mohammed is a rich man.

إِنَّ ٱلْإِمْرَأَةَ طَبَّاخَةٌ مَاهِرَةٌ *'inna ⌒li⌒mra'ata ṭabbā<u>kh</u>atun māhiratun*, The woman is a clever cook.

إِنَّ ٱلْوَلَدَيْنِ مَرِيضَانِ *'inna ⌒l-waladayni marīḍāni*, The two boys are sick.

إِنَّ ٱلْفَلَّاحِينَ مَشْغُولُونَ فِي ٱلْحَقْلِ *'inna ⁀l-fallāḥīna mashghūlūna fī ⁀l-ḥaqli,* The peasants are busy in the field.

A personal pronoun subject after إِنَّ *'inna* is, according to the above rule, in the accusative (i.e. a pronominal suffix), e.g.

إِنَّهُ ذُو فَضْلٍ عَظِيمٍ *'innahu dhū faḍlin ᶜaẓīmin,* He is the dispenser (lit. master) of great bounty.

إِنَّكُمْ ذَهَبْتُمْ إِلَى ٱلصَّيْدِ *'innakum dhahabtum 'ilā ⁀l-ṣaydi,* You went to the hunt.

'I' is either إِنِّي *'innī* or إِنَّنِي *'innanī* and 'we' either إِنَّا *'innā* or إِنَّنَا *'innanā*, the first word of each pair being more common than the second.

إِنَّ *'inna* has no translation in English, it being merely a device to introduce a nominal sentence. But if the predicate is prefixed by لَ *la* (emphatic '*lām*') then إِنَّ *'inna* acquires some force and is best translated by 'indeed', e.g.

إِنَّ ٱلْإِنْسَانَ لَفِي خُسْرٍ *'inna ⁀l-'insāna lafī khusrin,* Man is indeed in loss.

إِنَّ ٱلشَّابَّ لَشُجَاعٌ *'inna ⁀l-shābba lashujāᶜun,* The youth is indeed brave.

The particle إِنَّمَا *'innamā* 'only' takes both subject and predicate in the nominative. Note that 'only' qualifies the predicate and *not* the subject, e.g.

إِنَّمَا عَلِيٌّ نَجَّارٌ *'innamā ᶜalīyun najjārun,* Ali is only a carpenter.

The conjunction لٰكِنْ *lākin* or more commonly وَلٰكِنْ *walākin* when followed by a nominal sentence generally becomes وَلٰكِنَّ *walākinna* and has the same construction after it as إِنَّ *'inna*, e.g.

(أَنَا) ذَهَبْتُ إِلَى ٱلْمَحْكَمَةِ وَلٰكِنَّ مُحَمَّدًا ذَهَبَ إِلَى بَيْتِهِ

('anā) dhahabtu 'ilā ⁀l-maḥkamati walākinna Muḥammadan dhahaba 'ilā baytihi,

I went to the law-court but Mohammed went home.

هُوَ بِلَا شَكٍّ كَثِيرُ ٱلْمَالِ وَلٰكِنَّهُ بَخِيلٌ

huwa bilā shakkin kathīru ‿l-māli walākinnahu bakhīlun,
He is without doubt wealthy but he is miserly.

The conjunction فَإِنَّ *fa'inna*, for, is merely فَ *fa*, and, so + إِنَّ *'inna*.

Lastly the two particles لَعَلَّ *laʿalla*, perhaps, in the hope that, it is to be hoped that, and (يَا) لَيْتَ (*yā*) *layta*, would that! both take the same construction after them as إِنَّ *'inna*, e.g.

ذَهَبْتُ إِلَى زَيْدٍ لَعَلَّهُ عَثَرَ عَلَى قَلَمِي

dhahabtu 'ilā Zaydin laʿallahu ʿathara ʿalā qalamī,
I went to Zayd hoping that he *had* found my pen.

(N.B. عَثَرَ عَلَى *ʿathara ʿalā*, he found by chance, lit. he tripped over).

(يَا) لَيْتَ هِنْدًا حَاضِرَةٌ ٱلْيَوْمَ !

(*yā*) *layta Hindan ḥāḍiratuni ‿l-yawma!*
Would that Hind were present to-day!

36. Construction after أَمَّا *'ammā*, as for

Finally, if the subject of a nominal sentence is introduced by أَمَّا *'ammā*, as for, then the predicate *must* be prefixed by فَ *fa*, e.g.

أَمَّا ٱلْحَاكِمُ فَرَجُلٌ قَوِيٌّ

'ammā ‿l-ḥākimu farajulun qawīyun or

أَمَّا ٱلْحَاكِمُ فَهُوَ رَجُلٌ قَوِيٌّ

'ammā ‿l-ḥākimu fahuwa rajulun qawīyun,
The Governor is a strong man (lit. as for the Governor...),

أَمَّا أَنَا فَخَرَجْتُ فِي ٱلْحَالِ

'ammā 'anā fakharajtu fi ‿l-ḥāli,
As for me, I went out immediately (lit. in the instant).

Examples:

هَلْ كُنْتُمْ شَرِبْتُمُ ٱلْقَهْوَةَ قَبْلَ وُصُولِهِ ؟

hal kuntum sharibtumu ⁀l-qahwata qabla wuṣūlihi?
Had you drunk coffee before his arrival?

مَا كُنَّا شَرِبْنَاهَا

mā kunnā sharibnāhā,
We had not drunk it.

كَانَ ٱلْمَنْظَرُ مِنْ قِمَّةِ ٱلْجَبَلِ جَمِيلًا

kāna ⁀l-manẓaru min qimmati ⁀l-jabali jamīlan,
The view from the top of the mountain was beautiful.

كَانَتْ طُفُولَتُهُمْ سَعِيدَةً جِدًّا

kānat ṭufūlatuhum saعīdatan jiddan,
Their childhood was very happy.

قَدْ غَسَلَتِ ٱلْبِنْتُ ٱلْفَنَاجِينَ جَيِّدًا

qad ghasalati ⁀l-bintu ⁀l-fanājīna jayyidan,
The girl washed the cups well.

أَنَا مَشْغُولٌ كُلَّ يَوْمٍ بِكِتَابَةِ كِتَابٍ

'anā mashghūlun kulla yawmin bikitābati kitābin,
I am busy every day with the writing of a book.

فَرِحْنَا فَرَحًا عَظِيمًا لِزَوَاجِهَا

fariḥnā farahan عaẓīman lizawājihā,
We rejoiced greatly at her marriage.

سَرَقَ ٱللُّصُوصُ ذَهَبَ ٱلْبَخِيلِ وَفِضَّتَهُ وَلٰكِنَّهُمْ تَرَكُوا لَهُ كُلَّ كُتُبِهِ

saraqa ⁀l-luṣūṣu dhahaba ⁀l-bakhīli wafiḍḍatahu walākinnahum tarakū lahu kulla kutubihi,
The thieves stole the miser's gold and silver but they left him all (of) his books.

SUPPLEMENTARY VOCABULARY

كَيْفَ؟ *kayfa?* how?

وَالِدٌ *wālidun*, a begetter (i.e. father).

أَمْسِ *'amsi*, yesterday.

عِنْدَمَا ع*indamā*, when (conj.).

اِمْتِحَانٌ *imtiḥānun*, an examination.

خَبَرٌ <u>kh</u>*abarun* (pl. أَخْبَارٌ *'a<u>kh</u>bārun*), (piece of) news.

مَكْتُوبٌ *maktūbun*, written.

نَجَحَ *najaḥa*, he succeeded.

EXERCISE IX

أَيْنَ كُنْتَ بَعْدَ ٱلظُّهْرِ؟ كُنْتُ فِي ٱلْجُنَيْنَةِ مَعَ أَخَوَيَّ مَحْمُودٍ وَعُمَرَ. كَيْفَ كَانَتْ
حَالُ ٱلسَّيِّدَةِ وَالِدَتِكَ أَمْسِ؟ كَانَتْ بِخَيْرٍ وَلِلّٰهِ ٱلْحَمْدُ. أَفَرِحْتُنَّ عِنْدَمَا نَجَحْتُنَّ فِي
ٱمْتِحَانِكُنَّ؟ نَعَمْ، فَرِحْنَا فَرَحًا كَبِيرًا. هَلْ كَانَتْ أُخْتُكَ عَطْشَى عِنْدَمَا قَدِمَتْ مِن
دِمَشْقَ؟ لَا، كَانَ مَعَهَا قَلِيلٌ مِنَ ٱلْمَاءِ فِي ٱلسَّفَرِ. إِنَّ ٱلرَّجُلَيْنِ لَمَشْهُورَانِ. إِنِّى
كُنْتُ مَسْرُورًا جِدًّا عِنْدَمَا سَمِعْتُ ٱلْخَبَرَ. إِنَّمَا كَانُوا فَلَّاحِينَ فُقَرَاءَ. يَا لَيْتَكَ كُنْتَ
حَاضِرًا عِنْدَمَا ضَرَبُونِى! أَمَّا ٱلْبِنْتُ ٱلْمَرِيضَةُ فَشَرِبَتْ قَلِيلًا مِنَ ٱلْمَاءِ. كَانَتْ كُلُّ
كُتُبِ ٱلْعَالِمِ مَكْتُوبَةً بِٱللُّغَةِ ٱلْأَلْمَانِيَّةِ.

TRANSLITERATION

*'ayna kunta ba*ع*da ⌒l-ẓuhri? kuntu fī ⌒l-junaynati ma*ع*a 'a<u>kh</u>awayya,
Maḥmūdin wa*ع*Umara. kayfa kānat ḥālu ⌒l-sayyidati wālidatika 'amsi?
kānat bi<u>kh</u>ayrin wali⌒llāhi ⌒l-ḥamdu. 'afariḥtunna* ع*indamā najaḥtunna fī
⌒mtiḥānikunna? na*ع*am, fariḥnā farahan kabīran. hal kānat 'u<u>kh</u>tuka*
ع*aṭshā* ع*indamā qadimat min Dima<u>sh</u>qa? lā, kāna ma*ع*ahā qalīlun mina*

⁀l-mā'i fī ⁀l-safari. 'inna ⁀l-rajulayni lamashhūrāni. 'innī kuntu masrūran jiddan ʿindamā samiʿtu ⁀l-khabara. 'innamā kānū fallāḥīna fuqarā'a. yā laytaka kunta ḥāḍiran ʿindamā ḍarabūnī! 'ammā ⁀l-bintu ⁀l-marīḍatu fasharibat qalīlan mina ⁀l-mā'i. kānat kullu kutubi ⁀l-ʿālimi maktūbatan bi⁀l-lughati ⁀l-'almānīyati.

Translation

Where were you in the afternoon? I was in the garden with my (two) brothers, Mahmud and Omar. How was your mother (lit. the condition of the lady, your mother) yesterday? She was well (lit. in good), praise be to God. Did you (fem. pl.) rejoice when you passed your examination (lit. succeeded in...)? Yes, we were very happy. Was your sister thirsty when she arrived from Damascus? No, she had a little water with her on the journey. The two men are indeed famous. I was indeed very pleased when I heard the news. They were only poor peasants. Would that you had been present when they struck me! As for the sick girl, she drank a little water. All the scholar's books were written in the German language.

LESSON X

37. Demonstrative Pronouns

The demonstrative pronouns are:

this, that	ذَا	*dhā* masc. sing. (all three cases).
this, that	ذِي	*dhī*, or, more commonly ذِهِ *dhihi* fem. sing. (all three cases).
these, those (two)	ذَانِ	*dhāni* masc. nom.
these, those (two)	ذَيْنِ	*dhayni* masc. acc. and gen.
these, those (two)	تَانِ	*tāni* fem. nom.
these, those (two)	تَيْنِ	*tayni* fem. acc. and gen.
these, those	أُولَاءِ	*'ulā'i* masc. and fem. plur. (all three cases).

Note that the '*u*' of أُولَاءِ *'ulā'i*, although written long, is pronounced *short*.

These pronouns are rarely used as above, being more commonly prefixed by هَا *hā* (written هٰـ...) to denote propinquity, e.g.

هٰذَا *hā<u>dh</u>ā*, this (masc.),

هٰذِهِ *hā<u>dh</u>ihi*, this (fem.),

هٰؤُلَاءِ *hā'ulā'i*, these (masc. and fem.),

or suffixed by كَ *ka* or لِكَ *lika* to denote distance, e.g.

ذَاكَ *<u>dh</u>āka* or, more commonly, ذٰلِكَ *<u>dh</u>ālika*, that (masc.).

ذَانِكَ *<u>dh</u>ānika*, those two (masc. nom.).

أُولٰئِكَ *'ulā'ika*, those (masc. and fem. plur.).

Note especially تِلْكَ *tilka*, that (fem.).

38. Demonstrative Adjectives

If one of these demonstrative pronouns is immediately followed by the definite article, then the two combined form a demonstrative adjective, e.g.

هٰذَا ٱلْكِتَابُ *hā<u>dh</u>ā ◠l-kitābu*, this book.

هٰذِهِ ٱلِٱمْرَأَةُ *hā<u>dh</u>ihi ◠li◠mra'atu*, this woman.

هٰؤُلَاءِ ٱلنَّاسُ *hā'ulā'i ◠l-nāsu*, these people.

ذٰلِكَ ٱلْبَيْتُ *<u>dh</u>ālika ◠l-baytu*, that house.

تِلْكَ ٱلشَّجَرَةُ *tilka ◠l-<u>sh</u>ajaratu*, that tree.

أُولٰئِكَ ٱلرِّجَالُ *'ulā'ika ◠l-rijālu*, those men.

هٰذَانِ ٱلْخَيَّاطَانِ *hā<u>dh</u>āni ◠l-<u>kh</u>ayyāṭāni*, these (two) tailors.

تَانِكَ ٱلْبِنْتَانِ *tānika ◠l-bintāni*, those (two girls).

If the word one wishes to qualify by the demonstrative adjective is definite *without* the definite article, i.e. if it is a proper name or followed by a genitive, then the demonstrative adjective must *follow* the noun or genitive construction it qualifies, being really a pronoun in apposition, e.g.

مُحَمَّدٌ هٰذَا *Muḥammadun hādhā*, this Mohammed.

عَائِشَةُ هٰذِهِ *ʿā'ishatu hādhihi*, this Ayisha.

كُتُبُ ٱلْمُدَرِّسِ هٰذِهِ *kutubu ͡l-mudarrisi hādhihi*, these books of the teacher.

أَسَاتِذَةُ ٱلْجَامِعَةِ أُولٰئِكَ *'asātidhatu ͡l-jāmiʿati 'ulā'ika*, those university professors.

If the predicate of a demonstrative pronoun begins with the definite article the corresponding personal pronoun must be inserted between the two since, as noted above, the personal pronoun immediately followed by the definite article becomes the demonstrative adjective, e.g.

هٰذَا هُوَ ٱلسَّيْفُ *hādhā huwa ͡l-sayfu*, This is the sword.

تِلْكَ هِيَ ٱلْخَدَّامَةُ *tilka hiya ͡l-khaddāmatu*, That is the servant-girl.

هٰؤُلَاءِ هُمُ ٱلْكِرَامُ *hā'ulā'i humu ͡l-kirāmu*, These are the generous ones.

هٰذِهِ هِيَ ٱلنِّهَايَةُ *hādhihi hiya ͡l-nihāyatu*, This is the end.

If the predicate is definite by reason of a following genitive then the insertion of the personal pronoun is optional, e.g.

هٰذَا (هُوَ) بَيْتِي *hādhā (huwa) baytī*, This is my house.

هٰذِهِ (هِيَ) زَوْجَةُ ٱلضَّابِطِ *hādhihi (hiya) zawjatu ͡l-ḍābiṭi*, This is the officer's wife.

هٰؤُلَاءِ (هُمْ) ضُبَّاطُ ٱلْجَيْشِ *hā'ulā'i (hum) ḍubbāṭu ͡l-jayshi*, These are the officers of the army.

39. Relative Pronouns

The relative pronouns are:

that, which, who ٱلَّذِي *alladhī* masc. sing. (all three cases).

that, which, who ٱلَّتِي *allatī* fem. sing. (all three cases).

that, which, who اَللَّذَانِ *al-ladhāni* masc. dual nom.

that, which, whom اَللَّذَيْنِ *al-ladhayni* masc. dual acc. and gen.

that, which, who اَللَّتَانِ *al-latāni* fem. dual nom.

that, which, whom اَللَّتَيْنِ *al-latayni* fem. dual acc. and gen.

that, which, who اَلَّذِينَ *alladhīna* masc. plur. (all three cases).

that, which, who اَللَّاتِي *al-lātī* or اَللَّوَاتِي *al-lawātī* or اَللَّائِي *al-lā'ī* fem. plur. (all three cases).

Note that in the forms which occur most frequently, اَلَّذِي *alladhī*, اَلَّتِي *allatī* and اَلَّذِينَ *alladhīna*, there is only one '*l*', whereas the other forms have two '*l*'s. The initial *hamza* is *hamzat-al-waṣl*.

If the subject of a subordinate relative clause is other than the noun or pronoun qualified by it then the relative must be resumed by a personal pronoun, e.g.

اَلرَّجُلُ ٱلَّذِي ضَرَبَ مُحَمَّدًا *al-rajulu ⁀lladhī ḍaraba Muḥammadan*, The man who struck Mohammed.

but اَلرَّجُلُ ٱلَّذِي قَتَلُوهُ *al-rajulu ⁀lladhī qatalūhu*, The man whom they killed.

اَلْبِنْتُ ٱلَّتِي ذَهَبْتُ مَعَهَا إِلَى ٱلسُّوقِ *al-bintu ⁀llatī dhahabtu maʿahā 'ilā ⁀l-sūqi*, The girl with whom I went to the market.

اَلْخِطَابُ ٱلَّذِي كَتَبَتْهُ *al-khiṭābu ⁀lladhī katabathu*, The letter which she wrote.

اَلْكُتُبُ ٱلَّتِي فَرِحْنَا بِهَا *al-kutubu ⁀llatī fariḥnā bihā*, The books in which we rejoiced.

اَلنَّاسُ ٱلَّذِينَ وَثِقْتَ بِهِمْ *al-nāsu ⁀lladhīna wathiqta bihim*, The people in whom you trusted.

But note that if the noun qualified by the relative is indefinite the relative pronoun is omitted altogether, e.g.

رَجُلٌ قَتَلُوهُ *rajulun qatalūhu*, A man whom they killed.

رَجُلٌ ضَرَبَ مُحَمَّدًا *rajulun ḍaraba Muḥammadan*, A man who struck Mohammed.

بِنْتٌ ذَهَبْتُ مَعَهَا *bintun dhahabtu maɛahā*, a girl with whom I went.

هُمْ نَاسٌ وَثِقْنَا بِهِمْ *hum nāsun wathiqnā bihim*, They are people in whom we trusted.

40. Interrogative Pronouns

The most common interrogative pronouns are:

مَنْ ؟ *man?* who?

مَا ؟ *mā?*, more commonly مَاذَا ؟ *mādhā?* what?

أَيْنَ ؟ *'ayna?* where?

كَيْفَ ؟ *kayfa?* how?

مَتَى ؟ *mátā?* when?

كَمْ ؟ *kam?* how much, many?

أَيٌّ ؟ *'ayyun?* (fem. أَيَّةٌ ؟ *'ayyatun?*) which? any.

These are all, with the exception of أَيٌّ *'ayyun*, indeclinable, e.g.

مَنْ حَضَرَ مَعَكَ ؟ *man ḥaḍara maɛaka?* Who came with you?

مَنْ ضَرَبْتَ ؟ *man ḍarabta?* Whom did you strike?

كِتَابُ مَنْ هٰذَا ؟ *kitābu man hādhā?* Whose book is this?

مَاذَا كَتَبْتُمْ ؟ *mādhā katabtum?* What did you write?

مِنْ أَيْنَ لَكَ هٰذَا ؟ *min 'ayna laka hādhā?* Where did you get this from?

مَتَى سَمِعْتُمْ ذٰلِكَ ؟ *mátā samiɛtum dhālika?* When did you hear that?

After a preposition مَا *mā* as an interrogative is generally shortened to مَ *ma* and written attached to the preposition, e.g.

لِمَ ؟ *lima?* for what, why?

إِلَامَ ؟ *'ilāma?* till when?

عَلَامَ؟ *ɛalāma?* for what?

مِمَّ؟ *mimma?* from what?

Note that the noun qualified by كَمْ *kam?* how much, many? is in the *accusative singular*, e.g.

كَمْ كِتَابًا؟ *kam kitāban?* how many books?

كَمْ وَلَدًا؟ *kam waladan?* how many boys?

كَمْ سَاعَةً؟ *kam sāɛatan?* what many hours?

but كَمِ ٱلسَّاعَةُ؟ *kami ◠l-sāɛatu?* what time is it? (lit. how much is the hour?).

أَيٌّ *'ayyun* as an interrogative adjective governs a following genitive, e.g.

أَيُّ بَيْتٍ؟ *'ayyu baytin?* which house?

أَيُّ رَجُلٍ؟ *'ayyu rajulin?* which man?

أَيُّ ٱلرِّجَالِ؟ *'ayyu ◠l-rijāli?* which (one) of the men?

أَيٌّ *'ayyun* is very often used as common gender and its feminine أَيَّةٌ *'ayyatun* neglected, e.g.

أَيُّ أَمِيرَةٍ؟ *'ayyu 'amīratin?* which princess?

When a sentence begins with one of these interrogative pronouns the spoken question mark أَ *'a* or هَلْ *hal* cannot be used.

Note that مَنْ *man* and مَا *mā* are very often used as relative pronouns equalling ٱلَّذِي *alladhī*, e.g.

مَنْ قَتَلَ قُتِلَ *man qatala qutila*, He who killed was killed or he who kills will be killed.

قَدْ فَهِمْتُ مَا كَتَبُوهُ فِي خِطَابِهِمْ *qad fahimtu mā katabūhu fī khiṭābihim*, I understood what they wrote in their letter.

Examples:

كَمْ تِلْمِيذًا فِي هٰذِهِ ٱلْمَدْرَسَةِ؟

kam tilmīd̲h̲an fī hād̲h̲ihi ⌒l-madrasati?
How many pupils are in this school?

يَدُ ٱلْوَلَدِ هٰذِهِ نَظِيفَةٌ وَلٰكِنَّ تِلْكَ وَسِخَةٌ

yadu ⌒l-waladi hād̲h̲ihi naẓīfatun walākinna tilka wasik̲h̲atun,
This hand of the boy is clean but that one is dirty.

لِمَاذَا مَا ضَرَبْتَ ٱلْخَادِمَ ٱلَّذِي شَتَمَكَ؟

limād̲h̲ā mā ḍarabta ⌒l-k̲h̲ādima ⌒llad̲h̲ī s̲h̲atamaka?
Why did you not strike the servant who insulted you?

هٰذَا خِطَابٌ بَعَثَتْهُ سَيِّدَةٌ شَهِيرَةٌ

hād̲h̲ā k̲h̲iṭābun baʿat̲h̲athu sayyidatun s̲h̲ahīratun,
This is a letter which was sent by a famous lady.

أَيْنَ ٱلطَّبِيبُ ٱلَّذِي بَعَثْتُمْ فِي طَلَبِهِ؟

'ayna ⌒l-ṭabību ⌒llad̲h̲ī baʿat̲h̲tum fī ṭalabihi?
Where is the doctor you sent for? (lit. in search of whom you sent).

أَيَّ طَبِيبٍ طَلَبْتُمُوهُ؟

'ayya ṭabībin ṭalabtumūhu?
Which doctor did you ask for?

مَتَى تُرْجِمَ ذٰلِكَ ٱلْكِتَابُ؟

mátā turjima d̲h̲ālika ⌒l-kitābu?
When was that book translated?

Supplementary Vocabulary

شُبَّاكٌ *s̲h̲ubbākun* (pl. شَبَابِيكُ *s̲h̲abābīku*), a window.

حَلِيبٌ *ḥalībun*, milk.

ضَابِطٌ *ḍābiṭun* (pl. ضُبَّاطٌ *ḍubbāṭun*), an officer.

مُسِنٌّ *musinnun*, old.

خَالٌ *k̲h̲ālun*, a (maternal) uncle.

رِسَالَةٌ *risālatun* (pl. رَسَائِلُ *rasā'ilu*), a message, letter.

Exercise X

هٰذَا ٱلْأَمِيرُ أَعْدَلُ مِنْ ذٰلِكَ ٱلْمَلِكِ. هٰؤُلَاءِ ٱلرِّجَالُ مَشْغُولُونَ فِي مَكَاتِبِهِمْ. لِمَطْبَخِ ذٰلِكَ ٱلْبَيْتِ شُبَّاكَانِ. بُيُوتُ ٱلرَّجُلِ ٱلْغَنِيِّ تِلْكَ عَلَى نَهْرٍ. أَيْنَ أُولَائِكَ ٱلْأَوْلَادُ ٱلَّذِينَ شَرِبُوا ٱلْحَلِيبَ؟ هُمْ فِي جُنَيْنَةِ هٰذِهِ ٱلسَّيِّدَةِ. هٰذَا كِتَابٌ جَيِّدٌ. مَنْ كَتَبَهُ؟ كَتَبَهُ رَجُلٌ ٱسْمُهُ أَحْمَدُ. إِنَّ أُولَائِكَ ٱلسَّادَةَ ٱلَّذِينَ شَرِبْتُمْ مَعَهُمُ ٱلشَّايَ كَانُوا ضُبَّاطًا فِي ٱلْجَيْشِ ٱلْمِصْرِيِّ. سَمِعَتِ ٱلسَّيِّدَاتُ ٱللَّوَاتِي ذَهَبْنَ إِلَى ٱلْجُنَيْنَةِ مَعَ هٰذَا ٱلْأُسْتَاذِ ٱلْمُسِنِّ خَبَرَ زَوَاجِ ٱبْنِهِ. كُتُبُنَا هٰذِهِ هَدِيَّةٌ مِنْ خَالَتِنَا ٱلَّتِي بَعَثَتْهَا لَنَا بِٱلْبَرِيدِ. أَفَهِمْتُمْ مَا كَانَ مَكْتُوبًا فَوْقَ بَابِ ٱلْقَصْرِ؟ نَعَمْ، وَكَتَبْنَاهُ فِي رِسَالَةٍ بَعَثْنَاهَا إِلَى أَصْدِقَائِنَا فِي ٱلْهِنْدِ.

Transliteration

hād̲h̲ā ⌒l-'amīru 'aʿdalu min d̲h̲ālika ⌒l-maliki. hā'ulā'i ⌒l-rijālu mas̲h̲g̲h̲ūlūna fī makātibihim. limaṭbak̲h̲i d̲h̲ālika ⌒l-bayti s̲h̲ubbākāni. buyūtu ⌒l-rajuli ⌒l-g̲h̲anīyi tilka ʿalā nahrin. 'ayna 'ulā'ika ⌒l-'awlādu ⌒llad̲h̲īna s̲h̲aribū ⌒l-ḥalība? hum fī junaynati hād̲h̲ihi ⌒l-sayyidati. hād̲h̲ā kitābun jayyidun. man katabahu? katabahu rajuluni ⌒smuhu 'Aḥmadu. 'inna 'ulā'ika ⌒l-sādata ⌒llad̲h̲īna s̲h̲aribtum maʿahumu ⌒l-s̲h̲āya kānū ḍubbāṭan fī ⌒l-jays̲h̲i ⌒l-miṣrīyi. samiʿati ⌒l-sayyidātu ⌒l-lawātī d̲h̲ahabna 'ilā ⌒l-junaynati maʿa hād̲h̲ā ⌒l-'ustād̲h̲i ⌒l-musinni k̲h̲abara zawāji ⌒bnihi. kutubunā hād̲h̲ihi hadīyatun min k̲h̲ālatinā ⌒llatī baʿat̲h̲athā lanā bi⌒l-barīdi. 'afahimtum mā kāna maktūban fawqa bābi ⌒l-qaṣri? naʿam, wakatabnāhu fī risālatin baʿat̲h̲nāhā 'ilā 'aṣdiqā'inā fī ⌒l-Hindi.

Translation

This prince is more just than that king. These men are busy in their offices. The kitchen of that house has two windows. Those houses of the rich man are on a river. Where are those boys who drank the milk? They are in this lady's garden. This is an excellent book. Who wrote it? It was written by a man whose name is Ahmad. Those gentlemen with whom you (pl.) drank tea were officers in the Egyptian Army. The ladies who went to the garden with this old professor heard the news of his son's marriage. These books of ours are a gift from our (maternal) aunt who sent them to us by post. Did you understand what was written above the palace door? Yes, and we wrote it in a letter which we sent to our friends in India.

LESSON XI

As it is presumed that the student is by now thoroughly familiar with the Arabic script, the transliteration will be dispensed with in this and subsequent lessons except for words and letters underlined, the construction or vowelling of which should be specially emphasized.

41. Derivatives of Verbs

The following are the most common derivatives from simple verbs:

(i) *The Verbal Noun* or Noun of Action.

As stated in Lesson IX there exist many patterns of the verbal noun each one being most conveniently learned along with its root verb. The most common patterns from simple three-radical verbs are فُعُولٌ, فَعْلٌ, فَعَالٌ and فَعَالَةٌ, e.g.

خَرَجَ	he went out.	دُخُولٌ	entrance.
خُرُوجٌ	going out, exit.	قَتَلَ	he killed.
دَخَلَ	he entered.	قَتْلٌ	killing, being killed.

(N.B. The verbal noun of a transitive verb may be either active or passive.)

ذَهَبَ	he went.	كَتَبَ	he wrote.
ذَهَابٌ	going.	كِتَابَةٌ	writing.

The verbal noun very often expresses the English infinitive or subordinate clause, e.g.

قَصَدْتُ ٱلْخُرُوجَ I intended (made) to go out.

عَزَمَ عَلَى قَتْلِهِ he decided to kill him.

مَاذَا فَعَلْتُمْ بَعْدَ وُصُولِهِمْ ؟ What did you do after they had arrived?

The verbal noun of simple four-radical verbs is of the pattern فَعْلَلَةٌ, e.g.

تَرْجَمَةٌ translating, translation.

دَنْدَنَةٌ humming, buzzing.

(ii) *The Active Participle*

This is of the pattern فَاعِلٌ in simple three-radical verbs. Used adjectivally it generally, though not always, takes the sound plural endings, used nominally it may take one or more of the numerous broken plural patterns, e.g.

دَاخِلٌ entering, one who enters. قَاتِلٌ killing, a murderer.

خَارِجٌ one who goes out. كَاتِبٌ writing, a writer, clerk.

The active participle of simple four-radical verbs is مُفَعْلِلٌ *mufaعlilun*, e.g.

مُتَرْجِمٌ translating, a translator.

مُدَنْدِنٌ humming, buzzing.

If the middle radical of the simple verb is one of the weak letters و and ي (i.e. if the verb is a hollow verb, see Lesson XVII), it changes into *hamzat-al-qaṭع*, e.g.

كَانَ he was (for كَوَنَ). بَاعَ he sold (for بَيَعَ).

كَائِنٌ being, existing. بَائِعٌ selling, a salesman.

قَالَ he said (for قَوَلَ). سَالَ it flowed (for سَيَلَ).

قَائِلٌ saying. سَائِلٌ flowing, liquid.

If the *third* radical of the simple verb is one of the weak letters و and ي then note the following important phonetic changes:

...ُوْ, ...ِيْ, ...ُو, and ...ِي become ... ٍ *in* and ...ِوًا becomes ...ِيًا. Thus from قَضَى (for قَضَيَ), he decided, we have:

Nom. قَاضٍ (for قَاضِيٌ) a judge.

Acc. قَاضِيًا a judge.

Gen. قَاضٍ (for قَاضِيٍ) a judge.

From دَعَا (for دَعَوَ) he called, invited, we have:

Nom. دَاعٍ (for دَاعِوٌ) a caller, inviter, propagandist.

Acc. دَاعِيًا (for دَاعِوًا) a caller, inviter, propagandist.

Gen. دَاعٍ (for دَاعِوٍ) a caller, inviter, propagandist.

When these become definite ... ٍ becomes ...ِي, e.g.

اَلْقَاضِي the judge. اَلدَّاعِي the propagandist.

Active participles of verbs ending in و or ى when used adjectivally take the sound plural endings in which case ...ِيُو and ...ِوُو become ...ُو and ...ِيِي and ...ِوِي become ...ِي, e.g.

قَاضُونَ nom. judging (plur.).

قَاضِينَ acc. and gen. judging (plur.).

دَاعُونَ nom. calling (plur.).

دَاعِينَ acc. and gen. calling (plur.).

When they refer to rational male beings and are used as nouns they always make their plurals according to the pattern فُعَلَةٌ. But ...َيَ and ...َوَ generally become ...َا so we have:

قُضَاةٌ (for قُضَيَةٌ) judges.

دُعَاةٌ (for دُعَوَةٌ) propagandists.

The feminine (فَاعِلَةٌ) is regular in the singular, e.g.

جَارِيَةٌ a servant-girl (lit. a running girl), from جَرَى (for جَرَيَ) he ran.

The pattern فَاعِلَةٌ takes the broken plural form فَوَاعِلُ, but note that in the *indefinite only* final ...ِيُ (nom.) and, quite irregularly, ...ِيِ (gen.) become ... *in*. Thus

Nom.	جَوَارٍ	اَلْجَوَارِي
Acc.	جَوَارِيَ	اَلْجَوَارِيَ
Gen.	جَوَارٍ	اَلْجَوَارِي

Although the pattern فَوَاعِلُ is of the 2nd declension it seems to become of the 1st declension when the third radical is و or ي.

(iii) *The Passive Participle*

From simple three-radical verbs this is, as noted earlier, of the pattern مَفْعُولٌ, e.g.

مَضْرُوبٌ beaten. مَفْهُومٌ understood.

مَقْتُولٌ killed, murdered. مَكْتُوبٌ written.

If the middle radical is و or ي note the following changes:

(*a*) If و then this disappears altogether, e.g.

مَقُولٌ said, from قَالَ (for قَوَلَ), he said.

(*b*) If ي then *ū* changes to *ī* and the middle radical falls out, e.g.

مَبِيعٌ sold, from بَاعَ (for بَيَعَ), he sold.

If the third radical is ي then *ū* in the pattern مَفْعُولٌ becomes *ī*, e.g.

مَقْضِيٌّ (for مَقْضُويٌ) decided,

مَرْمِيٌّ (for مَرْمُويٌ from رَمَى he threw) thrown,

but quite regular مَدْعُوٌّ called, invited.

The passive participle of a simple four-radical verb is formed according to the pattern مُفَعْلَلٌ *mufaɛlalun*, e.g.

مُتَرْجَمٌ translated.

(iv) *The Noun of Place and/or Time*

This occurs in three patterns مَفْعَلٌ, مَفْعِلٌ and مَفْعَلَةٌ. Which one of these is derived from a given verb can only be learned through practice or reference to a dictionary, e.g.

مَكْتَبٌ a place of writing, desk, office.

مَجْلِسٌ a place of sitting, council.

مَدْرَسَةٌ a place of study or reading, school.

All three forms make their plurals according to the pattern مَفَاعِلُ, e.g.

مَكَاتِبُ desks, offices.

مَجَالِسُ councils.

مَدَارِسُ schools,

but note مَكْتَبَاتٌ plural of مَكْتَبَةٌ a book-shop, library.

If the second radical is و or ي then the vowel of the middle weak radical is thrown forward to the preceding vowelless first radical and becomes *long*, e.g.

مَقَامٌ (for مَقْوَمٌ from قَامَ he arose), a standing place.

مَضِيقٌ (for مَضْيِقٌ from ضَاقَ it was narrow), a strait.

If the third radical is و or ي then final ...َوٌ, ...َوًا, ...َوٍ and ...َيٌ, ...َيًا, ...َيٍ become *'alif maqṣūra* (written ...ًى) and the word is indeclinable, e.g.

مَعْنًى (from عَنَى he meant) (place or) idea intended, meaning.

In the plural of nouns of place and time the third radical of which is

و or ي the same phenomena occur, as we noted in the last paragraph on the active participle above, e.g.

Nom.	مَعَانٍ	ideas	اَلْمَعَانِي.
Acc.	مَعَانِيَ	ideas	اَلْمَعَانِيَ.
Gen.	مَعَانٍ	ideas	اَلْمَعَانِي.

(v) *The Noun of Instrument*

This is formed according to the patterns مِفْعَالٌ and مِفْعَلَةٌ (occasionally مِفْعَلٌ), e.g.

مِفْتَاحٌ (from فَتَحَ he opened) an instrument for opening, a key.

مِيزَانٌ (for مِوْزَانٌ from وَزَنَ he weighed) a balance.

مِكْنَسَةٌ (from كَنَسَ he swept) a broom.

مِرْسَاةٌ (for مِرْسَوَةٌ from رَسَا it anchored) an anchor.

مِبْرَدٌ (from بَرَدَ he filed) a file.

These take the broken plural patterns مَفَاعِلُ and مَفَاعِيلُ according to whether the vowel between the second and third radicals is short or long, e.g.

مَفَاتِيحُ	keys.	مَوَازِينُ	balances.
مَكَانِسُ	brooms.	مَرَاسٍ	anchors.
مَبَارِدُ	files.		

42. Derivatives of Nouns

The most common derivatives of nouns are:

(i) *The Relative Adjective*

This is formed by adding ...ِيّ to the noun, e.g.

اَلْعَرَبُ	the Arabs.	عِلْمٌ	knowledge, science.
عَرَبِيّ	Arabic, Arabian.	عِلْمِيّ	scientific.

The feminine of this is very commonly used in modern Arabic for forming abstract ideas, e.g.

مَسْؤُولٌ	asked, responsible.	عَقْلِيٌّ	mental.
مَسْؤُولِيَّةٌ	responsibility.	عَقْلِيَّةٌ	mentality.
عَقْلٌ	mind.		

(ii) *The Diminutive* which is rarely used is formed according to the patterns فُعَيْلٌ and, if there is a long vowel between the second and third radicals, فُعَيِّلٌ, e.g.

وُلَيْدٌ a small boy, urchin.

كُتَيِّبٌ a small book.

بُنَيَّةٌ a little girl.

وُرَيْقَةٌ (from وَرَقَةٌ a leaf, sheet of paper), a small leaf.

The diminutive, even though it may refer to males, generally takes the sound feminine plural ending, e.g.

وُلَيْدَاتٌ	small boys.	كُتَيِّبَاتٌ	small books.

Examples:

اَلدُّخُولُ صَعْبٌ وَلٰكِنَّ ٱلْخُرُوجَ أَصْعَبُ

It is difficult to go in but it is more difficult to come out.

مَنْ هُوَ مُتَرْجِمُ هٰذَا ٱلْكِتَابِ؟

Who is the translator of this book?

إِنَّ ٱلْقَاضِيَ قَضَى بِبَرَاءَتِهِ

The judge pronounced him innocent (lit. decided (the matter) with his innocence).

كُنْتُ مَدْعُوًّا إِلَى حَفْلَةٍ وَلٰكِنْ ذَهَبْتُ إِلَى ٱلْمَدْرَسَةِ

I was invited to a party, but I went to school.

مَا مَعْنَى هٰذِهِ ٱلْكَلِمَةِ؟ لَهَا مَعَانٍ عَدِيدَةٌ

What is the meaning of this word? It has numerous meanings.

(*Note*: At this stage of his studies it is essential for the student to acquire a good Arabic dictionary. The best Arabic-English dictionaries for beginners are those published by the Catholic Press of Beirut, Lebanon. In the remaining exercises in this book the supplementary vocabularies will be dispensed with, but the student will find the translation of unfamiliar words in the subsequent key. The student should ascertain from his dictionary the singular or plural of new words and enter *both* in his vocabulary notebook.)

Exercise XI

١—مَا فَهِمَتْ مَعْنَايَ إِلَّا بَعْدَ خُرُوجِي مِنْ عِنْدِهَا فَضَحِكَتْ ضَحِكًا كَبِيرًا لِٱرْتِبَاكِي.

٢—ذَهَبْنَا إِلَى مِصْرَ بَحْرًا عَنْ طَرِيقِ مَضِيقِ جَبَلِ طَارِقٍ حَيْثُ نَزَلْنَا لِمُدَّةِ يَوْمٍ.

٣—هَلْ ضُرِبَ وَلَدُكَ ٱلصَّغِيرُ فِي ٱلْمَدْرَسَةِ أَمْسِ؟ لَا، مَا كَانَتْ فِي كُرَّاسَتِهِ أَغْلَاطٌ كَثِيرَةٌ فَمَا ضُرِبَ.

٤—أَكُنْتُمَا مَشْغُولَيْنِ فِي مَكْتَبِكُمَا قَبْلَ ٱلظُّهْرِ؟ لَا، مَا كَانَ لَدَيْنَا شُغْلٌ كَثِيرٌ.

٥—بَرَدَ ٱلْعَامِلُ مِفْتَاحَ ٱلْحَدِيدِ بِٱلْمِبْرَدِ ٱلَّذِي كَانَ مَعَهُ فِي جَيْبِهِ.

٦— ٱلْعَرَبُ قَوْمٌ كِرَامٌ وَكُلُّ عَرَبِيٍّ مُسْتَعِدٌّ لِلْمَوْتِ دُونَ ضَيْفِهِ.

٧—حَكَمَ ٱلْقَاضِي بِإِعْدَامِ ٱلْقَاتِلِ ٱلَّذِي قَتَلَ زَوْجَتَهُ.

٨—أَمَرَتْ سَيِّدَةُ ٱلْبَيْتِ ٱلْخَدَّامَتَيْنِ بِكَنْسِ كُلِّ ٱلْغُرَفِ بِٱلْمَكَانِسِ ٱلْجَدِيدَةِ.

٩—يَا لَيْتَنَا غَيْرُ مَسْؤُولِينَ عَنْ تَقَدُّمِ إِخْوَتِنَا فِي ٱلْجَامِعَةِ!

١٠—لَمَّا ذَهَبَ ٱلْأَمِيرُ إِلَى ضَيْعَتِهِ فِي ٱلرِّيفِ ذَهَبَتْ بُنَيَّتُهُ مَعَهُ.

Translation

1. She only understood my meaning after I had left her (lit. my exit from her place) and laughed heartily at my confusion.

2. We went to Egypt by sea by way of the Strait of Gibraltar where we alighted for (the space of) one day.

3. Was your little boy beaten in school yesterday? No, there were not many mistakes in his exercise book and so he was not beaten.

4. Were you (two) busy in your office in the forenoon? No, we did not have much work.

5. The workman filed the iron key with the file which he had in his pocket.

6. The Arabs are a generous people and every Arab is prepared to die for his guest.

7. The judge condemned the murderer to be executed who had killed his wife.

8. The lady of the house ordered the two maidservants to sweep all the rooms with the new brooms.

9. Would that we were not responsible for our brothers' progress in the university!

10. When the prince went to his estate in the country his little daughter went with him.

LESSON XII

43. The Imperfect of the Simple Verb

The imperfect indicative active of the simple verb, denoting an action which is still incomplete or was incomplete at a stated or implied time, is formed according to the following paradigm:

1st person sing.	أَفْعَُِلُ
2nd person sing. masc.	تَفْعَُِلُ
2nd person sing. fem.	تَفْعَُِلِينَ
3rd person sing. masc.	يَفْعَُِلُ
3rd person sing. fem.	تَفْعَُِلُ
1st person plur.	نَفْعَُِلُ
2nd person plur. masc.	تَفْعَُِلُونَ

2nd person plur. fem.	تَفْعُلْنَ
2nd person dual masc. and fem.	تَفْعُلَانِ
3rd person plur. masc.	يَفْعُلُونَ
3rd person plur. fem.	يَفْعُلْنَ
3rd person dual masc.	يَفْعُلَانِ
3rd person dual fem.	تَفْعُلَانِ

Taking our stock verb كَتَبَ he wrote, we have:

أَكْتُبُ	I write, am writing, shall write.
تَكْتُبُ	you (masc.) write.
تَكْتُبِينَ	you (fem.) write.
يَكْتُبُ	he writes.
تَكْتُبُ	she writes.
نَكْتُبُ	we write.
تَكْتُبُونَ	you (masc.) write.
تَكْتُبْنَ	you (fem.) write.
تَكْتُبَانِ	you (dual) write.
يَكْتُبُونَ	they (masc.) write.
يَكْتُبْنَ	they (fem.) write.
يَكْتُبَانِ	they (dual masc.) write.
تَكْتُبَانِ	they (dual fem.) write.

If the vowel after the middle radical of the perfect is '*u*' then the vowel following the middle radical of the imperfect is likewise '*u*', e.g.

كَرُمَ	he was generous.	شَرُفَ	he was noble.
يَكْرُمُ	he is (will be) generous.	يَشْرُفُ	he is noble..

If the vowel after the middle radical of the perfect is '*i*' then the vowel following the middle radical of the imperfect is '*a*', e.g.

فَرِحَ	he rejoiced.	سَمِعَ	he heard.
يَفْرَحُ	he rejoices.	يَسْمَعُ	he hears.

An exception to this rule is the verb حَسِبَ he thought, considered the imperfect of which is either يَحْسَبُ or يَحْسِبُ.

But if the vowel after the middle radical of the perfect is '*a*' then the middle vowel of the imperfect can only be determined through practice or by reference to a dictionary, e.g.

كَتَبَ	he wrote.	يَقْطَعُ	he cuts.
يَكْتُبُ	he writes.	جَلَسَ	he sat (down).
قَطَعَ	he cut.	يَجْلِسُ	he sits (down).

The negative of the imperfect is made by prefixing لَا or مَا, the latter being more common when the imperfect is present tense, e.g.

لَا أَجْلِسُ عَلَى ٱلْأَرْضِ	I do not sit on the ground.
لَا نَقْطَعُ ٱللَّحْمَ بِالشَّوْكَةِ	We do not cut meat with a fork.
مَا يَفْهَمُ قَوْلِي	He does not understand what I am saying (lit. my speech).

When a person of the perfect كَانَ, he was, is followed by the corresponding person of the imperfect of another verb, the resultant combination equals the past continuous tense of European languages, e.g.

كُنْتُ أَكْتُبُ خِطَابًا لَمَّا دَخَلُوا عَلَيَّ

I was writing a letter when they came in to me.

كَانَ يَذْهَبُ إِلَى ٱلسُّوقِ كُلَّ يَوْمٍ أَثْنَاءَ إِجَازَتِهِ

He used to go to market every day during his vacation.

44. The Future

The imperfect indicative is also used to express future action, but in this case it is generally strengthened by prefixing the future particle ...سَ or سَوْفَ, e.g.

سَأَذْهَبُ مَعَكَ غَدًا I shall go with you tomorrow.

سَوْفَ يَفْعَلُ مَا يَقْصِدُ He will do what he intends.

45. The Passive of the Imperfect

The imperfect indicative passive of all simple transitive verbs may be made according to the pattern يُفْعَلُ *yufeąlu* conjugated as above, e.g.

يُذْكَرُ ذٰلِكَ فِي كُتُبِ ٱلْمُؤَرِّخِينَ

That is mentioned in the books of the historians.

كَيْفَ تُكْتَبُ هٰذِهِ ٱلْحُرُوفُ بِٱلْخَطِّ ٱلْفَارِسِيِّ؟

How are these letters written in Persian script?

46. The Future or Imperfect of كَانَ

The future or imperfect indicative of كَانَ, he was, is conjugated as follows:

أَكُونُ I am, shall be.

تَكُونُ you (masc.) will be.

تَكُونِينَ you (fem.) will be.

يَكُونُ he will be.

تَكُونُ she will be.

نَكُونُ we shall be.

تَكُونُونَ you (masc.) will be.

(for تَكُونْنَ) تَكُنَّ you (fem.) will be.

تَكُونَانِ you (dual) will be.

يَكُونُونَ they (masc.) will be.

(for يَكُونْنَ) يَكُنَّ they (fem.) will be.

يَكُونَانِ they (dual masc.) will be.

تَكُونَانِ they (dual fem.) will be.

The imperfect of كَانَ followed by the perfect of another verb gives us the future perfect, e.g.

تَكُونُ سَمِعْتَ ذٰلِكَ You will have heard that.

أَكُونُ كَتَبْتُ ٱلْخِطَابَ قَبْلَ وُصُولِكُمْ I shall have written the letter before your arrival.

47. The Imperfect of the Simple Quadriliteral Verb

The imperfect indicative active of simple quadriliteral verbs is made according to the pattern يُفَعْلِلُ *yufaʿlilu* and their passive according to the pattern يُفَعْلَلُ *yufaʿlalu* and conjugated as above, e.g.

أُتَرْجِمُ I translate.

تُتَرْجِمُ you (masc.) translate.

تُتَرْجِمِينَ you (fem.) translate.

يُتَرْجِمُ he translates, يُتَرْجَمُ it is translated.

تُتَرْجِمُ she translates, etc.

Examples:

إِنَّ ٱلْعُمَّالَ يَقْطَعُونَ ٱلْخَشَبَ بِٱلْفُؤُوسِ (sings. فَأْسٌ and عَامِلٌ)

The workers cut the wood with axes.

لِمَ لَا تَكْتُبِينَ مَكَاتِيبَكِ بِقَلَمِ ٱلْحِبْرِ؟

Why do you (fem.) not write your letters with the fountain-pen (lit. the ink-pen)?

نَرْجِعُ إِلَى ٱلْبَيْتِ قَبْلَ غُرُوبِ ٱلشَّمْسِ

We return home before the setting of the sun.

يَحْسِبُونَنِي لَا أَفْهَمُهُمْ

They think I do not understand them. (Note construction.)

سَتَكُونُ ٱلْخَدَّامَةُ حَاضِرَةً فِي ٱلصَّبَاحِ

The servant will be present in the morning.

إِنَّ ذَيْنِكَ ٱلْوَلَدَيْنِ يَكُونَانِ قَدْ كَتَبَا خِطَابَاتِهِمَا

Those two boys will have written their letters.

هَلْ تُتَرْجَمُ كُتُبٌ كَثِيرَةٌ مِنَ ٱلْإِنْكِلِيزِيَّةِ إِلَى ٱلْعَرَبِيَّةِ؟

Are many books translated from English into Arabic?

قَدْ تُرْجِمَتْ كُتُبٌ كَثِيرَةٌ فِي ٱلسَّنَةِ ٱلْمَاضِيَةِ

Many books were translated last year.

إِنَّ ٱلتَّلَامِيذَ يَجْلِسُونَ عَلَى كَرَاسِيَّ أَمَامَ ٱلْمُدَرِّسِ

The pupils sit on chairs in front of the teacher.

سَوْفَ يَكُونُ ٱلْمُدَرِّسَانِ فِي ٱلْمَدْرَسَةِ بَعْدَ ٱلظُّهْرِ

The (two) teachers will be in the school in the afternoon.

تَغْسِلُ ٱلْبَنَاتُ ثِيَابَهُنَّ بِٱلْمَاءِ وَٱلصَّابُونِ ثُمَّ يَعْصِرْنَهَا

The girls wash their clothes with soap and water then wring them out.

Exercise XII

١—أَتَكْتُبُ خِطَابًا لِأُمِّكَ مَرَّةً فِي ٱلْأُسْبُوعِ؟ نَعَمْ، وَهِيَ تَكْتُبُ لِي مَرَّتَيْنِ فِي ٱلْأُسْبُوعِ.

٢—يَذْهَبُ ٱلتَّلَامِذَةُ إِلَى ٱلْمَدْرَسَةِ فِي ٱلصَّبَاحِ وَيَرْجِعُونَ بَعْدَ ٱلظُّهْرِ لِلْغَدَاءِ.

٣—يَفْرَحُ كُلَّمَا يَسْمَعُ بِتَقَدُّمِ صَدِيقِهِ ٱلسَّرِيعِ فِي دِرَاسَاتِهِ.

٤—سَوْفَ نَكُونُ مُسْتَعِدِّينَ لِلْخُرُوجِ مَعَكُمْ عِنْدَ مَا تَحْضُرُونَ فِي ٱلْمَسَاءِ. (حَضَرَ)

٥—هَلْ تُبْعَثُ رَسَائِلُ كَثِيرَةٌ إِلَى فَرَنْسَا بِٱلْبَرِيدِ ٱلْجَوِّيِّ؟ نَعَمْ، لَا تُبْعَثُ رَسَائِلُ إِلَى هُنَاكَ بِٱلْبَرِيدِ ٱلْعَادِيِّ.

٦—كَمْ كِتَابًا تُرْجِمَ إِلَى ٱللُّغَةِ ٱلْعَرَبِيَّةِ فِي ٱلسَّنَةِ ٱلْمَاضِيَةِ؟ تُتَرْجَمُ كُتُبٌ عَدِيدَةٌ كُلَّ سَنَةٍ.

٧—لَا تَغْسِلُ يَدَيْهَا قَبْلَ ٱلْأَكْلِ وَذٰلِكَ عَيْبٌ كَبِيرٌ.

٨—مَا أَسْمَعُ كَلَامَهُ بِسَبَبِ ٱلضَّوْضَاءِ ٱلْكَبِيرَةِ ٱلَّتِي تَعْمَلُهَا ٱلْبَنَاتُ فِي ٱلْفَصْلِ. (عَمِلَ)

٩—أَيْنَ تَذْهَبَانِ لِقَضَاءِ فَصْلِ ٱلصَّيْفِ؟ نَذْهَبُ عَادَةً إِلَى شَاطِئِ ٱلْبَحْرِ.

١٠—لِمَ لَا تَكْتُبِينَ رَسَائِلَكِ بِوُضُوحٍ أَكْثَرَ؟

Translation

1. Do you write a letter to your mother once a week? Yes, and *she* writes to me twice a week.

2. The pupils go to school in the morning and return in the afternoon for lunch.

3. He rejoices whenever he hears of his friend's swift progress in his studies.

4. We shall be ready to go out with you (pl.) when you come in the evening.

5. Are many letters sent to France by air mail? Yes, no letters are sent there by ordinary mail.

6. How many books were translated into Arabic last year? Numerous books are translated every year.

7. She does not wash her hands before eating which is a great disgrace.

8. I do (can) not hear what he is saying (lit. his speech) because (by reason) of the great noise the girls are making in class.

9. Where do you (two) go to spend the summer season? We generally go to the sea-side.

10. Why do you (fem.) not write your letters more clearly (lit. with more clarity)?

LESSON XIII

48. The Subjunctive Mood

There are three moods of the imperfect of the verb, the indicative which we studied in the preceding lesson, the subjunctive mood and the jussive mood.

The subjunctive, active and passive, of the imperfect is formed from the indicative as follows:

Those persons which end with the last radical, i.e. which have no adjunct letters following the last radical, change the final vowel '*u*' into '*a*'. Those persons which end with نَ preceded by a long vowel after the last radical lose their نَ and if the preceding long vowel is '*ū*' an extra '*alif* is added. The 2nd and 3rd person plural feminines which end with نَ immediately after the last radical are the same in all three moods.

Thus the imperfect subjunctive active of كَتَبَ he wrote, is:

أَكْتُبَ	I (may) write.
تَكْتُبَ	you (masc.) (may) write.
تَكْتُبِي	you (fem.) (may) write.
يَكْتُبَ	he (may) write.
تَكْتُبَ	she (may) write.
نَكْتُبَ	we (may) write.
تَكْتُبُوا	you (masc.) (may) write.
تَكْتُبْنَ	you (fem.) (may) write.
تَكْتُبَا	you (dual) (may) write.
يَكْتُبُوا	they (masc.) (may) write.
يَكْتُبْنَ	they (fem.) (may) write.
يَكْتُبَا	they (dual masc.) (may) write.
تَكْتُبَا	they (dual fem.) (may) write.

The same changes in the verbal endings occur in the imperfect subjunctive of كَانَ, quadriliteral verbs and passives, e.g.

يَكُونَ he (may) be.

يُتَرْجِمَ he (may) translate.

يُكْتَبَ it (may) be written.

The subjunctive is used in subordinate clauses after the following common conjunctions:

أَنْ that, أَلَّا (or أَنْ لَا) that not, لِ, كَيْ, لِكَيْ and لِأَنْ so that, كَيْلَا, لِكَيْلَا and لِئَلَّا so that not, حَتَّى until, so that, e.g.

قَصَدْتُ أَنْ أَذْهَبَ مَعَهُ

I intended to go with him.

كُنْت جَالِسًا فِي ٱلْمَقْهَى حَتَّى تَحْضُرَ أُخْتِي

I was sitting in the café until my sister should come.

نَدْرُسُ لِكَيْ نَنْجَحَ (لِنَنْجَحَ) فِي ٱلِٱمْتِحَانِ

We study so that we may succeed in the examination.

نَظَرَ ٱلشَّيْخُ إِلَى سَاعَتِهِ لِئَلَّا يَتَأَخَّرَ (derived verb) عَنِ ٱلْمِيعَادِ

The shaykh looked at his watch so that he should not be late for the appointment.

49. The Negative of the Future

The subjunctive preceded by the particle لَنْ (a contraction for لَا يَكُونُ أَنْ) is used to express the negative of the future = 'never', e.g.

لَنْ تَذْهَبِي مَعَنَا You (fem.) will never go with us.

لَنْ نَقْبَلَ ٱلضَّيْمَ We shall never accept (submit to) oppression.

50. Subordinate Clauses after 'that'

If a subordinate clause is a factual statement and not a wish or purpose it is turned into a nominal clause and introduced by the conjunction أَنَّ 'that'. The construction after أَنَّ is the same as that after إِنَّ, i.e. the subject is in the accusative, e.g.

بَلَغَنِي أَنَّ عَلِيًّا قَتَلَ أَخَاهُ It reached me (I heard) that Ali killed his brother.

سَمِعْنَا أَنَّ ٱلرَّجُلَ ضَرَبَ وَلَدَ جَارِهِ We have heard that the man struck his neighbour's child.

زَعَمَ أَنَّهُ لَا يَفْهَمُ تِلْكَ ٱللُّغَةَ He asserted that he did not understand that language.

Note the tense sequence of the last sentence. At the time when he made his assertion he said: 'I *do* not understand.'

After the hollow verb قَالَ he said (conjugated in the perfect and imperfect exactly like كَانَ), 'that' must be translated by إِنَّ and *not* أَنَّ. In classical Arabic this إِنَّ had to be followed by direct speech but in modern Arabic we often find it followed by indirect speech. Thus the sentence 'he said he would go to Egypt' is translated classically by قَالَ إِنِّي سَوْفَ أَذْهَبُ إِلَى مِصْرَ and in modern Arabic by قَالَ إِنَّهُ سَوْفَ يَذْهَبُ إِلَى مِصْرَ. Once more note the tense sequence.

Examples:

لَنْ أَكْتُبَ لَهُ خِطَابًا بَعْدَ ٱلْيَوْمِ

I shall never write him a letter after today.

هَلْ قَرَأْتُمْ جَرِيدَةَ ٱلصَّبَاحِ؟ نَقْرَؤُهَا ٱلْآنَ لِكَيْ نَعْلَمَ أَخْبَارَ ٱلدُّنْيَا (sing. خَبَرٌ)

Have you read the morning newspaper? We are reading it now so that we may know the world news.

كَيْفَ حَالُ صَدِيقِكَ؟ قَالَ لَهُ ٱلطَّبِيبُ إِنَّهُ (إِنَّكَ) مَرِيضٌ جِدًّا

How is (the state of) your friend? The doctor told him he was very ill.

لَنْ نَقْبَلَ أَنْ يَذْهَبَ مَعَنَا إِلَى ٱلرِّيفِ

We shall not accept (agree to) his going with us to the country.

زَعَمُوا أَنَّ ٱلرَّجُلَ قَدْ سَرَقَ مِنْهُمْ مَبْلَغًا كَبِيرًا

They asserted that the man had robbed them of a large sum (of money).

أَتَحْسِبِينَ أَنِّي (أَنَّنِي) لَا أَقْدِرُ أَنْ أَقْرَأَ خَطَّكِ؟

Do you (fem.) think that I cannot read your handwriting?

هَلْ كَسَرْتَ ٱلزُّجَاجَةَ ٱلَّتِي كَانَتْ أُمُّكَ تَقْصِدُ أَنْ تَمْلَأَهَا بِٱلْحَلِيبِ؟

Have you broken the bottle which your mother intended to fill with milk?

قَضَى ٱلْقَاضِي بِأَنْ يُضْرَبَ ٱللُّصُوصُ حَتَّى يَعْرِفُوا أَنَّ مَالَ ٱلنَّاسِ حَرَامٌ

The judge decreed that the robbers should be beaten so that they should know that peoples' property is sacred.

Exercise XIII

١—طَلَبَ مِنِّي (إِلَيَّ) أَنْ أَكْتُبَ خِطَابًا لِمُدِيرِ شَرِكَتِهِ ٱلتِّجَارِيَّةِ لِأَنَّ يَمِينَهُ (يَدَهُ ٱلْيُمْنَى) كَانَتْ مَجْرُوحَةً. (جَرَحَ)

٢—أَتَقْصِدُونَ أَنْ تَقْرَؤُوا كُلَّ يَوْمٍ هٰذِهِ ٱلْجَرِيدَةَ ٱلَّتِي تَنْشُرُ يَوْمِيًّا مِثْلَ هٰذِهِ ٱلْأَخْبَارِ؟ (نَشَرَ)

٣—قَالَ إِنَّ خَبَرَ وَفَاةِ أَبِيهِ بَلَغَهُ مُنْذُ أُسْبُوعٍ.

٤—أَتَقْبَلِينَ أَنْ تَذْهَبِي مَعَنَا إِلَى شَاطِئِ ٱلْبَحْرِ لِكَيْ نَسْبَحَ فِي ٱلْمَاءِ ٱلدَّافِئِ؟ (سَبَحَ)

٥—هَلْ تَحْسِبْنَ أَنَّ مُحَمَّدًا وَلَدٌ مُجْتَهِدٌ؟ كَانَ مُجْتَهِدًا فِي ٱلسَّنَةِ ٱلْمَاضِيَةِ وَلٰكِنَّهُ ٱلْآنَ كَسْلَانُ جِدًّا.

٦—قَالَ ٱلْقَاضِي إِنَّهُ مُضْطَرٌّ إِلَى رَفْضِ أَقْوَالِهِمُ ٱلْكَاذِبَةِ. (رَفَضَ...)

٧—ضَرَبَ ٱلطَّبَّاخُ ٱلْجَوْزَةَ بِٱلشَّاكُوشِ لِيَكْسِرَ قِشْرَهَا.

٨—يَكُونُ خَيْرًا لَكُمْ أَنْ تَذْهَبُوا إِلَى ٱلْعِرَاقِ بِٱلطَّائِرَةِ لِأَنَّ ٱلسَّفَرَ بِٱلْبَحْرِ طَوِيلٌ جِدًّا.

٩—كَيْفَ تَجْرُؤُ أَنْ تَجْلِسَ عَلَى كُرْسِيٍّ وَأُمُّكَ ٱلْعَجُوزُ جَالِسَةٌ عَلَى ٱلْأَرْضِ؟ (جَرُؤَ)

١٠—لَقَدْ كَتَبَ هٰذَا ٱلْمُؤَرِّخُ ٱلشَّهِيرُ كُتُبًا عَدِيدَةً يَشْرَحُ فِيهَا نَظَرِيَّاتِهِ ٱلْغَرِيبَةَ. (شَرَحَ)

Translation

1. He asked me to write a letter to the director of his commercial company because his right hand was wounded.

2. Do you (pl.) intend to read every day this newspaper which publishes such (lit. the like of this) news daily?

3. He said that the news of his father's death (had) reached him a week ago.

4. Do you (fem.) accept to go with us to the sea-side to swim in the warm water?

5. Do you (fem. pl.) think that Mohammed is an industrious boy? He was industrious last year but now (adv. acc.) he is very lazy.

6. The judge said that he was compelled to reject their false (lit. lying) statements.

7. The cook struck the walnut with the hammer in order to break its shell.

8. It will be better (best) for you to go to Iraq by air because the journey by sea is very long.

9. How do you dare to sit on a chair when your old mother is sitting on the ground?

10. This famous historian has written many books in which he explains his strange theories.

LESSON XIV

51. The Jussive Mood

The jussive mood, active and passive, of the imperfect is formed from the indicative as follows:

Those persons which end with the last radical, i.e. which have no adjunct letters following the last radical, lose their final vowel altogether and take *sukūn*. The other persons are the same as in the subjunctive given in the preceding lesson.

Thus the jussive active of كَتَبَ is:

أَكْتُبْ may I write, let me write.

تَكْتُبْ may you (masc.) write.

تَكْتُبِي may you (fem.) write.

يَكْتُبْ may he write.

تَكْتُبْ may she write.

نَكْتُبْ may we write.

تَكْتُبُوا may you (masc.) write.

تَكْتُبْنَ may you (fem.) write.

تَكْتُبَا may you (dual) write.

يَكْتُبُوا may they (masc.) write.

يَكْتُبْنَ may they (fem.) write.

يَكْتُبَا may they (dual masc.) write.

تَكْتُبَا may they (dual fem.) write.

The same changes in the verbal endings occur in the jussive mood of quadriliteral verbs and passives, e.g.

يُتَرْجِمْ may he translate,

يُكْتَبْ may it be written,

but note that in the hollow verb كَانَ those persons mentioned above which end with the last radical and become vowelless have the preceding long vowel shortened since, according to Arabic phonetics, a long vowel cannot be followed by a vowelless consonant, e.g.

أَكُنْ may I be, let me be.

تَكُنْ may you (masc.) be.

تَكُونِي	may you (fem.) be.
يَكُنْ	may he be.
تَكُنْ	may she be, etc.

The jussive mood is rarely used standing alone, being generally preceded by the particle لِ. If the conjunction فَ 'and so' is prefixed to لِ this latter becomes vowelless, e.g.

لِتُضْرَبْ عُنُقُهُ !	may his neck be struck!
لِيَفْرَحْ طُولَ حَيَاتِهِ !	may he rejoice throughout his life! (lit. the length of his life).
فَلْيَذْهَبُوا مَعَكَ إِلَى بَارِيسَ !	let them (may they) go with you to Paris!
فَلْتَطْبُخْ لَنَا لَحْمًا !	let her (may she) cook meat for us!

The jussive mood may be strengthened by adding ـَنْ... or ـَنَّ... to the various persons, e.g.

أَكْتُبَنْ !	or	أَكْتُبَنَّ !	I shall certainly write!
تَكْتُبَنْ !	or	تَكْتُبَنَّ !	you shall certainly write! (masc.).
تَكْتُبِنْ !	or	تَكْتُبِنَّ !	you shall certainly write? (fem.).
يَكْتُبَنْ !	or	يَكْتُبَنَّ !	he shall certainly write!
تَكْتُبَنْ !	or	تَكْتُبَنَّ !	she shall certainly write!
تَكْتُبُنْ !	or	تَكْتُبُنَّ !	you shall certainly write! (plur.)
—		يَكْتُبَانِّ !	they shall certainly write! (dual).

For the use of the jussive mood in conditional sentences see § 90.

52. Prohibition

The 2nd persons of the jussive mood preceded by لَا give us the prohibition, e.g.

لَا تَكْتُبْ !	do not write! (masc.).
لَا تَذْهَبِي !	do not go! (fem.).

(from حَزِنَ) لَا تَحْزَنُوا ! do not grieve (be sad)! (masc. plur.).

لَا تَغْسِلْنَ ! do not wash! (fem. plur.).

لَا تَحْضُرَا ! do not come! (dual).

لَا تَكُنْ غَبِيًّا do not be stupid!

53. Negation of the Perfect

One most important use of the jussive mood has nothing imperative about it! This is when it is preceded by the particle لَمْ. In this case it is the *negation of the perfect* and is equal to and, if anything, as common as مَا + the perfect, e.g.

لَمْ أَكْتُبْ لَهُ خِطَابًا I *did not* write him a letter.

لَمْ يَذْهَبْ مَعَ أَخِيهِ He did not go with his brother.

لَمْ تَغْسِلِي يَدَيْكِ You (fem.) have not washed your hands.

(from صَدَقَ) لَمْ يَصْدُقُوا They have not spoken the truth.

If لَمْ is strengthened by adding مَا it is then equal to 'not yet', e.g.

لَمَّا يَفْهَمْ مَعْنَى هٰذِهِ ٱلْكَلِمَةِ He has not yet understood the meaning of this word.

لَمَّا نُتَرْجِمْ كِتَابَكَ We have not yet translated your book.

لَمَّا يَبْلُغْهُمْ هٰذَا ٱلْخَبَرُ This news has not yet reached them.

54. The Imperative

The imperative proper is derived from the second persons of the jussive mood active by cutting off the prefixed ت and its vowel, thus: تَكْتُبْ, تَكْتُبِي, تَكْتُبُوا, تَكْتُبْنَ, تَكْتُبَا. If what remains begins with a vowelless consonant it must be given an initial *hamzat-al-waṣl* the vowel of which is '*u*' if the next vowel following is '*u*' or '*i*' if it is '*i*' *or* '*a*', e.g.

اُكْتُبْ ! write! (masc.).

اُكْتُبِي ! write! (fem.).

اُكْتُبُوا ! write! (masc. plur.).

اُكْتُبْنَ ! write! (fem. plur.).

اُكْتُبَا ! write! (dual).

اِرْجِعْ ! return!

اِسْمَعْ ! hear, listen!

If after cutting off the prefixed ت what remains does not begin with a vowelless consonant then no prefixed *hamzat-al-waṣl* is necessary, e.g.

تَرْجِمْ ! translate! (masc.).

تَرْجِمِي ! translate! (fem.).

تَرْجِمُوا ! translate! (masc. plur.).

تَرْجِمْنَ ! translate! (fem. plur.).

تَرْجِمَا ! translate! (dual).

كُنْ ! be! (masc.).

كُونِي ! be! (fem.).

كُونُوا ! be! (masc. plur.).

كُنَّ ! be! (fem. plur.).

كُونَا ! be! (dual).

55. The Vocative

The vocative is introduced by the interjection يَا O! and is the same as the nominative. A word of the 1st declension loses its nūnation, e.g.

يَا وَلَدُ ! O boy! يَا مُحَمَّدُ ! O Mohammed!

The vocative is the same as the accusative if the word is governed by a genitive, e.g.

يَا سَيِّدَ ٱلنَّاسِ ! O Lord of the people!

(*al-fāḍila*) ! يَا سَيِّدِي ٱلْفَاضِلَ (my) excellent Sir!

! يَا عَبْدَ ٱللّٰهِ O Abdallah (Servant of God)!

A rhetorical and rather pompous way of introducing the vocative equal to the nominative is to prefix أَيُّهَا (يَا) (masc. sing. and plur.), أَيَّتُهَا (يَا) (fem. sing. and plur.) which must be immediately followed by the definite article. This is the usual mode of introducing the vocative qualified by an adjective, e.g.

! يَا أَيُّهَا ٱلشَّيْخُ O shaykh!

! يَا أَيُّهَا ٱلنَّاسُ O people!

! يَا أَيَّتُهَا ٱلْأَمِيرَةُ O princess!

!. يَا أَيُّهَا ٱلضَّابِطُ ٱلشُّجَاعُ O brave officer!

Examples:

! فَلْيُتَرْجَمْ هٰذَا ٱلْكِتَابُ إِلَى ٱلْعَرَبِيَّةِ

Let this book be translated into Arabic!

لَمْ يَقْتُلِ ٱللُّصُوصُ ٱلْمُسَافِرَ وَلٰكِنَّهُمْ سَرَقُوا مَالَهُ

The robbers did not kill the traveller but they stole his property.

! لَا تَكُونِي حَزِينَةً (لَا تَحْزَنِي)، يَا بِنْتِي

Do not be sad, my girl!

لَمَّا نَسْمَعْ أَخْبَارَهُمْ

We have not yet heard news of them.

لَمْ يَفْهَمُوا مَا كُنْتُ أَقْصِدُهُ

They did not understand my meaning (lit. what I was intending).

! يَا عَلِيُّ، ٱعْمَلْ لَنَا مَعْرُوفًا وَٱكْتُبْ لِأَبِينَا

O Ali! Do us the kindness and write to our father!

! يَا أَخِي، ٱقْرَأْ مَا هُوَ مَكْتُوبٌ فِي خِطَابِ أُخْتِنَا

O my brother! Read what is written in our sister's letter!

يَا أَيُّهَا ٱلْقَاضِي ٱلْفَاضِلُ، لَا تَحْكُمْ عَلَى هٰذَا ٱلرَّجُلِ ٱلْمِسْكِينِ !

O excellent judge! Do not condemn this wretched man!

أُخْرُجْ مِنْ عِنْدِنَا وَلَا تَقْرُبْ مِنَّا بَعْدَ هٰذَا ٱلْيَوْمِ !

Go out from our presence and do not come near us after this day!

Exercise XIV

١—فَلْنَرْجِعْ عَلَى ٱلْفَوْرِ إِلَى وَطَنِنَا لِنَسْمَعَ مِنْ أَفْوَاهِ أَصْدِقَائِنَا مَا حَدَثَ هُنَاكَ فِي غِيَابِنَا.

٢—يَا وَلَدِي ٱلْعَزِيزَ، لَا تَحْزَنْ لِعَدَمِ نَجَاحِكَ لِأَنَّكَ كُنْتَ مَرِيضًا أَثْنَاءَ ٱلِٱمْتِحَانِ وَسَوْفَ تَنْجَحُ فِي ٱلسَّنَةِ ٱلْمُقْبِلَةِ إِنْ شَاءَ ٱللّٰهُ.

٣—يَا حَضْرَةَ ٱلْقَاضِي، ٱكْتُبْ فِي ٱلْكَشْفِ أَسْمَاءَ هٰؤُلَاءِ ٱلْمُجْرِمِينَ، ٱلَّذِينَ دَخَلُوا ٱلْبَنْكَ لَيْلًا وَسَرَقُوا أَمْوَالَ ٱلنَّاسِ ٱلصَّالِحِينَ، حَتَّى تَنْظُرَ ٱلْحُكُومَةُ فِي عُقُوبَتِهِمْ.

٤—لَا تَكُونَا غَائِبَتَيْنِ يَا بِنْتَيَّ عِنْدَمَا تَحْضُرُ خَالَتُكُمَا لِزِيَارَتِنَا لِأَنَّهَا قَدْ قَالَتْ لِأُمِّكُمَا إِنَّهَا مُشْتَاقَةٌ إِلَى رُؤْيَتِكُمَا.

٥—اِذْهَبْ إِلَى ٱلْبَابِ وَٱسْمَحْ لِلزَّائِرِ أَنْ يَدْخُلَ لِيَشْرَبَ كُوبَ حَلِيبٍ. (سَمَحَ)

٦—يَا طَبَّاخُ، هٰذَا ٱللَّحْمُ غَيْرُ مَطْبُوخٍ. اُطْبُخْهُ جَيِّدًا وَٱبْعَثْهُ إِلَى ٱلِٱمْرَأَةِ ٱلْفَقِيرَةِ ٱلَّتِي تَسْكُنُ بِجَانِبِ مَكْتَبِ ٱلْبَرِيدِ ٱلْعُمُومِيِّ. (سَكَنَ)

٧—لِمَ لَمْ تَغْسِلْ وَجْهَكَ؟ لَمْ أَغْسِلْهُ لِأَنَّ ٱلصَّابُونَ كَانَ مَفْقُودًا. اِغْسِلْهُ حَالًا !

٨—لَا تُتَرْجِمِ ٱلرَّسَائِلَ ٱلْمَكْتُوبَةَ بِلُغَةٍ أَقْدِرُ أَنْ أَفْهَمَهَا. (قَدَرَ)

٩—لَنْ يَعْمَلُوا أَكْثَرَ مِنْ وَاجِبِهِمْ لِأَنَّهُمْ نَاسٌ كَسَالَى.

١٠—لَا تَضْرِبِي ذٰلِكَ ٱلْكَلْبَ ٱلْمِسْكِينَ يَا سَيِّدَتِي، لِأَنَّ صَاحِبَهُ سَرِيعُ ٱلْغَضَبِ.

Translation

1. Let us return immediately to our country (patria) in order to hear from the mouths of our friends what has happened there in our absence.

2. My dear boy, do not be sad at your lack of success for you were sick during (prepositional acc.) the examination and you will succeed next year, if God wills.

3. Your Honour the Judge (lit. honour of the Judge), write in the list the names of these criminals who entered the bank by night and stole the property of the honest people, so that the Government may look into their punishment.

4. Do not be absent, my daughters (dual), when your aunt comes to visit us for she has said to your mother that she is longing to see you (lit. to your seeing).

5. Go to the door and allow the visitor to come in and drink a glass of milk.

6. Cook, this meat is not cooked. Cook it well and send it to the poor woman who lives beside the General Post Office.

7. Why have you not washed your face? I did not wash it because the soap was missing. Wash it at once.

8. Do not translate the letters which are written in a language which I can understand.

9. They will never do more than they must (their duty) because they are lazy people.

10. Do not beat that wretched dog, madam, for its master is quick to get angry (of anger).

LESSON XV

56. The Simple Doubled Verb

A doubled verb is one of which the second and third radicals are identical. This class presents no great difficulty but the following two points should be noted:

If the form of the word in terms of فَعَلَ requires that the last radical be *vowelled and not separated from its preceding twin by a long vowel*, then the two identical radicals are run together without any separating vowel, e.g.

جَرَّ (for جَرَرَ) he pulled.

وَدَّ (for وَدِدَ) he wished, would have liked.

If such contraction takes place and the first radical is vowelless the vowel of the second radical is moved forward to the first, e.g.

يَجُرُّ (for يَجْرُرُ) he pulls.

يَوَدُّ (for يَوْدَدُ) he wishes, would like.

As an example of the conjugation of the perfect active of a doubled verb we have the following paradigm:

	جَرَرْتُ	I pulled.
	جَرَرْتَ	you (masc.) pulled.
	جَرَرْتِ	you (fem.) pulled.
(for جَرَرَ)	جَرَّ	he pulled.
(for جَرَرَتْ)	جَرَّتْ	she pulled.
	جَرَرْنَا	we pulled.
	جَرَرْتُمْ	you (masc. plur.) pulled.
	جَرَرْتُنَّ	you (fem. plur.) pulled.
	جَرَرْتُمَا	you (dual) pulled.
(for جَرَرُوا)	جَرُّوا	they (masc.) pulled.
	جَرَرْنَ	they (fem.) pulled.
(for جَرَرَا)	جَرَّا	they (masc. dual) pulled.
(for جَرَرَتَا)	جَرَّتَا	they (fem. dual) pulled.

The perfect passive is.

	جُرِرْتُ	I was pulled.
(for جُرِرَ)	جُرَّ	he was pulled, etc.

The imperfect indicative active is:

أَجُرُّ	I pull.
تَجُرُّ	you (masc.) pull.

تَجُرِّينَ you (fem.) pull.

يَجُرُّ he pulls.

تَجُرُّ she pulls.

نَجُرُّ we pull.

تَجُرُّونَ you (masc. plur.) pull.

تَجْرُرْنَ you (fem. plur.) pull.

تَجُرَّانِ you (dual) pull.

يَجُرُّونَ they (masc.) pull.

يَجْرُرْنَ they (fem.) pull.

يَجُرَّانِ they (masc. dual) pull.

تَجُرَّانِ they (fem. dual) pull.

Doubled verbs are mostly of the pattern فَعَلَ and generally take '*u*' as their middle vowel in the imperfect. A few, however, take '*i*' in the imperfect.

The imperfect indicative passive is:

أُجَرُّ I am pulled.

يُجَرُّ he is pulled, etc.

The same rules for the subjunctive as have already been given apply to the doubled verbs, e.g.

أَجُرَّ I (may) pull.

تَجُرَّ you (masc.) (may) pull.

تَجُرِّي you (fem. (may) pull.

يَجُرَّ he (may) pull.

تَجُرَّ she (may) pull.

يَجُرُّوا they (masc.) (may) pull, etc.

Note that the jussive mood has two alternative forms. The first of these is perfectly regular in accordance with the rules given in the preceding lesson and at the beginning of this one, e.g.

أَجْرُرْ ! may I pull!

تَجْرُرْ ! may you (masc.) pull!

تَجُرِّي ! may you (fem.) pull!

يَجْرُرْ ! may he pull!

تَجْرُرْ ! may she pull! etc.

But by far the more common form of the jussive mood of doubled verbs is *identical with the subjunctive mood*, e.g.

أَجُرَّ ! may I pull!

تَجُرَّ ! may he pull! etc.

Thus it will be seen that we also have two forms of the imperative proper in the masculine singular, viz.

أُجْرُرْ ! or more commonly جُرَّ ! pull! (masc.).

جُرِّي ! pull! (fem.).

جُرُّوا ! pull! (masc. plur.).

أُجْرُرْنَ ! pull! (fem. plur.).

جُرَّا ! pull! (dual).

57. The Active Participle of a Doubled Verb

The active participle (فَاعِل) is جَارٌّ (for جَارِرٌ) pulling. It should be noted that it is only in derivatives of doubled verbs in which the two twin consonants are run together that we sometimes find a long vowel, always 'ā', followed by a vowelless consonant as above.

The passive participle (مَفْعُول) is مَجْرُورٌ.

Examples:

يَلْزَمُ (perf. لَزِمَ) أَنْ يَكُونَ ٱلْحِصَانُ ٱلَّذِي يَجُرُّ ٱلْعَرَبَةَ قَوِيًّا

The horse that draws the carriage must be strong (lit. it is necessary that...).

يَا فَاطِمَةُ، رُدِّي ٱلْجَرِيدَةَ لِصَاحِبِهَا ! لَقَدْ رَدَدْتُهَا

O Fatima, return the newspaper to its owner! I have already returned it.

أَلَمْ تَسُنَّ ٱلسِّكِّينَ قَبْلَ مَا (قَبْلَ أَنْ) قَطَعْتَ ٱللَّحْمَ؟ بَلَى، هِيَ حَادَّةٌ جِدًّا

Did you not sharpen the knife before you cut the meat? Yes, it is very sharp. (Note that 'yes' in answer to a negative question is بَلَى, not نَعَمْ.

لِمَاذَا يَقِلُّ ٱلْمَطَرُ فِي ٱلصَّيْفِ؟ لَا شَكَّ أَنَّهُ يَقِلُّ بِسَبَبِ قِلَّةِ ٱلسَّحَابِ

Why does the rain decrease in summer? There is no doubt that it decreases by reason of the sparseness of the clouds. (Note that لَا which denies that such and such a class of thing exists, as لَا شَكَّ there is no doubt, is followed by the indefinite accusative *without* nūnation.)

لَنْ نَفِرَّ أَمَامَ ٱلْأَعْدَاءِ (sing. عَدُوٌّ) لِأَنَّنَا شُجْعَانٌ

We shall never flee before the enemy because we are brave.

يَا بُنَيَّةُ، لَا تَكُبِّي كُوزَ ٱلْحَلِيبِ ٱلَّذِي وَضَعْتُهُ عَلَى ٱلْمَائِدَةِ؟

Little girl, do not upset the jug of milk which I have put on the table!

يَوَدُّ مُحَمَّدٌ أَنْ يَذْهَبَ إِلَى حَدِيقَةِ ٱلْحَيَوَانَاتِ

Mohammed would like (lit. likes) to go to the Zoological Garden.

ٱلْجَبَانُ مَذْمُومٌ (يُذَمُّ) لِجُبْنِهِ

The coward is censured for his cowardice.

اَلشَّمْسُ أَحَرُّ فِي ٱلصَّيْفِ مِنْهَا فِي ٱلشِّتَاءِ

The sun is warmer in summer than (it is) in winter.

لَا تَسُدُّوا طَرِيقَنَا، يَا أَيُّهَا ٱلنَّاسُ، فَإِنَّا نَوَدُّ أَنْ نَذْهَبَ إِلَى قَصْرِ ٱلْمَلِكِ

Do not block our way, you people, for we wish to go to the king's palace.

Exercise XV

١—أَتَوَدِّينَ أَنْ تَنْظُرِينِي رَاكِبًا جَمَلًا؟ أَوَدُّ أَنْ أَرْكَبَ جَمَلًا بِنَفْسِي. (رَكِبَ)

٢—فِي ٱلشَّرْقِ يَجُرُّ ٱلْمِحْرَاثَ ثَوْرٌ أَمَّا فِي ٱلْغَرْبِ فَيَجُرُّهُ حِصَانٌ وَفِي بَعْضِ ٱلْأَقْطَارِ تَجُرُّهُ جَرَّارَةٌ.

٣—طَلَبْتُ مِنْهُمْ أَنْ يَبُتُّوا فِي ٱلْأَمْرِ بِسُرْعَةٍ وَلٰكِنَّهُمْ لَمْ يَعْمَلُوا شَيْئًا بَعْدُ.

٤—أَرَشَشْتُمْ أَرْضَ ٱلْفِنَاءِ بِٱلْمَاءِ لِئَلَّا يَصْعَدَ ٱلْغُبَارُ؟ نَعَمْ، قَدْ رَشَشْنَاهَا وَكَنَسْنَا ٱلسُّلَّمَ. (صَعِدَ)

٥—أَتَشُكُّكُنَّ فِي صِدْقِهِ؟ لَا، لَا نَشُكُّ فِي أَنَّهُ يَصْدُقُ دَائِمًا.

٦—مَدَدْتُ لَهُ يَدِي وَلٰكِنَّهُ لَمْ يَمُدَّ لِي يَدَهُ. مُدَّهَا لَهُ مَرَّةً ثَانِيَةً.

٧—لَا يَفِرُّ مِثْلُ هٰذَا ٱلْجَيْشِ ٱلْبَاسِلِ أَمَامَ ٱلْعَدُوِّ مَهْمَا كَثُرَ عَدَدُهُ.

٨—يَنُصُّ ٱلْقَانُونُ عَلَى أَنْ تُنْشَرَ أَسْمَاءُ جَمِيعِ ٱلْمُفْلِسِينَ فِي ٱلصَّحِيفَةِ ٱلرَّسْمِيَّةِ.

٩—لَمْ نَقْدِرْ أَنْ نَحُلَّ ٱلْعُقْدَةَ وَلِذٰلِكَ قَطَعْنَا ٱلدُّوبَارَةَ بِهٰذَا ٱلسِّكِّينِ ٱلْحَادِّ.

١٠—رَقَّ قَلْبُهُ عِنْدَمَا سَمِعَ أَنَّ ٱلْعَجُوزَ قَدْ ضُرِبَتْ أَمَامَ ٱلْمَحْكَمَةِ.

Translation

1. Would you like to see me riding a camel? I should like to ride a camel myself (lit. with myself).

2. In the east the plough is drawn by an ox but in the west it is drawn by a horse and in some (lit. a part of the) countries it is drawn by a tractor.

3. I requested them to take steps in the matter quickly but they have not done anything yet.

4. Have you sprinkled the ground of the courtyard with water so that the dust may not rise? Yes, we have sprinkled it and swept the stairs.

5. Do you (fem. pl.) doubt his honesty? No, we do not doubt that he always speaks the truth.

6. I stretched out my hand to him but he did not stretch out his (hand) to me. Stretch it out to him again (lit. a second time).

7. Such a brave army does not flee before the enemy however great his number may be (lit. however it has become great).

8. The law stipulates (lays down) that the names of all bankrupts shall be published in the Official Journal.

9. We were not able to untie the knot and so (therefore) we cut the string with this sharp knife.

10. His heart became tender (he was touched) when he heard that the old woman had been beaten in front of the law-court.

LESSON XVI

58. Verbs which have *Hamza* as a Radical

(i) *Verbs with* hamza *as 1st radical.*

These are conjugated perfectly regularly, full consonantal value being given to the *hamza* with the following exceptions:

In the imperative proper *hamza* becomes the weak consonant cognate to the vowel of the prefixed *hamzat-al-waṣl*, e.g.

إِيذَنْ ! (for إِئْذَنْ from أَذِنَ) allow, permit!

إِيسِرْ ! (for إِئْسِرْ from أَسَرَ) capture!

أُومُلْ ! (for أُؤْمُلْ from أَمَلَ) hope!

However, when the vowel of the prefixed *hamzat-al-waṣl* is elided by reason of a word preceding it, the first radical *hamza* reverts to its original consonantal value. Note that if the word which causes the vowel of the *hamzat-al-waṣl* to be elided is فَ or وَ 'and', 'so' then the *'alif* carrying the *hamzat-al-waṣl* is also elided, e.g.

وَأْذَنْ ! and permit!

وَأْسِرْ ! and capture!

فأمُلْ ! and so hope!

but قُلْتُ: آئْذَنْ ! I said: permit!

قُلْتُ: آئْسِرْ ! I said: capture!

قُلْتُ: آؤْمُلْ ! I said: hope!

Note that the three common verbs أَكَلَ he ate, أَخَذَ he took and أَمَرَ he commanded, in all of which the vowel of the middle radical is '*u*' in the imperfect, lose their first radical *hamza* altogether in the imperative proper, e.g.

كُلْ، كُلِي، كُلُوا، كُلْنَ، كُلَا ! eat!

خُذْ، خُذِي، خُذُوا، خُذْنَ، خُذَا ! take!

مُرْ، مُرِي، مُرُوا، مُرْنَ، مُرَا ! command!

(ii) *Verbs with* hamza as *2nd radical.*

These are all perfectly regular with the exception of سَأَلَ he asked, which has two forms of the jussive mood in the more common of which the middle radical *hamza* is elided and its vowel moved forward to the first radical, e.g.

أَسْأَلْ ! or more commonly	أَسَلْ !	may I ask!
تَسْأَلْ ! or more commonly	تَسَلْ !	may you (masc.) ask!
تَسْأَلِي ! or more commonly	تَسَلِي !	may you (fem.) ask!
etc.	etc.	etc.

Thus we have two forms of the imperative proper, viz.

إِسْأَلْ ! or more commonly	سَلْ !	ask! (masc. sing.).
إِسْأَلِي ! or more commonly	سَلِي !	ask! (fem. sing.).
etc.	etc.	etc.

(iii) *Verbs with* hamza *as 3rd radical.*

These are perfectly regular in all cases, full consonantal value being given to the *hamza*, e.g.

قَرَأَ he read. يَقْرَأُ he reads.

قُرِئَ	it was read.	يُقْرَأُ	it is read.
لَمْ يَقْرَأْ	he did not read.	أَنْ يَقْرَأَ	that he may read.
إِقْرَأْ !	read!	مَقْرُوءٌ	read.

59. Verbs with و as 1st radical

The peculiarity of the *most common* of this class of verbs which are otherwise quite regular is that the 1st radical falls out altogether in the imperfect *active*, e.g.

	وَصَلَ	he arrived.	يَصِلُ	he arrives.	صِلْ !	arrive!
	وَعَدَ	he promised.	يَعِدُ	he promises.	عِدْ !	promise!
	وَضَعَ	he placed.	يَضَعُ	he places.	ضَعْ !	place!
	وَقَعَ	he fell.	يَقَعُ	he falls.	قَعْ !	fall!
but	يُوعَدُ	he *is* promised.	يُوضَعُ	it *is* placed.		

In some less common verbs the initial و is retained, e.g.

وَجِلَ he was afraid, timid.

يَوْجَلُ he is afraid.

إِيجَلْ ! (for إِوْجَلْ) be afraid!

Note that eight verbs of the pattern فَعِلَ of which the following are the most common retain the '*i*' of the 2nd radical in the imperfect contrary to the rule given in Lesson XII:

	وَرِثَ	he inherited.	يَرِثُ	he inherits.
	وَثِقَ بِـ...	he trusted (in).	يَثِقُ	he trusts.
	وَرِمَ	it swelled.	يَرِمُ	it swells.
(weak verb)	وَلِيَ	he was near, in charge of.	يَلِي (for يَلِيُ)	he is near, in charge of.

If the verb is doubled no elision of the initial و takes place, e.g.

وَدَّ (for وَدِدَ) he liked, wished.

يَوَدُّ he likes, wishes.

Verbs which have ي as 1st radical are regular in all respects, e.g.

يَئِسَ he despaired.

يَيْأَسُ he despairs.

إِيْأَسْ ! despair!

Examples:

هَلْ تَأْذَنُونَ لِي بِٱلْخُرُوجِ ؟ سَنَأْذَنُ لَكَ بَعْدَ قَلِيلٍ

Do you permit me to go out? We shall permit you shortly. (Note the construction after أَذِنَ).

إِيذَنْ لِي بِٱلسَّفَرِ، يَا أَبِي، وَأْمُلْ مِنْهُ خَيْرًا !

Father, permit me to travel and hope that good will come of it!

سَوْفَ نَسْأَلُهُمْ عَنْ مِيعَادِ حُضُورِهِمْ . لَا تَسْلُوهُمْ عَنْهُ !

We shall ask them about the time fixed for (lit. the appointed time of) their coming. Do not ask them about it!

خُذُوا هٰذَا ٱلْخُبْزَ ٱلْجَيِّدَ وَكُلُوهُ !

Take this excellent bread and eat it!

لَقَدْ أَخَذْنَاهُ وَسَوْفَ نَأْكُلُ مِنْهُ حَتَّى نَشْبَعَ

We have taken it and shall eat of it until we are satisfied.

هَلْ بَرِئَتِ ٱلسَّيِّدَةُ حَرَمُكَ مِنْ مَرَضِهَا ؟ لَا، لِلْأَسَفِ لَمْ تَبْرَأْ بَعْدُ

Has your wife (lit. the lady your wife) recovered from her illness? No, unfortunately (lit. to the regret) she has not yet recovered.

هَلْ وَصَلَ إِخْوَتُنَا مِنَ ٱلْإِسْكَنْدَرِيَّةِ ؟ لَا، يُؤَمَّلُ أَنْ يَصِلُوا بَعْدَ ٱلظُّهْرِ

Have our brothers arrived from Alexandria? No, it is hoped that they will (may) arrive in the afternoon.

ثِقْ بِٱللّٰهِ وَٱعْمَلْ مَا تَظُنُّهُ خَيْرًا

Trust in God and do what you think best (good).

يَا أُخْتِي، ٱحْذَرِي أَنْ تَقَعِي فِي ٱلنَّهْرِ!

Sister, be careful not to fall into the river!

مَنْ سَيَرِثُ هٰذَا ٱلْمَالَ ٱلْكَثِيرَ؟ يَا لَيْتَنِي وَارِثُهُ!

Who will inherit this fortune? Would that I were heir to it! (Note that لَيْتَ (يَا) 'would that' takes the same construction after it as إِنَّ and أَنَّ.)

Exercise XVI

(Note: In the remaining exercises the vowelling will be given less and less, especially in prepositions and nouns with which the student should be by now thoroughly familiar.)

١—خُذْ هذا الصُّنْدوقَ الأَخْضَرَ الكبيرَ وضَعْهُ في السَّيَّارةِ التي سَتَصِلُ عند الظُّهْرِ تَمامًا.

٢—لَمْ تَأْذَنْ لي حَرَمُكَ بالجُلوسِ في الصَّالُونِ حتّى آخُذَ بَعْضَ الراحةِ.

٣—لم يَسْأَلُوها عن صِحّةِ أبيها لأنّ رِسالةً وصلتْهم مِنْهُ في نَفْسِ اليومِ.

٤—ألم تَقَعِي عن فَرَسِكِ عندما ذهبْتِ إلى صَيْدِ الثَّعْلَبِ؟ بَلَى، وكسرْتُ ذِراعي.

٥—ابْحَثُوا لي عن رجلٍ أَثِقُ بِهِ لِمُساعَدَتي في أَعْمالي.

٦—يا شابُّ، لا تَيْأَسْ من أَنْ تَرِثَ مالَ عَمِّكَ بالرَّغْمِ مِنْ أنّ مَوْقِفَهُ منكَ ومن أمِّكَ لم يَكُنْ مَوْقِفَ رجلٍ كريمٍ.

٧—يا بِنْتي، كُلي خُبْزَكِ وٱشْرَبي حليبَكِ بِسُرْعةٍ لِكَيْ تَصِلي المدرسةَ قبلَ فَتْحِ البابِ.

٨—يُؤْمَلُ أنْ ياذَنُوا لنا بالذَهابِ معهم إلى المَسْرَحِ.

٩—إنَّ الخادمةَ لم تَضَعْ قُمْصاني في دُرْجي بَلْ وضَعَتْها على السَرِيرِ.

١٠—لا تَسْأَلُوا عمّا (عن ما) لا يَخُصُّكم ! يا لَيْتَنَا لم نَسَلْ !

Translation

1. Take this large green box and put it in the motor-car which will arrive at noon exactly.

2. Your wife did allow me to sit in the sitting-room to take some rest.

3. They did not ask her about her father's health because they had received a letter from him the same day.

4. Did you (fem.) not fall from your mare when you went fox-hunting? Yes, and I broke my arm.

5. Look for a man for me in whom I can trust to help me (lit. for my help) in my work.

6. Young man, do not despair of inheriting your uncle's próperty although his attitude to you and your mother was not that of a generous man.

7. Daughter, eat your bread and drink your milk quickly so that you may arrive at school before the door opens.

8. It is to be hoped that they will allow us to go with them to the theatre.

9. The servant did not put my shirts in my drawer but (she put them) on the bed.

10. Do not ask about what does not belong to you (pl.)! Would that we had not asked!

LESSON XVII

60. Hollow Verbs

The hollow verbs are those of which the middle radical is one of the weak consonants و and ي. They fall into four categories to the first of which the student has already been introduced in the paragraphs on the conjugation of كَانَ.

Group I. This consists of verbs of the pattern فَعَلَ the middle radical of which is و. Their characteristic is a long '*ū*' between the first and last radicals in the imperfect, e.g.

زَارَ (for زَوَرَ) he visited.

يَزُورُ (for يَزْوُرُ) he visits.

This verb fully conjugated in the perfect active is:

zurtu	زُرْتُ	I visited.
	زُرْتَ	you (masc.) visited.
	زُرْتِ	you (fem.) visited.
	زَارَ	he visited.
	زَارَتْ	she visited.
	زُرْنَا	we visited.
	زُرْتُمْ	you (masc. plur.) visited.
	زُرْتُنَّ	you (fem. plur.) visited.
	زُرْتُمَا	you (dual) visited.
	زَارُوا	they (masc.) visited.
	زُرْنَ	they (fem.) visited.
	زَارَا	they (masc. dual) visited.
	زَارَتَا	they (fem. dual) visited.

The imperfect indicative active is:

'azūru	أَزُورُ	I visit.
	تَزُورُ	you (masc.) visit.
	تَزُورِينَ	you (fem.) visit.
	يَزُورُ	he visits.
	تَزُورُ	she visits.

	نَزُورُ	we visit.
tazūrūna	تَزُورُونَ	you (masc. plur.) visit.
tazŭrna	تَزُرْنَ	you (fem. plur.) visit.
	تَزُورَانِ	you (dual) visit.
yazūrūna	يَزُورُونَ	they (masc.) visit.
yazŭrna	يَزُرْنَ	they (fem.) visit.
	يَزُورَانِ	they (masc. dual) visit.
	تَزُورَانِ	they (fem. dual) visit.

The imperfect subjunctive active is:

'azūra	أَزُورَ	I (may) visit.
	تَزُورَ	you (masc.) (may) visit.
	تَزُورِي	you (fem.) (may) visit, etc.

Now note again the shortening of the long vowel preceding the final radical when this is vowelless, e.g.

The jussive active is:

'azŭr!	أَزُرْ !	may I visit!
	تَزُرْ !	may you (masc.) visit!
	تَزُورِي !	may you (fem.) visit!

The imperative proper is:

زُرْ !	visit! (masc.).
زُورِي !	visit! (fem.).
زُورُوا !	visit! (masc. plur.).
زُرْنَ !	visit! (fem. plur.).
زُورَا !	visit! (dual).

The active participle (see Lesson XI) is:

زَائِرٌ (for زَاوِرٌ) visiting, a visitor.

The passive participle (see Lesson XI) is:

مَزُورٌ (for مَزْوُورٌ) visited.

Group II. This consists of verbs of the pattern فَعِلَ the middle radical of which is و. Their characteristic is a long '*ā*' between the first and last radicals in the imperfect, e.g.

نَالَ (for نَوِلَ) he obtained.

يَنَالُ (for يَنْوَلُ) he obtains.

This verb fully conjugated in the perfect active is:

niltu	نِلْتُ	I obtained.
	نِلْتَ	you (masc.) obtained.
	نِلْتِ	you (fem.) obtained.
	نَالَ	he obtained.
	نَالَتْ	she obtained.
	نِلْنَا	we obtained.
	نِلْتُمْ	you (masc. plur.) obtained.
	نِلْتُنَّ	you (fem. plur.) obtained.
	نِلْتُمَا	you (dual) obtained.
	نَالُوا	they (masc.) obtained.
	نِلْنَ	they (fem.) obtained.
	نَالَا	they (masc. dual) obtained.
	نَالَتَا	they (fem. dual) obtained.

The imperfect indicative active is:

'anālu	أَنَالُ	I obtain.
	تَنَالُ	you (masc.) obtain.
	تَنَالِينَ	you (fem.) obtain.
	يَنَالُ	he obtains.
	تَنَالُ	she obtains.
	نَنَالُ	we obtain.
tanālūna	تَنَالُونَ	you (masc. plur.) obtain.
tanălna	تَنَلْنَ	you (fem. plur.) obtain.
	تَنَالَانِ	you (dual) obtain.
yanālūna	يَنَالُونَ	they (masc.) obtain.
yanălna	يَنَلْنَ	they (fem.) obtain.
	يَنَالَانِ	they (masc. dual) obtain.
	تَنَالَانِ	they (fem. dual) obtain.

The imperfect subjunctive active is:

'anāla	أَنَالَ	I (may) obtain.
	تَنَالَ	you (masc.) (may) obtain.
	تَنَالِي	you (fem.) (may) obtain. etc.

The jussive active is:

'anăl!	أَنَلْ !	may I obtain!
	تَنَلْ !	may you (masc.) obtain!
	تَنَالِي !	may you (fem.) obtain! etc.

The imperative proper is:

نَلْ ! obtain! (masc.).

نَالِي ! obtain! (fem.).

نَالُوا ! obtain! (masc. plur.).

نَلْنَ ! obtain! (fem. plur.).

نَالَا ! obtain! (dual).

The active participle is:

نَائِلٌ (for نَاوِلٌ) obtaining).

The passive participle is:

مَنُولٌ (for مَنْوُولٌ) obtained.

Group III. This consists of verbs of the pattern فَعَلَ the middle radical of which is ي. Their characteristic is a long '*ī*' between the first and last radicals of the imperfect, e.g.

بَاعَ (for بَيَعَ) he sold.

يَبِيعُ (for يَبْيِعُ) he sells.

This verb fully conjugated in the perfect active is:

biʿtu بِعْتُ I sold.

بِعْتَ you (masc.) sold.

بِعْتِ you (fem.) sold.

بَاعَ he sold.

بَاعَتْ she sold.

بِعْنَا we sold.

بِعْتُمْ you (masc. plur.) sold.

بِعْتُنَّ you (fem. plur.) sold.

	بِعْتُمَا	you (dual) sold.
	بَاعُوا	they (masc.) sold.
	بِعْنَ	they (fem.) sold.
	بَاعَا	they (masc. dual) sold.
	بَاعَتَا	they (fem. dual) sold.

The imperfect indicative active is:

'abīعu	أَبِيعُ	I sell.
	تَبِيعُ	you (masc.) sell.
	تَبِيعِينَ	you (fem.) sell.
	يَبِيعُ	he sells.
	تَبِيعُ	she sells.
	نَبِيعُ	we sell.
tabīعūna	تَبِيعُونَ	you (masc. plur.) sell.
tabiعna	تَبِعْنَ	you (fem. plur.) sell.
	تَبِيعَانِ	you (dual) sell.
yabīعūna	يَبِيعُونَ	they (masc.) sell.
yabiعna	يَبِعْنَ	they (fem.) sell.
	يَبِيعَانِ	they (masc. dual) sell.
	تَبِيعَانِ	they (fem. dual) sell.

The imperfect subjunctive active is:

'abīعa	أَبِيعَ	I (may) sell.
	تَبِيعَ	you (masc.) (may) sell.
	تَبِيعِي	you (fem.) (may) sell, etc.

The jussive active is:

'abīʿ!	أَبِعْ !	may I sell!
	تَبِعْ !	may you (masc.) sell!
	تَبِيعِي !	may you (fem.) sell! etc.

The imperative proper is:

بِعْ ! sell! (masc.).

بِيعِي ! sell! (fem.).

بِيعُوا ! sell! (masc. plur.).

بِعْنَ ! sell! (fem. plur.).

بِيعَا ! sell! (dual).

The active participle is:

بَائِعٌ (for بَايِعٌ) selling.

The passive participle is:

مَبِيعٌ (for مَبْيُوعٌ) sold.

Group IV. This consists of verbs of the pattern فَعِلَ the middle radical of which is ي, e.g.

هَابَ (for هَيِبَ) he feared, was in awe of.

يَهَابُ (for يَهْيَبُ) he fears.

Verbs in this group are identical in conjugation with verbs of Group II, e.g.

هِبْتُ I feared, etc.

أَهَابُ I fear, etc.

أَهَابَ I (may) fear, etc.

أَهَبْ ! may I fear! etc.

هَبْ ! fear! etc.

هَائِبٌ fearing.

The only exception is that the passive participle is as that of Group III, e.g.

مَهِيبٌ feared, held in awe.

61. The Passive of Hollow Verbs

The passives of transitive verbs of all four preceding groups are identical, e.g.

زِيرَ (for زُوِرَ) he was visited.

يُزَارُ (for يُزْوَرُ) he is visited.

نِيلَ (for نُوِلَ) it was obtained.

يُنَالُ (for يُنْوَلُ) it is obtained.

بِيعَ (for بُيِعَ) it was sold.

يُبَاعُ (for يُبْيَعُ) it is sold.

هِيبَ (for هُيِبَ) he was feared.

يُهَابُ (for يُهْيَبُ) he is feared.

Thus the perfect passive is:

زِرْتُ I was visited.

زِرْتَ you (masc.) were visited.

زِرْتِ you (fem.) were visited.

زِيرَ he was visited.

زِيرَتْ she was visited, etc.

The imperfect indicative passive is:

أُزَارُ I am visited.

تُزَارُ you (masc.) are visited.

تُزَارِينَ you (fem.) are visited.

يُزَارُ he is visited.

تُزَارُ she is visited, etc.

Examples:

إِنِّي لَمْ أَزُرْ صَدِيقِي مُنْذُ أُسْبُوعَيْنِ فَأَوَدُّ أَنْ أَزُورَهُ غَدًا

I have not visited my friend for (lit. since) two weeks and so I should like to visit him to-morrow.

مَتَى جِئْتُمْ (from جَاءَ Group III) مِنَ ٱلْقَاهِرَةِ؟ جِئْنَا أَمْسِ

When did you come from Cairo? We came yesterday.

لَنْ تَمُوتَ ذِكْرَى أُولَائِكَ ٱلْأَبْطَالِ (sing. بَطَلٌ)

The memory of those heroes will never die.

يَا وَلَدِي، لَا تَخَفْ (from خَافَ Group II) مِنَ ٱلظُّلْمَةِ!

My boy, don't be afraid of the darkness!

لِمَاذَا يُقَالُ إِنَّهُ لَنْ يَبِيعَ كُتُبَهُ؟

Why is it said that he will never sell his books?

لَا يَنَالُ ٱلتِّلْمِيذُ ٱلْكَسْلَانُ ٱلْجَائِزَةَ

The lazy pupil does not win the prize.

يَا صَدِيقَيَّ، قُومَا فَلْنَذْهَبْ مَعًا إِلَى ٱلْجُنَيْنَةِ!

My (two) friends, arise and let us go together to the garden!

هَلْ سِرْتُمْ (from سَارَ Group III) عَلَى أَقْدَامِكُمْ مِنَ ٱلْفَجْرِ حَتَّى ٱلظُّهْرِ؟

لَا، رَكِبْنَا عَرَبَةً

Did you walk (lit. travel on your feet) from dawn until noon? No, we rode (in) a carriage.

كَانَ مِنَ ٱللَّازِمِ أَنْ يَعُودُوا إِلَى بُيُوتِهِمْ قَبْلَ وُصُولِ ٱلْمُفَتِّشِ

It was (of the) necessary that they should return to their homes before the inspector's arrival.

كُلْ وَٱشْرَبْ مِنْ رِزْقِ ٱللّٰهِ، ثُمَّ نَمْ (from نَامَ Group II) حَتَّى ٱلصَّبَاحِ !

Eat and drink of the sustenance of God, then sleep until the morning!

Exercise XVII

١—قُلْنَا لِصديقِنا محمدٍ إنّنا نَوَدُّ أن نَزُورَ القاضِيَ ولكنّه قال إنّهُ يَخَافُ من غَضَبِهِ.

٢—لَنْ تَنالي رِضَا والِدَيْكِ بِدُونِ طاعةٍ كاملةٍ

٣—بِكَمْ تَبيعُ لي هذا الكتابَ؟ أَبيعُهُ لَكَ بِقِرْشَيْنِ. إنّه لَرَخيصٌ.

٤—يُقَالُ إنّ هذا الولدَ الصغيرَ يَخافُ مِنَ الظَّلامِ فإذا هو شُجاعٌ مِثْلَ الأَسَدِ!

٥—أَوَدُّ أن أَنامَ على سَريري الوَثيرِ حتّى تَجيئَني الخادمةُ بالشاي.

٦—يَقُولُونَ إنّهم لا يَجِدُونَ ما يَسُرُّهم في هذه المدينةِ الوَسِخةِ. (وَجَدَ)

٧—لَقَدْ بِيعَتْ هذه السَّيّارةُ بِثَمَنٍ غالٍ. لِمَاذا؟ هل مَاتَ صاحِبُها؟ لا، ولكنّه سوف يَمُوتُ عَنْ قريبٍ.

٨—تَذْهَبُ النِّساءُ إلى السُّوقِ في الصباحِ ويَعُدْنَ إلى بُيوتِهِنَّ بَعْدَ شِراءِ ما يَلْزَمُهُنَّ. (لَزِمَ)

٩—يا بَنَاتُ قُمْنَ فَٱذْهَبْنَ إلى أُمِّكُنَّ التي هي في الجُنَيْنةِ في ٱنْتِظارِ زِيارةِ عَمّتِكُنَّ.

١٠—أَتَوْدَدْنَ أَنْ تَسِرْنَ معي إلى مَحَطّةِ السِّكّةِ الحَديديّةِ؟ لا، نَحْنُ تَعِبَاتٌ جدًّا.

Translation

1. We said to our friend Mohammed that we should like to visit the Judge but he said he was afraid of his anger.

2. You (fem.) will never get your parents' approval without complete obedience.

3. For how much will you sell me this book? I will sell it to you for two piastres. It is indeed cheap.

4. It is said that this little boy is afraid of the dark but lo! he is as brave as a lion!

5. I should like to sleep in my comfortable bed until the servant brings me (lit. comes to me with) tea.

6. They say that they do not find anything which (lit. what) pleases them in this dirty city.

7. This motor-car has been sold for a high (lit. dear) price. Why? Has its owner died? No, but he will die soon.

8. The women go to the market in the morning and return home after purchasing (lit. the purchase of) what they require (lit. what is necessary to them).

9. Girls, rise and go to your mother who is in the garden awaiting (lit. in expectation of) your aunt's visit.

10. Would you (fem. pl.) like to walk with me to the railway station? No, we are very tired.

LESSON XVIII

62. Weak Verbs

The weak verbs are those of which the last radical is one of the weak letters و and ي. Like the hollow verbs they fall into four categories which resolve themselves into three groups.

Group I. This consists of verbs of the pattern فَعَلَ the last radical of which is و. Weak verbs of pattern فَعُلَ are rare. Their characteristic is a long '*ū*' after the middle radical in the imperfect, e.g.

دَعَا (for دَعَوَ) he called, invited.

يَدْعُو (for يَدْعُوُ) he calls.

(N.B. دَعَا لِـ... he called (God) for, he blessed.

دَعَا عَلَى ... he called (God) against, he cursed.)

This verb fully conjugated in the perfect active is:

	دَعَوْتُ	I called, invited.
	دَعَوْتَ	you (masc.) called.
	دَعَوْتِ	you (fem.) called.
(for دَعَوَ)	دَعَا	he called.
(for دَعَاتْ)	دَعَتْ	she called.
	دَعَوْنَا	we called.
	دَعَوْتُمْ، دَعَوْتُنَّ	you (plur.) called.
	دَعَوْتُمَا	you (dual) called.
(for دَعَوُوا)	دَعَوْا	they (masc.) called.
	دَعَوْنَ	they (fem.) called.
	دَعَوَا	they (masc. dual) called.
	دَعَتَا	they (fem. dual) called.

The imperfect indicative active is:

(for أَدْعُوُ)	أَدْعُو	I call.
	تَدْعُو	you (masc.) call.
(for تَدْعُوِينَ)	تَدْعِينَ	you (fem.) call.
	يَدْعُو	he calls.
	تَدْعُو	she calls.
	نَدْعُو	we call.
(for تَدْعُوُونَ)	تَدْعُونَ	you (masc. plur.) call.
	تَدْعُونَ	you (fem. plur.) call.
	تَدْعُوَانِ	you (dual) call.

(for يَدْعُوُونَ)	يَدْعُونَ	they (masc.) call.
	يَدْعُونَ	they (fem.) call.
	يَدْعُوَانِ، تَدْعُوَانِ	they (dual) call.

The imperfect subjunctive active is:

	أَدْعُوَ	I (may) call.
	تَدْعُوَ	you (masc.) (may) call.
(for تَدْعُوِي)	تَدْعِي	you (fem.) (may) call.
	يَدْعُوَ	he (may) call.
	تَدْعُوَ	she (may) call, etc.
Note (for يَدْعُوُوا)	يَدْعُوا	they (masc.) (may) call.

Those persons of the *jussive mood of weak verbs* which end with the last radical drop this latter altogether, e.g.

أَدْعُ !	may I call!
تَدْعُ !	may you (masc.) call!
تَدْعِي !	may you (fem.) call! etc.

The imperative proper is:

أُدْعُ، أُدْعِي، أُدْعُوا، أُدْعُونَ، أُدْعُوَا ! call!

For the active and passive participles of *all* weak verbs see Lesson XI.

Group II. This consists of verbs of the pattern فَعِلَ the last radical of which is و. Owing to the preceding '*ī*' the و changes into ي. Their characteristic is a long '*ā*' after the middle radical in the imperfect. This is written as ـَى ('*alif maqṣūra biṣūrat al-yā*') owing to the ي of the perfect, e.g.

رَضِيَ (for رَضِوَ)	he was pleased, satisfied.
يَرْضَى (for يَرْضَيُ for يَرْضَوُ)	he is pleased.

This verb fully conjugated in the perfect active is:

	رَضِيتُ	I was pleased, contented.
	رَضِيتَ	you (masc.) were pleased.
	رَضِيتِ	you (fem.) were pleased.
(for رَضِوَ)	رَضِيَ	he was pleased.
	رَضِيَتْ	she was pleased.
	رَضِينَا	we were pleased.
	رَضِيتُمْ، رَضِيتُنَّ	you (plur.) were pleased.
	رَضِيتُمَا	you (dual) were pleased.
(for رَضِيُوا)	رَضُوا	they (masc.) were pleased.
	رَضِينَ	they (fem.) were pleased.
	رَضِيَا، رَضِيَتَا	they (dual) were pleased.

The imperfect indicative active is:

(for أَرْضَيُ)	أَرْضَى	I am pleased.
	تَرْضَى	you (masc.) are pleased.
(for تَرْضَيِينَ)	تَرْضَيْنَ	you (fem.) are pleased.
	يَرْضَى	he is pleased.
	تَرْضَى	she is pleased.
	نَرْضَى	we are pleased.
(for تَرْضَيُونَ)	تَرْضَوْنَ	you (masc. plur.) are pleased.
	تَرْضَيْنَ	you (fem. plur.) are pleased.
	تَرْضَيَانِ	you (dual) are pleased.
(for يَرْضَيُونَ)	يَرْضَوْنَ	they (masc.) are pleased.

يَرْضَيْنَ they (fem.) are pleased.

يَرْضَيَانِ، تَرْضَيَانِ they (dual) are pleased.

Since both ـَيُ... and ـَيِ... become ـَى... the subjunctive is the same as the indicative except for those persons which in the latter mood end in نَ *originally* preceded by a long vowel after the last radical (see Lesson XIII), e.g.

أَرْضَى I (may) be pleased.

تَرْضَى you (masc.) (may) be pleased.

(for تَرْضَيِي) تَرْضَيْ you (fem.) (may) be pleased, etc.

The jussive active is:

أَرْضَ ! may I be pleased!

تَرْضَ ! may you (masc.) be pleased!

تَرْضَيْ ! may you (fem.) be pleased! etc.

The imperative proper is:

إِرْضَ، إِرْضَيْ، إِرْضَوْا، إِرْضَيْنَ، إِرْضَيَا ! be pleased!

Group III. This consists of verbs of the pattern فَعَلَ the last radical of which is ي. Their characteristic is a long 'ī' after the middle radical in the imperfect, e.g.

رَمَى (for رَمَيَ) he threw.

N.B. رَمَاهُ he threw it.

يَرْمِي (for يَرْمِيُ) he throws.

This verb fully conjugated in the perfect active is:

رَمَيْتُ I threw.

رَمَيْتَ، رَمَيْتِ you threw.

(for رَمَيَ) رَمَى he threw.

رَمَتْ she threw. (for رَمَاتْ)

رَمَيْنَا we threw.

رَمَيْتُمْ، رَمَيْتُنَّ، رَمَيْتُمَا you threw.

رَمَوْا they (masc.) threw. (for رَمَيُوا)

رَمَيْنَ they (fem.) threw.

رَمَيَا، رَمَتَا they (dual) threw.

The imperfect indicative active is:

أَرْمِي I throw. (for أَرْمِيُ)

تَرْمِي you (masc.) throw.

تَرْمِينَ you (fem.) throw. (for تَرْمِيِينَ)

يَرْمِي he throws.

تَرْمِي she throws.

نَرْمِي we throw.

تَرْمُونَ you (masc. plur.) throw. (for تَرْمِيُونَ)

تَرْمِينَ you (fem. plur.) throw.

تَرْمِيَانِ you (dual) throw.

يَرْمُونَ they (masc.) throw. (for يَرْمِيُونَ)

يَرْمِينَ they (fem.) throw.

يَرْمِيَانِ، تَرْمِيَانِ they (dual) throw.

The imperfect subjunctive active is:

أَرْمِيَ I (may) throw.

تَرْمِيَ you (masc.) (may) throw.

تَرْمِي you (fem.) (may) throw, etc. (for تَرْمِيِي)

The jussive active is:

أَرْمِ !	may I throw!
تَرْمِ !	may you (masc.) throw!
تَرْمِي !	may you (fem.) throw! etc.

The imperative proper is:

اِرْمِ، اِرْمِي، اِرْمُوا، اِرْمِينَ، اِرْمِيَا ! throw!

Group IV. This consists of verbs of the pattern فَعِلَ the last radical of which is ي. They are the same in every respect as verbs of Group II, e.g.

	لَقِيَ	he met.
(for يَلْقَيُ)	يَلْقَى	he meets.

N.B. Some verbs of the pattern فَعَلَ whose last radical is ي have their imperfect according to the pattern يَفْعَلُ. In the perfect these are conjugated regularly, i.e. like those of Group III. In the imperfect they are conjugated like those of Group II, e.g.

سَعَيْتُ	I ran, strove.
سَعَيْتَ، سَعَيْتِ	you ran.
سَعَى	he ran, etc.
أَسْعَى	I run, strive.
تَسْعَى	you (masc.) run.
تَسْعَيْنَ	you (fem.) run.
يَسْعَى	he runs, etc.

63. The Passive of Weak Verbs

The passives of transitive verbs of all four preceding groups are identical, e.g.

دُعِيَ	he was called, invited.
يُدْعَى	he is called.

رُمِيَ he was thrown.

يُرْمَى he is thrown.

The passives are conjugated in the perfect and imperfect like verbs of Group II, e.g.

دُعِيتُ I was called.

دُعِيتَ، دُعِيتِ you were called.

دُعِيَ he was called.

دُعِيَتْ she was called, etc.

أُدْعَى I am called.

تُدْعَى، تُدْعَيْنَ you are called.

يُدْعَى he is called.

تُدْعَى she is called, etc.

64. Doubly Weak Verbs

If a verb contains more than one weak radical note the following:

(i) If the two weak radicals come together the first of these becomes strong retaining its full consonantal value, e.g.

نَوَى	he intended.	يَنْوِي	he intends.
(for حَيِيَ) حَيَّ	he lived.	يَحْيَا	he lives.

Note that *'alif maqṣūra* after ي is written ا..., not ى....

(ii) If the two weak radicals are separated by a strong one, then all the rules given in this lesson and in Lesson XVI obtain, e.g.

وَعَى he learned by heart, understood.

يَعِي he learns by heart, understands.

وَلِيَ he was near, in charge of.

يَلِي he is near.

Note especially the following two important verbs:

65. لَيْسَ he is not

Although this verb is conjugated like a perfect it is always *present indicative*, e.g.

لَسْتُ	I am not.
لَسْتَ، لَسْتِ	you are not.
لَيْسَ	he is not.
لَيْسَتْ	she is not.
لَسْنَا	we are not.
لَسْتُمْ، لَسْتُنَّ، لَسْتُمَا	you are not.
لَيْسُوا، لَسْنَ	they are not.
لَيْسَا، لَيْسَتَا	they (dual) are not.

The predicate after لَيْسَ is in the accusative like that after كَانَ or more commonly introduced by ...بِ, e.g.

لَيْسَ عَالِمًا	he is not learned.
لَيْسَ بِغَنِيٍّ	he is not rich.
لَسْتُ بِغَافِلٍ	I am not heedless.
لَسْتُمْ فَلَّاحِينَ	you are not peasants.

66. رَأَى he saw, considered

This verb, conjugated like سَعَى, though perfectly regular in the perfect, drops its middle radical *hamza* in the imperfect and moves its vowel forward to the first radical, e.g.

رَأَيْتُ	I saw.
رَأَيْتَ، رَأَيْتِ	you saw.
رَأَى	he saw.

	رَأَتْ	she saw, etc.
but	أَرَى	I see.
	تَرَى، تَرَيْنَ	you see.
	يَرَى	he sees.
	تَرَى	she sees, etc.
	أَنْ أَرَى	that I may see.
	لَمْ أَرَ	I did not see.
(rarely used)	رَ !	see!
	رُئِيَ	it was seen.
but	يُرَى	it is seen.

Examples:

يُقَالُ إِنَّ قَبِيلَةً مِنْ قَبَائِلِ ٱلْعَرَبِ غَزَتْ (Group I) قَبِيلَةً أُخْرَى (آخَرُ .masc)

It is said that a certain Arab tribe (lit. a tribe of the tribes of the Arabs) raided another tribe.

كَانُوا يَوَدُّونَ أَنْ يَقْفُوا (Group I) آثَارَ (أَثَرٌ .sing) جِيرَانِهِمْ وَلٰكِنَّهُمْ ضَلُّوا ٱلطَّرِيقَ

They wanted to follow their neighbours' tracks but they went astray on the way. (Note the accusative of place.)

إِنَّنَا لَمْ نَجْنِ ثِمَارَ هٰذِهِ ٱلشَّجَرَةِ لِأَنَّهَا لَيْسَتْ نَاضِجَةً

We have not gathered the fruits of this tree because they are not ripe.

بَكَتِ (Group III) ٱلْبَنَاتُ وَزَعَمْنَ أَنَّهُنَّ لَا يَقْوَيْنَ (Group IV) عَلَى ٱلْمَشْيِ

The girls wept and asserted that they were not strong enough to walk (lit. are not strong on walking).

إِبْقَوْا (Group IV) هُنَا حَتَّى يَأْتِيَ خَبَرٌ مِنَ ٱلْجَاسُوسِ !

Remain (plur.) here until word (lit. news) comes from the spy!

لَسْتُ غَضْبَانَ وَلٰكِنِّي أَرْجُوكَ أَلَّا تَجِيءَ بِدُونِ إِذْنِي

I am not angry but I beg you not to come without my permission.

مَا رَأْيُهُمْ فِي هٰذِهِ ٱلْمَسْأَلَةِ؟ يَرَوْنَ أَنَّهُ غَيْرُ لَائِقٍ أَنْ يَقُولُوا شَيْئًا

What is their opinion about this matter? They consider (lit. see) that it is not seemly that they should say anything. (Note آرَاء plur of رَأْي a view, opinion in which the first two radicals are transposed.)

يُرْجَى أَنْ نَرَاهُمْ بِخَيْرٍ بَعْدَ سَفَرِهِمُ ٱلطَّوِيلِ

It is hoped that we may see them well after their long journey.

كَانَتْ أُخْتِي تَنْوِي أَنْ تَقْرَأَ عَلَيَّ ذٰلِكَ ٱلْكِتَابَ، غَيْرَ أَنَّ أَشْغَالَهَا ٱلْكَثِيرَةَ حَالَتْ (Group I) دُونَ ذٰلِكَ

My sister intended to read that book to me, however, her many occupations prevented her from doing that (lit. interposed themselves in front of that).

دَعْهُمْ يَأْتُونَ (from أَتَى Group III) مَعَنَا إِلَى ٱلْحَفْلَةِ وَإِنْ لَمْ يُدْعَوْا رَسْمِيًّا

Let them come to the party with us although they have not been invited officially. (Note the construction after (وَدَعَ) imperfect يَدَعُ he lets, permits, the perfect of which is seldom used.)

Exercise XVIII

١—مَعَ أَنّ الرجلَيْنِ دَعَوَاه لم يَدْنُ منهُما لأنّه ما كان يودُّ أن يَلْقَاهُما.

٢—كُلَّمَا يأْتينا سَاعِي البَرِيدِ الّذي يُدْعَى عَلِيًّا بِخطاباتٍ يَدُقُّ البابَ الخَلْفِيَّ مرّتَيْنِ.

٣—هل تَنْوِيَانِ أن تأْخُذا بنتَكُمَا الكُبْرَى معكما عندما تَقْضِيَانِ إجازةَ الصَّيْفِ في إِسْبَانِيَا الجَنُوبِيَّةِ؟

٤—لَيْسَ خالُنا بغَنِيٍّ فلا نَرْجُو أن نَرِثَ منه شَيْئًا.

٥—اِرْمِ هذا الكتابَ القديمَ في سَلَّةِ المُهْمَلاتِ وٱشْرِ نُسْخَةً جديدةً منه.

٦—عِ ما قُلْتُهُ لَكَ لأنّه سوف يَنْفَعُكَ في المُسْتَقْبَلِ

٧—لَسْنَا فُقَرَاءَ ولٰكِنْ لا نَقْدِرُ أن نَصْرِفَ هذا المَبْلَغَ الكبيرَ وَعِلَاوَةً على ذٰلك نَرَى الثَّمَنَ غالِيًا جدًّا.

٨—ما رَأَيْتُ قَطُّ سيّدةً أَجْمَلَ منها تَمْشِي في الحَدِيقةِ العُمُومِيَّةِ. يَقُولُ صديقي إنّها زَوْجَةُ وزيرِ (ٱلشُّؤُونِ) الخَارِجِيَّةِ

٩—سَعَوْا للحُصُولِ لي على تَذْكِرَةِ دُخُولٍ ولٰكِنْ عَبَثًا لأنّ كُلَّ التَّذَاكِرِ قد بِيعَتْ مُنْذُ أُسبوعٍ. (حَصَلَ...عَلَى)

١٠—أَلَسْتَ أَبا مَحْمُودٍ؟ بَلَى، وأَظُنُّ حَضْرَتَكَ أُسْتاذَهُ. أَمَلِي أن تَرْضَى عَنْهُ دائِمًا.

Translation

1. Although the (two) men called him he did not approach them because he did not want to meet them.

2. Whenever the postman who is called ʿAli brings us letters he knocks twice on the back door.

3. Do you (dual) intend to take your eldest daughter with you when you spend the summer holiday in southern Spain?

4. Our uncle is not rich so we do not hope to inherit anything from him.

5. Throw this old book into the waste-paper basket (lit. basket of neglected things) and buy a new copy of it.

6. Keep in mind what I have said to you for it will benefit you in the future.

7. We are not poor but we cannot spend this large sum, and, moreover, we think the price is very high.

8. I have never seen a more beautiful lady walking in the public garden. My friend says she is the wife of the Minister of Foreign Affairs.

9. They used their offices (lit. strove) to get an entrance card for me but in vain because all the cards had been sold a week before.

10. Are you not Maḥmūd's father? Yes, and I think you (lit. your honour) are his professor. I hope (lit. my hope is) that you are always pleased with him.

LESSON XIX

67. Derived Verbs

So far the student has dealt with simple verbs of three or four radicals only and it is now time to discuss the derived verbs. These derived forms are mainly from three-radical verbs, only two of them being from three- and four-radical verbs.

Taking the letters ف, ع and ل to represent the first or original form we have the following patterns:

I.	فَعَلَ	*faعala, faعula, faعila.*			
II.	فَعَّلَ	*faععala.*	IX.	اِفْعَلَّ	*ifعalla.*
III.	فَاعَلَ	*fāعala.*	X.	اِسْتَفْعَلَ	*istafعala.*
IV.	أَفْعَلَ	*'afعala.*	XI.	اِفْعَالَّ	*ifعālla.*
V.	تَفَعَّلَ	*tafaععala.*	XII.	اِفْعَوْعَلَ	*ifعawعala.*
VI.	تَفَاعَلَ	*tafāعala.*	XIII.	اِفْعَوَّلَ	*ifعawwala.*
VII.	اِنْفَعَلَ	*infaعala.*	XIV.	اِفْعَنْلَلَ	*ifعanlala.*
VIII.	اِفْتَعَلَ	*iftaعala.*	XV.	اِفْعَنْلَى	*ifعanlā.*

As the last five derived forms are exceedingly rare and present no especial difficulty in their vowel patterns they may be ignored by the beginner.

Note that the prefixed *hamza* in form IV is *hamzat-al-qaṭع* and that the prefixed *hamza* in forms VII–XV is *hamzat-al-waṣl.*

It is most convenient to deal with the derived verbs in four groups, but before preceding to this I advise the student to learn the meanings of the derived verbs he comes across in his reading without troubling himself unduly about the original or first form.

68. Verbal Form II. فَعَّلَ

This is formed by doubling the middle radical so that the verb becomes a quadriliteral (stock verb تَرْجَمَ) of which the second and third radicals are identical. This form is conjugated ***in exactly the same manner as a simple quadriliteral verb.***

Taking عَلَّمَ, he taught, as an example we have:

Perfect active	عَلَّمْتُ	I taught.
	عَلَّمْتَ، عَلَّمْتِ	you taught.
	عَلَّمَ	he taught.
	عَلَّمَتْ	she taught, etc.
Perfect passive	عُلِّمَ	he was taught, etc.
Imperfect active	أُعَلِّمُ	I teach.
	تُعَلِّمُ، تُعَلِّمِينَ	you teach.
	يُعَلِّمُ	he teaches.
	تُعَلِّمُ	she teaches, etc.
Imperfect passive	يُعَلَّمُ	he is taught, etc.
Imperative	عَلِّمْ !	teach! etc.
Active participle	مُعَلِّمٌ	teaching, a teacher.
Passive participle	مُعَلَّمٌ	taught.

N.B. The active and passive participles of *all* derived verbs begin with prefixed ...مُـ *mu*, the characteristic of the *active* participle being a short '*i*' *before the last radical* and the characteristic of the *passive* participle being a short '*a*' *before the last radical.*

Verbal noun	تَعْلِيمٌ	teaching, instruction.

N.B. If all three radicals are sound the verbal noun of the 2nd form may be of any one of three patterns تَفْعِيلٌ, تَفْعَالٌ or تَفْعِلَةٌ. The first of these is by far the most common. Which verb takes which pattern of the verbal noun can only be learned through reading or reference to a dictionary. But if the last radical is *hamza*, و or ي, then the pattern of the verbal noun is *always* تَفْعِلَةٌ, e.g.

	هَنَّأَ	he congratulated.
	تَهْنِئَةٌ	congratulation.
(for عَلَّوَ)	عَلَّى	he raised, exalted.
(for تَعْلِوَةٌ)	تَعْلِيَةٌ	raising, exaltation.

The 2nd form denotes:

(1) Intensity of action, e.g.

كَسَرَ	he broke.
كَسَّرَ	he smashed.
قَطَعَ	he cut.
قَطَّعَ	he cut up, tore up.

(2) Causation, e.g.

عَلِمَ	he knew.
عَلَّمَ	he taught.
شَرُفَ	he was noble.
شَرَّفَ	he honoured.

(3) Estimation, e.g.

صَدَقَ	he spoke the truth.
صَدَّقَ	he considered s.o. truthful, believed.
كَذَبَ	he lied.
كَذَّبَ	he considered s.o. a liar, disbelieved.

(4) It is often formed from nouns, e.g.

خَيْمَةٌ	a tent.
خَيَّمَ	he pitched his tent.

سِلَاحٌ a weapon.

سَلَّحَ he armed.

If a verb is doubled or *hamzated* or if the 1st or 2nd radical is و or ي the 2nd form is perfectly regular, e.g.

رَدَّ he returned (trans.).

رَدَّدَ يُرَدِّدُ he repeated (over and over).

تَرْدِيدٌ (constant) repetition.

أَلَّفَ يُؤَلِّفُ he composed, compiled, formed.

تَأْلِيفٌ composition, compilation, a (literary) work.

هَنَّأَ يُهَنِّئُ he congratulated.

تَهْنِئَةٌ congratulation.

وَفَّقَ يُوَفِّقُ He (God) gave success.

تَوْفِيقٌ success.

قَوَّمَ يُقَوِّمُ he straightened.

تَقْوِيمٌ straightening, (a calendar).

Note the softening of *hamza* into a long '*ā*' in the verbal noun of أَرَّخَ he dated, wrote history, viz. تَارِيخٌ (pl. تَوَارِيخُ) dating, a date, a history.

All derived forms of weak verbs, i.e. those the last radical of which is و or ي, change the last radical into '*alif maqṣūra*, written ـَى.... They, with the exception of forms V and VI, are conjugated exactly like weak verbs of Group III (i.e. like رَمَى) of the preceding lesson, e.g.

(root سمو) سَمَّى he named.

سُمِّيَ he was named.

يُسَمِّي he names.

يُسَمَّى he is named.

	سَمِّ !	name!
Active participle	مُسَمٍّ	naming (cf. قَاضٍ).
Passive participle	مُسَمًّى	named.
Verbal noun	تَسْمِيَةٌ	naming.
(root ولي)	وَلَّى	he put in charge of.
	وُلِّيَ	he was put in charge of.
	يُوَلِّي	he puts in charge of.
	يُوَلَّى	he is put in charge of.
	وَلِّ !	put in charge!
Active participle	مُوَلٍّ	putting in charge.
Passive participle	مُوَلًّى	put in charge.
Verbal noun	تَوْلِيَةٌ	appointment.

69. Verbal Form III فَاعَلَ

This is formed by lengthening the '*a*' of the first radical. Verbs of this form are conjugated exactly like those of the form فَعَّلَ, e.g.

Perfect active	قَاتَلْتُ	I fought s.o.
	قَاتَلْتَ، قَاتَلْتِ	you fought.
	قَاتَلَ	he fought.
	قَاتَلَتْ	she fought, etc.
Perfect passive	قُوتِلَ	he was fought, etc.
Imperfect active	أُقَاتِلُ	I fight.
	تُقَاتِلُ، تُقَاتِلِينَ	you fight.
	يُقَاتِلُ	he fights.

	تُقاتِلُ	she fights, etc.
Imperfect passive	يُقاتَلُ	he is fought, etc.
Imperative	! قاتِلْ	fight! etc.
Active participle	مُقاتِلٌ	fighting, a warrior.
Passive participle	مُقاتَلٌ	fought.
Verbal noun	قِتالٌ or مُقاتَلَةٌ	fighting.

N.B. The pattern of the verbal noun of form III is either مُفاعَلَةٌ or فِعالٌ. Some verbs take one form, other verbs the other form. A few verbs, including the example above, take both, e.g.

مُلاقاةٌ (for مُلاقَيَةٌ) or لِقاءٌ meeting.

In لِقاءٌ note the change of the final weak radical *bearing the case ending* to *hamza* after a long '*ā*'.

The 3rd form denotes:

(1) The doing of an action to someone, e.g.

كاتَبَ he wrote to, corresponded with.

قاوَمَ he stood up to, opposed.

(2) The attempt to do something to someone, e.g.

قاتَلَ he tried to kill, fought with.

سَبَقَ he preceded.

سابَقَ he competed with.

Note that such verbs of form III usually take an explicit or implicit direct object which is always a person. Reciprocity is implied in both cases.

We occasionally find verbs of form III which have no idea of reciprocity behind them. The idea of effort is, however, apparent even in these, e.g.

سافَرَ he travelled.

بالَغَ he exaggerated.

If a verb is doubled note that in form III there is no contraction of the twin consonants after the long '*ū*' of the perfect passive, e.g.

(for شَادَدَ) شَادَّ he spoke violently to.

but شُودِدَ he was spoken to violently.

(for يُشَادِدُ) يُشَادُّ he speaks violently to.

(for يُشَادَدُ) يُشَادُّ he is spoken to violently.

Active *and* passive participles مُشَادٌّ,

Verbal noun مُشَادَّةٌ a noisy dispute.

If a verb is *hamzated* or contains one of the weak letters و or ي it is conjugated regularly in accordance with the rules already given, e.g. (see Introduction § 7)

آلَفَ (for أَالَفَ) يُؤَالِفُ he was familiar with.

سَاءَلَ يُسَائِلُ he questioned.

وَافَقَ يُوَافِقُ he agreed with, suited.

نَاوَلَ يُنَاوِلُ he handed s.t. to s.o.

بَايَعَ يُبَايِعُ he swore allegiance to.

لَاقَى يُلَاقِي he met.

70. Verbal Form IV أَفْعَلَ

This is formed by making the first radical vowelless and prefixing a short '*a*' *on hamzat-al-qaṭ* ع, e.g.

جَلَسَ he sat (down).

أَجْلَسَ he seated.

This verb is conjugated as follows:

Perfect active أَجْلَسْتُ I seated.

أَجْلَسْتَ، أَجْلَسْتِ you seated.

أَجْلَسَ he seated.

		أَجْلَسَتْ	she seated, etc.
Perfect passive		أُجْلِسَ	he was seated, etc.
Imperfect active	*'ujlisu,*	أُجْلِسُ	I seat.
		تُجْلِسُ، تُجْلِسِينَ	you seat.
		يُجْلِسُ	he seats.
		تُجْلِسُ	she seats, etc.
Imperfect passive	*yujlasu,*	يُجْلَسُ	he is seated, etc.
Imperative	*'ajlis!*	أَجْلِسْ !	seat!
Active participle		مُجْلِسٌ	seating.
Passive participle		مُجْلَسٌ	seated.
Verbal noun	*'ijlāsun,*	إِجْلَاسٌ	seating.

N.B. All verbs of the form أَفْعَلَ make their verbal nouns according to the pattern إِفْعَالٌ.

The 4th form of the verb is generally causative as in the above example.

When causation is intended sometimes the 2nd form is used, sometimes the 4th. Occasionally both forms occur with somewhat different meanings, e.g.

عَلَّمَ he caused to know, taught.

أَعْلَمَ he caused to know, informed.

Sometimes both are used with no difference in meaning, e.g.

نَجَا he escaped.

نَجَّى and أَنْجَى he caused to escape, saved.

Very often we find verbs of the 4th form in which the idea of causation is very remote, e.g.

أَصْبَحَ he became (lit. came or did in the morning).

أَشْكَلَ it became difficult.

If the root verb is doubled the 4th form presents no difficulties, the rules for the doubled verb being maintained, e.g.

	مَدَّ	he stretched.
	أَمَدَّ	he helped, supplied.
	أُمِدَّ	he was helped, supplied.
	يُمِدُّ	he helps, supplies.
	يُمَدُّ	he is helped, supplied.
Imperative	أَمْدِدْ !	help! supply!
Active participle	مُمِدٌّ	helping, supplying.
Passive participle	مُمَدٌّ	helped, supplied.
Verbal noun	إِمْدَادٌ	help(ing), supply(ing).

Similarly if the root verb is *hamzated* or if it has as its first or third radical و or ي, e.g.

	آلَفَ (for أَأْلَفَ) يُؤْلِفُ (بَيْنَ)	he reconciled.
Imperative	آلِفْ !	reconcile!
Verbal noun	إِيلَافٌ	reconciling, reconciliation.
	أَقْرَأَ يُقْرِئُ	he taught to read.
Imperative	أَقْرِئْ !	teach to read!
Verbal noun	إِقْرَاءٌ	teaching to read.
	يَقِظَ	he was awake.
	أَيْقَظَ يُوقِظُ (for يُيْقِظُ)	he awakened s.o.
	أُوقِظَ (for أُيْقِظَ)	he was awakened.
Imperative	أَيْقِظْ !	awaken!
Verbal noun	إِيقَاظٌ	awakening.

	أَوْصَلَ يُوصِلُ	he caused to arrive, brought, sent, forwarded.
Imperative	أَوْصِلْ	bring! send!
Verbal noun	إِيصَالٌ (for إِوْصَالٌ)	bringing, sending.
	أَلْقَى يُلْقِي	he threw, delivered (a speech, lecture).
Imperative	أَلْقِ !	throw! deliver! (a speech).
Verbal noun	إِلْقَاءٌ	throwing, delivery.

If the middle radical in the pattern أَفْعَلَ is و or ي note that its vowel is thrown forward to the first radical and *becomes long*, the weak middle radical dropping out, e.g.

(for أَخْوَفَ)	أَخَافَ	he frightened.
(for يُخْوِفُ)	يُخِيفُ	he frightens.
(for أُخْوِفَ)	أُخِيفَ	he was frightened.
(for يُخْوَفُ)	يُخَافُ	he is frightened.
(for أَذْيَعَ)	أَذَاعَ	he broadcast.
(for يُذْيِعُ)	يُذِيعُ	he broadcasts.
(for أُذْيِعَ)	أُذِيعَ	it was broadcast.
(for يُذْيَعُ)	يُذَاعُ	it is broadcast.

The usual shortening of long vowels before vowelless consonants takes place, e.g.

Perfect active	أَخَفْتُ	I frightened.
	أَخَفْتَ، أَخَفْتِ	you frightened.
	أَخَافَ	he frightened.
	أَخَافَتْ	she frightened, etc.
Perfect passive	أُخِفْتُ	I was frightened.

	أُخِيفَ	he was frightened, etc.
Imperfect active	أُخِيفُ	I frighten.
	تُخِيفُ، تُخِيفِينَ	you frighten.
	يُخِيفُ	he frightens.
	تُخِيفُ	she frightens, etc.
Imperfect passive	أُخَافُ	I am frightened.
	يُخَافُ	he is frightened, etc.
Imperative *'akhif!*	أَخِفْ !	frighten!
	أَخِيفِي !	frighten!
	أَخِيفُوا	frighten! etc.
Active participle	مُخِيفٌ	frightening.
Passive participle	مُخَافٌ	frightened.
Verbal noun *'ikhāfatun,*	إِخَافَةٌ	frightening.

Note that the verbal noun of the 4th form of hollow verbs receives an added *tā' marbūṭa.*

N.B. The 4th form of the verb رَأَى, he saw, presents the same phenomenon as occurs in the imperfect of the simple verb, namely the elision of the middle radical *hamza* and the moving of its vowel forward to the first radical, e.g.

(for أَرْأَى)	أَرَى	he showed.
(for أُرْئِيَ)	أُرِيَ	he was shown.
(for يُرْئِي)	يُرِي	he shows.
(for يُرْأَى)	يُرَى	he is shown.
(for يُرْءِ)	لَمْ يُرِ	he did not show.
(for أَرْءِ)	أَرِ !	show!

Causative verbs from transitive roots may take a double accusative, e.g.

أَرَانِي سَاعَتَهُ he showed me his watch.

أَرِنَا جَوَازَ سَفَرِكَ ! show us your passport!

Finally, the student should note that the vowel of the personal *prefixes* of the imperfect active of the three derived forms given in this lesson is '*u*', whereas in all other active forms of the verb it is '*a*'.

Examples:

يَجِبُ عَلَيْكَ أَنْ تُفَتِّحَ عَيْنَيْكَ عِنْدَمَا تَعْبُرُ ٱلشَّارِعَ

You must (lit. it is incumbent on you to) open your eyes wide when you cross the street.

مَتَى تُشَرِّفُونَنَا بِزِيَارَتِكُمْ ؟

When will you honour us with your visit?

لَا تُوَلِّنَا ظَهْرَكَ، فَإِنَّنَا نُرِيدُ أَنْ نَرَى وَجْهَكَ

Do not turn your back on us for we wish to see your face.

إِنَّ ٱلْقَاضِيَ لَمْ يُبَرِّئِ ٱلرَّجُلَ ٱلَّذِي قَتَلَ زَوْجَتَهُ

The judge did not acquit the man who (had) killed his wife.

أَنُصَدِّقُهُمْ أَمْ نُكَذِّبُهُمْ ؟ لَا أَرَى دَاعِيًا لِتَكْذِيبِهِمْ

Shall we believe them or disbelieve them? I see no reason for (lit. that which calls to) disbelieving them.

أَعْطِنِي كِتَابًا يُبَيِّنُ أَصْوَاتَ ٱللُّغَةِ ٱلْأَلْمَانِيَّةِ

Give me a book which explains the phonetics (lit. the sounds) of the German language.

أَهْدَيْتُ لَهَا خَاتَمَ ذَهَبٍ بِمُنَاسَبَةِ عِيدِ مِيلَادِهَا

I presented a gold ring to her on the occasion of her birthday (lit. the festival of her birth).

أُرَاجِعُ ٱلْقَامُوسَ عِنْدَمَا أَجْهَلُ مَعْنَى كَلِمَةٍ

I refer to the dictionary when I do not know the meaning of a word.

يُرِيدُونَ أَنْ يُوقَظُوا قَبْلَ ٱلْفَجْرِ بِقَلِيلٍ لِأَنَّهُمْ يَنْوُونَ أَنْ يُسَافِرُوا إِلَى ٱلضَّيْعَةِ ٱلْمُجَاوِرَةِ

They wish to be awakened shortly before dawn because they intend to travel to the neighbouring estate.

لَمْ يُرُونِي كَيْفَ أَلْقَوْا ٱلْحَبْلَ حَوْلَ رَقَبَةِ ٱلثَّوْرِ

They did not show me how they threw the rope around the bull's neck.

EXERCISE XIX

١—يُنْكِرُ ذلك ولٰكِنَّنا سوف نُثْبِتُ أنّه كاذبٌ.

٢—لا تُحَاوِلُوا أن تُقِيمُوا في تِلْكَ البِلادِ أَكْثَرَ من شَهْرٍ لِأَنّ الإقامةَ فيها لا تُلَائِمُ الجِنْسَ الأَبْيَضَ.

٣—أُرِيدُ أن تُوقِظِيني حالَمَا تُشْرِقُ الشَّمْسُ لأنّي قد سمِعْتُ أن المَنْظَرَ رَائِعٌ.

٤—مَنْ يُوصِلُ هذا الطَّرْدَ الثَّقِيلَ إلى المَحَطّةِ؟ أَعْطِ الحَمّالَ قِرْشَيْنِ فسوف يُوصِلُهُ.

٥—أَقْبَلَتِ ٱلوُفُودُ لِتُهَنِّئَ الرَّئِيسَ بنَجاحِهِ في المُفَاوَضَاتِ. (وَفْدٌ)

٦—أُرِيدُ أن أُسافِرَ إلى إِيرَانَ لِكَيْ أُشاهِدَ آثارَ الحَضارةِ الإيرانيّةِ القديمةِ. (أَثَرٌ)

٧—كان يَجِبُ علينا أن نُعْطِيَ بائعَ الصُّحُفِ قِرْشَيْنِ ولٰكِنْ نَسِينَا فلَمْ نُعْطِهِ إِلّا قِرْشًا واحدًا. (صَحِيفَةٌ)

٨—إنّ السَّادَةَ لم يَأْتُوا لَمَّا دُعُوا لأنّ الوَقْتَ كان ضَيِّقًا. (سَيِّدٌ)

٩—لقد وَعَدَ الوزيرُ بِإِلْقاء مُحَاضَرةٍ في نَادِي الشُّبَّانِ فيَجِبُ عليكم أن تُمِدُّوهُ بالمَعْلُومَاتِ اللّازِمةِ.

١٠—كُنتُ قد أَضَعْتُ جَوازَ سَفَرِي فأَكْرَهَني حارِسُ الحُدُودِ على النُّزُولِ مِنَ ٱلقِطَارِ لِأُرَافِقَهُ إلى مَكْتَبِ المَأْمُورِ. (أَضَاعَ)

Translation

1. He denies that but we shall prove that he is lying.

2. Do not try to reside in that country more than one month because residence there is not suitable for white people (lit. the white race).

3. I want you (fem.) to awaken me as soon as the sun rises because I have heard that the sight is glorious.

4. Who will take this heavy parcel to the station? Give the porter two piastres and he will take it.

5. The delegations came to congratulate the president on his success in the negotiations.

6. I wish to travel to Persia (Iran) in order to see the remains (lit. traces) of ancient Persian civilization.

7. We should have given the newspaper seller two piastres but we forgot and only gave him one piastre.

8. The gentlemen did not come when they were invited because the time was short (lit. narrow).

9. The minister has promised to deliver a lecture in the youth club and so you (pl.) must supply him with the necessary information.

10. I had lost my passport and so the frontier guard forced me to get out of the train in order to go with him to the (police) captain's office.

LESSON XX

71. Verbal Form V تَفَعَّلَ

Form V is made by prefixing تَ to form II of which it is the reflexive, e.g.

عَلَّمَ he taught.

تَعَلَّمَ he taught himself, learned.

شَرَّفَ he honoured.

تَشَرَّفَ he had the honour.

Form V is conjugated as follows:

Perfect active تَعَلَّمْتُ I learned.

تَعَلَّمْتَ، تَعَلَّمْتِ you learned.

تَعَلَّمَ he learned.

تَعَلَّمَتْ she learned, etc.

Perfect passive *tuعullima*, تُعُلِّمَ it was learned, etc.

Imperfect active *'ataعallamu*, أَتَعَلَّمُ I learn.

تَتَعَلَّمُ، تَتَعَلَّمِينَ you learn.

يَتَعَلَّمُ he learns.

تَتَعَلَّمُ she learns, etc.

Note the sequence of '*a*'s in the imperfect active.

Imperfect passive *yutaعallamu*, يُتَعَلَّمُ it is learned, etc.

Imperative تَعَلَّمْ learn! (masc.).

تَعَلَّمِي ! learn! (fem.).

تَعَلَّمُوا ! learn! (masc. plur.).

Active participle *mutaعallimun*, مُتَعَلِّمٌ learning.

Passive participle *mutaعallamun*, مُتَعَلَّمٌ learned.

Verbal noun *taعallumun*, تَعَلُّمٌ learning, study.

N.B. All verbs of the form تَفَعَّلَ make their verbal nouns according to the pattern تَفَعُّلٌ.

If the root verb is doubled or *hamzated* or if the 1st or 2nd radical is و or ي, form V is perfectly regular, e.g.

يَتَرَدَّدُ تَرَدَّدَ he hesitated.

تَرَدُّدٌ hesitation.

يَتَأَلَّفُ تَأَلَّفَ it became formed, composed.

تَأَلُّفٌ formation (intrans.).

يَتَرَأَّسُ تَرَأَّسَ he became head, president.

تَرَؤُّسٌ presiding.

يَتَنَبَّأُ بِـ...	تَنَبَّأَ	he prophesied.
	تَنَبُّؤٌ	prophesying, prophecy.
يَتَوَجَّهُ إِلَى	تَوَجَّهَ	he directed his face to, travelled towards.
	تَوَجُّهٌ	directing oneself.
يَتَخَيَّرُ	تَخَيَّرَ	he chose.
	تَخَيُّرٌ	choosing, choice.

If the 3rd radical is و or ي form V is conjugated like weak verbs of Group III (see Lesson XVIII) which are of the pattern يَفْعَلُ in the imperfect (i.e. like سَعَى), e.g.

	تَعَشَّى	he took supper, dined.
	تَعَشَّيْتُ	I dined.
	يَتَعَشَّى	he dines.
	أَتَعَشَّى	I dine.
Imperative	تَعَشَّ !	dine! (masc.).
	تَعَشَّيْ !	dine! (fem.).
	تَعَشَّوْا !	dine (masc. plur.), etc.
Active participle	مُتَعَشٍّ	dining (cf. قَاضٍ).
Passive participle	مُتَعَشًّى	taken as supper or place where supper is taken (see § 77).
Verbal noun	تَعَشٍّ (اَلتَّعَشِّي)	dining (for تَعَشِّيٍ for تَعَشُّيٌ).
	تَوَلَّى	he took charge of.
	تَوَلَّيْتُ	I took charge of.
	يَتَوَلَّى	he takes charge of.
	أَتَوَلَّى	I take charge of.

Imperative	تَوَلَّ !	take charge of! (masc.).
	تَوَلَّيْ !	take charge of! (fem.).
	تَوَلَّوْا !	take charge of! (masc. plur.). etc.
Active participle	مُتَوَلٍّ	taking charge of.
Passive participle	مُتَوَلًّى	taken charge of.
Verbal noun	تَوَلٍّ (اَلتَّوَلِّي)	taking charge of.

The Vth form given above is the first derived form of quadriliteral verbs, e.g.

زَعْزَعَهُ	he moved, shook it.
تَزَعْزَعَ	it moved, shook (intrans.).
يَتَزَعْزَعُ	it moves, shakes (intrans.).
مُتَزَعْزِعٌ	moving, shaking.
تَزَعْزُعٌ	movement, motion, shaking.

72. Verbal Form VI تَفَاعَلَ

Form VI is made by prefixing تَ to form III of which it is generally the reflexive, e.g.

قَاتَلَهُ	he fought with him.
تَقَاتَلَ ٱلْقَوْمُ	the people fought each other.
سَابَقَهُ	he vied with him.
تَسَابَقَا	they (two) ran a race.

In many verbs of form VI the idea of reciprocity contained in the two examples above is quite absent, e.g.

تَثَاءَبَ يَتَثَاءَبُ	he yawned.
تَثَاؤُبٌ	yawning, a yawn.

يَتَنَاوَلُ	تَنَاوَلَ	he took (in his hand).
	تَنَاوُلٌ	taking.
يَتَنَاوَمُ	تَنَاوَمَ	he pretended to be asleep.
	تَنَاوُمٌ	pretending to be asleep.

The VIth form is conjugated similarly to form V, e.g.

Perfect active		تَنَاوَلْتُ	I took (in my hand).
		تَنَاوَلْتَ، تَنَاوَلْتِ	you took.
		تَنَاوَلَ	he took.
		تَنَاوَلَتْ	she took, etc.
Perfect passive	*tunūwila*	تُنُووِلَ	it was taken, etc.
Imperfect active		أَتَنَاوَلُ	I take.
		تَتَنَاوَلُ، تَتَنَاوَلِينَ	you take.
		يَتَنَاوَلُ	he takes.
		تَتَنَاوَلُ	she takes, etc.
Imperfect passive	*yutanāwalu*	يُتَنَاوَلُ	it is taken, etc.
Imperative		تَنَاوَلْ !	take! (masc.).
		تَنَاوَلِي !	take! (fem.).
		تَنَاوَلُوا	take! (masc. plur.), etc.
Active participle		مُتَنَاوِلٌ	taking.
Passive participle		مُتَنَاوَلٌ	taken.
Verbal noun		تَنَاوُلٌ	taking.

N.B. All verbs of the form تَفَاعَلَ make their verbal nouns according to the pattern تَفَاعُلٌ.

If the root verb is doubled or *hamzated* or if the 1st or 2nd radical is و or ي the VIth form is perfectly regular, e.g.

	تَرَادَّا يَتَرَادَّانِ ٱلْبَيْعَ	they (two) rescinded the sale (by mutual agreement).
	تَرَادُّ بَيْعٍ	rescinding of a sale.
N.B.	تُرُودِدَ ٱلْبَيْعُ	the sale was rescinded where no contraction takes place. See the perfect passive of form III of doubled verbs.
	تَآلَفُوا يَتَآلَفُونَ	they became familiar with each other.
	تَآلُفٌ	mutual familiarity
	تَثَاءَبَ يَتَثَاءَبُ	he yawned.
	تَثَاؤُبٌ	yawning, a yawn.
	تَكَافَأَ يَتَكَافَأُ ٱلْقَوْمُ	the people were equal.
	تَكَافُؤٌ	being equal, equality.
	تَوَافَقَ يَتَوَافَقُ ٱلْقَوْمُ	the people agreed among themselves.
	تَوَافُقٌ	mutual agreement.
	تَعَاوَنَ يَتَعَاوَنُ ٱلْقَوْمُ	the people helped, co-operated with each other.
	تَعَاوُنٌ	co-operation.
	تَمَايَلَ يَتَمَايَلُ	he swayed (intrans.).
	تَمَايُلٌ	swaying.

If the 3rd radical is و or ي form VI is conjugated like form V above, e.g.

تَعَامَى	he pretended to be blind.
تَعَامَيْتُ	I pretended to be blind.
يَتَعَامَى	he pretends to be blind.

	أَتَعَامَى	I pretend to be blind.
Imperative	تَعَامَ !	pretend to be blind!
	تَعَامَيْ !	pretend to be blind.
	تَعَامَوْا !	pretend to be blind, etc.
Active participle	مُتَعَامٍ (اَلْمُتَعَامِي)	pretending to be blind.
Verbal noun	تَعَامٍ (اَلتَّعَامِي)	pretending to be blind,

(for تَعَامُيٌ for تَعَامِيٌ).

Note the verb تَعَالَى He (God) has made Himself exalted, the imperative of which (masc. ! تَعَالَ, fem. ! تَعَالَيْ, masc. plur. ! تَعَالَوْا, etc.) is applicable to any being and means 'come!'! This imperative is more common than the imperatives of the usual verbs of coming such as حَضَرَ, جَاءَ and أَتَى.

Examples:

مَتَى نَتَشَرَّفُ بِمُقَابَلَةِ ٱلْمَلِكِ؟ نَحْنُ مَدْعُوُّونَ لِزِيَارَةِ ٱلْقَصْرِ غَدًا

When shall we have the honour of meeting the king? We are invited to visit the palace to-morrow.

كَانَ مُتَوَجِّهًا إِلَى ٱلْبَابِ لَمَّا عَثَرَ فِي ٱلْبِسَاطِ

He was going to the door when he tripped on the carpet.

إِنَّ زَوْجَتِي لَا تَتَنَاوَلُ ٱلْغَدَاءَ قَبْلَ حُضُورِي

My wife will not take lunch before my arrival.

لَمَّا يَتَوَلَّ قِيَادَةَ ٱلْجَيْشِ مَعَ أَنَّهُ تَعَيَّنَ مُنْذُ أُسْبُوعٍ

He has not yet taken over command of the army although he was appointed a week ago.

تَخَيَّرُوا أَحْسَنَ ٱلتُّفَّاحِ لِيُهْدُوهُ لِأَصْدِقَائِهِمْ

They chose the best of the apples in order to present them (lit. it) to their friends.

تَعَلَّمِ ٱللُّغَةَ ٱلْعَرَبِيَّةَ لِأَنَّهَا نَافِعَةٌ جِدًّا

Learn the Arabic language because it is very useful!

كَيْفَ يَتَكَافَأُ ٱلْكَسْلَانُ وَٱلْمُجْتَهِدُ؟

How can (lit. are) the lazy man and the industrious man be equal?

تَعَاوُنُ ٱلْأُمَمِ (sing. أُمَّةٌ) مِفْتَاحُ ٱلسِّلْمِ

The co-operation of nations is the key to peace.

تَلَاقَى ٱلصَّدِيقَانِ بَعْدَ مُضِيِّ سَنَةٍ كَامِلَةٍ

The two friends met (each other) after the passing of a whole year.

تَعَالَيْ مَعِي لِكَيْ أُرِيَكِ مَا يُوجَدُ فِي جُنَيْنَتِي مِنْ زُهُورٍ جَمِيلَةٍ

Come (fem.) with me so that I may show you the beautiful flowers that are in my garden (lit. what is found (i.e. exists) in my garden of beautiful flowers).

Exercise XX

١—عَزَمَ الطَّلَبَةُ الهُنُودُ على أن يَتَوَجَّهُوا إلى مِصْرَ لكي يَتَلَقَّوا ٱلْعِلْمَ في الجامعِ الأَزْهَرِ الذي هو أَقْدَمُ جامعةٍ في العَالَمِ الإِسْلَامِيِّ. (طَالِبٌ هِنْدِيٌّ)

٢—أَرْجُو أن تُشَرِّفَنِي وتَتَعَشَّى معي هذا المَسَاء.

٣—أرادَ الرَّئيسُ أن يَتَعَاوَنَ مع أَعْضَاء المَجْلِسِ ولٰكِنَّهُمْ أَصَرُّوا على إِقَالَتِهِ من مَنْصِبِهِ. (عُضْوٌ، أَقَالَ)

٤—تعالَ معي لِنَتَفَرَّجَ على الحَيَوَانَاتِ الغريبةِ في حديقةِ الحيوانِ.

٥—هذا الشَّيْخُ مُتَوَاضِعٌ جدًّا مَعَ أَنَّه عَلَّامَةٌ مشهورٌ وقد كَتَبَ كُتُبًا عديدةً تُتَدَاوَلُ في الدَّوَائِرِ العِلْمِيَّةِ. (دَائِرَةٌ)

٦—يا بَنَاتُ، لِماذا تَتَشَاءَبْنَ كُلُّكُنَّ ٱليَوْمَ؟ أَلَمْ تَنَمْنَ هذه اللَّيلةَ؟

٧—رَاسَلْنَا أخانا في أمريكا عِدَّةَ سِنِينَ ولكِنَّنا لا نُرَاسِلُهُ الآن لأَنَّه قد عَزَمَ أَلَّا يَعُودَ إلى وَطَنِهِ أَبَدًا.

٨ــلا تَتَنَاوَل ذلك الصَّحْنَ لأنّه كان في الفُرْنِ أَكْثَر من نِصْفِ سَاعةٍ وهو حارٌّ جدًّا.

٩ــمَنْ يَتَوَلَّى تَنْفِيذَ هذه المُهِمَّة الصَّعْبَة؟ أنا أَتَوَلَّاهُ بِدُونِ تَرَدُّد. (نَفَّذَ)

١٠ــقَابَلُوا كَثِيرِينَ من شُيُوخِ ٱلْبَدْوِ عندما كانوا مُقِيمِينَ في الصَّحْرَاء قريبًا مِنَ الإِسْكَنْدَرِيَّة.

Translation

1. The Indian students decided to go to Egypt to study (lit. to receive knowledge) in the Azhar Mosque which is the oldest university in the Islamic world.

2. I hope you will do me the honour and dine with me this evening.

3. The president wanted to co-operate with the members of the council but they insisted on dismissing him from his post.

4. Come with me so that we may look at the strange animals in the Zoological Gardens.

5. This old man is very humble although he is a famous scholar and has written many books which are passed around in learned (scientific) circles.

6. Girls, why are you all yawning to-day? Did you not sleep last night.

7. We corresponded with our brother in America for many years but we do not correspond with him now because he has decided never to return to his country (patria).

8. Do not take that plate in your hand because it has been in the oven for more than half an hour and it is very hot.

9. Who will undertake to execute this difficult task? I shall undertake it without hesitation.

10. They met many Beduin shaykhs when they were living in the desert near Alexandria.

LESSON XXI

73. Verbal Form VII إِنْفَعَلَ

Form VII is made by prefixing a vowelless ن to the first or simple form of the verb. As no word in Arabic can begin with a vowelless consonant this ن must be preceded by *hamzat-al-waṣl* the vowel of which is '*i*'.

The VIIth form which is not very common is the passive or reflexive of the first form, e.g.

كَسَرَ	he broke (trans.).
إِنْكَسَرَ	it broke (intrans.), became broken.
قَلَبَ	he overturned, upset.
إِنْقَلَبَ	it became overturned, upset.

N.B. The VIIth form is not made from verbs of which the first radical is أ, ر, ل, ن, و or ي. A few exceptions to this rule exist in modern Arabic.

Form VII is conjugated as follows:

Perfect active	إِنْقَلَبْتُ	I became overturned.
	إِنْقَلَبْتَ، إِنْقَلَبْتِ	you became overturned.
	إِنْقَلَبَ	he became overturned.
	إِنْقَلَبَتْ	she became overturned, etc.
Perfect passive	non-existent in form VII.	
Imperfect active	أَنْقَلِبُ	I become overturned.
	تَنْقَلِبُ، تَنْقَلِبِينَ	you become overturned.
	يَنْقَلِبُ	he becomes overturned.
	تَنْقَلِبُ	she becomes overturned, etc.
Imperfect passive	non-existent in form VII.	
Imperative	إِنْقَلِبْ !	become overturned! (masc. sing.).
	إِنْقَلِبِي !	become overturned! (fem. sing.).
	إِنْقَلِبُوا !	become overturned! (masc. plur.), etc.
Active participle	مُنْقَلِبٌ	becoming overturned,

Passive participle as noun of place	مُنْقَلَبٌ	place of overturning.
Verbal noun	اِنْقِلَابٌ	becoming overturned, a revolution.

N.B. All verbs of the form اِنْفَعَلَ make their verbal nouns according to the pattern اِنْفِعَالٌ the *hamza* of which is *hamzat-al-waṣl.*

The student should note the vowel patterns of form VII which, with the following additions in brackets, are the same for forms VII–XV viz.

Perfect active	*(i)aaa.*
(Perfect passive	*(u)uia*).
Imperfect active	*aaiu.*
(Imperfect passive	*uaau*).
Imperative (masc. sing.)	*(i)ai.*
Active participle	*uaiun.*
(Passive participle	*uaaun*).
Verbal noun	*(i)iāun.*

The same phonetic changes which take place in the simple forms of the doubled, hollow and weak verbs take place in form VII of these, e.g.

	ضَمَّ يَضُمُّ	he collected, pressed.
	اِنْضَمَّ يَنْضَمُّ (إِلَى)	he was pressed, joined (a party, etc.).
Active participle	مُنْضَمٌّ	
Verbal noun	اِنْضِمَامٌ	
	قَادَ يَقُودُ	he led.
	اِنْقَادَ يَنْقَادُ	he was led, became docile.
Active participle	مُنْقَادٌ	being led, docile.
Verbal noun	اِنْقِيَادٌ (for اِنْقِوَادٌ)	docility.

Note that the imperfect of forms VII and VIII of hollow verbs takes a long '*ā*' between the 1st and 3rd radicals, the sound groups '*awi*' and '*ayi*' both becoming '*ā*'.

	حَنَى يَحْنِي	he bent (trans.).
	اِنْحَنَى يَنْحَنِي	he became bent, bowed.
Active participle	مُنْحَنٍ (اَلْمُنْحَنِي)	bowing.
Verbal noun	اِنْحِنَاءٌ	bowing.

Note once more that final radical و or ي bearing the case ending changes to *hamzat-al-qaṭ*ع after long '*ā*'.

74. Verbal Form VIII اِفْتَعَلَ

Form VIII is made by inserting تَ between the 1st and 2nd radicals. The 1st radical becoming vowelless it must be preceded by *hamzat-al-waṣl*. Form VIII is usually the reflexive of the 1st or root form but contrary to form VII it may take a direct object. Sometimes the Ist and VIIIth forms occur with no great difference in meaning, e.g.

جَمَعَ يَجْمَعُ	he collected (trans.).
اِجْتَمَعَ ٱلْمَاءُ	the water collected.
اِجْتَمَعَ ٱلنَّاسُ	the people collected, assembled.
فَرَقَ يَفْرِقُ	he separated (trans.).
اِفْتَرَقَ ٱلنَّاسُ	the people separated (intrans.).
لَمَسَ يَلْمِسُ	he touched, felt.
اِلْتَمَسَ	he sought.
شَرَى يَشْرِي	he bought.
اِشْتَرَى يَشْتَرِي	he bought.

The VIIIth form is conjugated as follows:

Perfect active	اِلْتَمَسْتُ	I sought.
	اِلْتَمَسْتَ، اِلْتَمَسْتِ	you sought.
	اِلْتَمَسَ	he sought.
	اِلْتَمَسَتْ	she sought, etc.

Perfect passive	*ultumisa*,	اُلْتُمِسَ	it was sought, etc.
Imperfect active		أَلْتَمِسُ	I seek.
	تَلْتَمِسِينَ ،	تَلْتَمِسُ	you seek.
		يَلْتَمِسُ	he seeks.
		تَلْتَمِسُ	she seeks, etc.
Imperfect passive		يُلْتَمَسُ	it is sought, etc.
Imperative		اِلْتَمِسْ !	seek! (masc. sing.).
		اِلْتَمِسِي !	seek! (fem. sing.).
		اِلْتَمِسُوا !	seek! (masc. plur.), etc.
Active participle		مُلْتَمِسٌ	seeking.
Passive participle		مُلْتَمَسٌ	sought.
Verbal noun		اِلْتِمَاسٌ	seeking, search, requesting.

The following phonetic changes of the inserted ت in form VIII are to be noted:

(i) If the 1st radical of the root verb is د, ذ or ز the inserted ت becomes د, e.g.

دَهَنَ يَدْهُنُ	he greased, oiled, painted.
اِدَّهَنَ يَدَّهِنُ	it became oiled.
ذَخَرَ يَذْخَرُ	he stored.
اِدَّخَرَ and اِذَّخَرَ	he stored.
زَادَ يَزِيدُ	he increased (trans.).
اِزْدَادَ يَزْدَادُ	he increased (intrans.).

(ii) If the 1st radical of the root verb is one of the emphatic consonants ص, ض and ط the inserted ت becomes ط, e.g.

صَفَا يَصْفُو	it was pure.
اِصْطَفَى يَصْطَفِي	he chose (as the purest).
ضَرَبَ	he struck.
اِضْطَرَبَ يَضْطَرِبُ	he became excited.
طَلَعَ يَطْلُعُ	he ascended, climbed.
اِطَّلَعَ عَلَى	he got knowledge of.

(iii) If the 1st radical is ظ the inserted ت becomes ظ, e.g.

ظَلَمَ يَظْلِمُ	he oppressed.
اِظَّلَمَ يَظَّلِمُ	he suffered oppression.

(iv) If the 1st radical is و this assimilates to the inserted ت, e.g.

	وَكَلَ (يَكِلُ) إِلَيْهِ ٱلْأَمْرَ	he entrusted the matter to him.
	اِتَّكَلَ عَلَى	he relied on.
	وَفِقَ يَفِقُ	it was suitable.
	اِتَّفَقَ ٱلْقَوْمُ	the people agreed (among themselves).
Note also	اِتَّفَقَ	it happened by chance.

Lastly note that in the VIIIth form of the verb أَخَذَ, he took, the initial *hamza* is assimilated to the inserted ت, viz.

اِتَّخَذَ يَتَّخِذُ	he took (for himself).

The VIIIth form of the doubled, hollow and weak verbs presents us with no special difficulty, e.g.

	مَدَّ يَمُدُّ	he stretched (trans.), spread.
	اِمْتَدَّ يَمْتَدُّ	it stretched (intrans.), extended.
Active participle	مُمْتَدٌّ	stretching.

Verbal noun	اِمْتِدَادٌ	stretching, expanse.
(root حوج)	اِحْتَاجَ يَحْتَاجُ إِلَى	he needed.
Active participle	مُحْتَاجٌ	needing.
Passive participle	مُحْتَاجٌ إِلَيْهِ	needed.
Verbal noun	اِحْتِيَاجٌ and حَاجَةٌ	needing, need.
	شَرَى يَشْرِي	he bought.
	اِشْتَرَى يَشْتَرِي	he bought.
Active participle	مُشْتَرٍ (اَلْمُشْتَرِي)	buying, a purchaser.
Passive participle	مُشْتَرًى	bought.
Verbal noun	اِشْتِرَاءٌ and شِرَاءٌ	buying, purchase.

Examples:

اِحْتَلَّ ٱلْحُلَفَاءُ أَلْمَانِيَا بَعْدَ ٱنْكِسَارِ ٱلْجَيْشِ ٱلْأَلْمَانِيِّ

The allies occupied Germany after the collapse (lit. the breaking) of the German Army.

لَا أُرِيدُ أَنْ أَنْضَمَّ إِلَى حِزْبٍ هٰذِهِ مَبَادِئُهُ (sing. مَبْدَأٌ)

I do not wish to join a party with such principles (lit. whose principles are these).

لَنْ نَنْحَنِيَ أَمَامَ أَحَدٍ لِأَنَّنَا أَحْرَارٌ (sing. حُرٌّ)

We shall never bow before anyone because we are free men.

مَتَى ٱجْتَمَعَتِ ٱلْوُفُودُ (sing. وَفْدٌ) ؟ لَمْ تَجْتَمِعْ بَعْدُ

When did the delegations meet? They have not yet met.

لِمَ لَا تُرِيدُ أَنْ تَشْتَرِيَ ذٰلِكَ ٱلْكِتَابَ ؟ إِنَّ أُخْتِي ٱشْتَرَتْهُ لِي أَمْسِ

Why do you not want to buy that book? My sister bought it for me yesterday.

تَمْتَدُّ ٱلْبِلَادُ ٱلْعَرَبِيَّةُ مِنَ ٱلْمَغْرِبِ ٱلْأَقْصَى إِلَى حُدُودِ إِيرَانَ

The Arab countries extend from the farthest West (i.e. Morocco) to the frontiers of Persia.

كَيْفَ تَحْتَاجُونَ إِلَى أَقْلَامٍ جَدِيدَةٍ ؟ أَلَمْ أُعْطِكُمْ كُلَّ مَا كَانَ عِنْدِي مِنْ أَقْلَامٍ جَيِّدَةٍ فِي ٱلْأُسْبُوعِ ٱلْمَاضِي؟

How is it that you need new pens? Did I not give you all the good pens I had last week? (Note the double accusative after أَعْطَى he gave.)

اِتَّكِلُوا عَلَى ٱللّٰهِ فِي ٱلسَّرَّاءِ وَٱلضَّرَّاءِ

Trust in God in happiness and affliction.

يَا رَبِّي ! زِدْنِي عِلْمًا لِكَيْ أَعْرِفَ مَا يُرْضِيكَ

O my Lord! Increase my knowledge (lit. increase me as regards knowledge) so that I may know what will please Thee.

لَمَّا ٱنْتَهَتْ (masc. اِنْتَهَى) خُطْبَةُ ٱلْخَطِيبِ قَامَ رَجُلٌ يَنْفِي مَا كَانَ ٱدَّعَاهُ

When the speaker's speech ended a man got up to deny what he had claimed.

Exercise XXI

١—كُنْتُ أَظُنُّكُم تَحْتَاجُونَ إلى مُساعَدَتِي ولكن قد ٱتَّضَحَ لي أنّه يُمْكِنُكُم ٱلِاتِّفاقُ مع هؤلاء النّاسِ بِدونِ وَساطَتِي.

٢—عندما ٱقْتَحَمَ اللِّصّانِ بَيْتي (acc.) أَطْلَقْتُ علَيْهِما ٱلنّارَ فٱنْهَزَمَا ولم يَسْرِقَا شيئًا ذَا قِيمَةٍ.

٣—اِلْتَمِسِي مِنْهُ ٱلعَفْوَ فَرُبَّمَا يَنْسَى ما مَضَى ويُعَلِّمُكِ كيف تَتَّكِلِينَ عليهِ في المُسْتَقْبَلِ. (نَسِيَ)

٤—عندما رَأَى البُولِيسُ ٱجْتِمَاعَ المُتَظَاهِرِينَ الهائِجِينَ ظَنُّوا أنهم لَنْ يَتَمَكَّنُوا مِنْ أَنْ يَمْنَعُوهم مِنَ التَّقَدُّمِ نَحْوَ القَصْرِ المَلَكِيِّ. (هَاجَ يَهِيجُ، N.B. *malakīyun*)

٥—اِحْتَاجَتِ ٱلسَّيِّدتانِ إلى بيتٍ في شارعٍ هادئٍ وبَعْدَ بَحْثٍ طويلٍ ٱشْتَرَتَا بيتًا صغيرًا في ضاحيةٍ من ضَوَاحِي لَنْدَنَ ٱلشَّماليَّةِ.

٦—لَمْ تَمْتَدَّ سُلْطةُ القوّاتِ المُحْتَلَّةِ إلى جميعِ أَنْحاءِ البِلادِ كَمَا يَزْعُمُ بَعْضُ النّاسِ بَلِ ٱقْتَصَرَتْ على المُدُنِ الكبيرةِ فَقَطْ. (نَحْوٌ)

٧—أُضْطُرَّ المُجْرِمُ إلى الاِعْتِرافِ بالجَريمةِ التي ٱرْتَكَبَهَا فَحَكَمَ عليه القاضي بالسَّجْنِ لِمُدَّةِ سَنَتَيْنِ.

٨—سَقَطَتْ أَمْطارٌ غزيرةٌ أَثْنَاءَ اللَّيْلِ فَٱمْتَلَأَتْ جميعُ الأَحْوَاضِ بالمَاءِ فَفَرِحَ الفَلّاحُونَ فَرَحًا عظيمًا. (حَوْضٌ)

٩—لا يُحْتَمَلُ ان تَتَّصِلَ أُخْتِي بي بالتِّلِفُونِ قَبْلَ الظُّهْرِ لأنّها تَخْرُجُ كُلَّ صَباحٍ لِشِرَاءِ لَوَازِمِ بيتِها.

١٠—لا تَخْتَلِطُوا بِهؤلاءِ الرِّجالِ فقد سَمِعْتُ أنَّ ناسًا صالحِينَ كثيرِينَ مُسْتَاءُونَ مِن تَصَرُّفَاتِهِمْ. (سوء)

Translation

1. I thought you needed my help but it has become clear to me that it is possible for you to come to an agreement with these people without my mediation.

2. When the (two) burglars forced their way into my house I fired at them and they fled and did not steal anything of value.

3. Seek (fem.) his pardon and perhaps he will forget what has passed and teach you how to rely on him in the future.

4. When the police saw the assembling of the excited demonstrators they thought they would never be able to prevent them from advancing in the direction of the royal palace.

5. The two ladies needed a house in a quiet street and after a long search they bought a small house in one of London's northern suburbs.

6. The authority of the occupying forces did not extend to all regions of the country, as some people assert, but was confined to the large towns only.

7. The criminal was compelled to confess the crime he had committed and the judge sentenced him to be imprisoned for two years.

8. Heavy (abundant) rains fell during the night and all the water-troughs became filled with water and the peasants were very happy.

9. It is not probable that my sister will ring me up (lit. get in touch with me by telephone) in the forenoon because she goes out every morning to purchase her household requirements (lit. the necessary things of her house).

10. Do not mix with these men for I have heard that many good people are offended by their behaviour (lit. actions).

LESSON XXII

75. Verbal Form IX إِفْعَلَّ

Form IX is made by doubling the 3rd radical and dropping the vowel of the 1st with consequent prefixing of *hamzat-al-waṣl*. This verbal form is made from those adjectives of the pattern أَفْعَلُ, fem. فَعْلَاءُ, pl. فُعْلٌ which denote colours or defects of the body (see Lesson VI), e.g.

أَحْمَرُ	red.
إِحْمَرَّ	he became red, blushed.
أَصْفَرُ	yellow.
إِصْفَرَّ	he became yellow, pale.
أَخْضَرُ	green.
إِخْضَرَّ	it became green.
أَعْوَجُ	bent, twisted.
إِعْوَجَّ	it became bent.

The last radical of form IX being doubled it is conjugated like a doubled verb, e.g.

Perfect active	إِحْمَرَرْتُ	I blushed.
	إِحْمَرَرْتَ، إِحْمَرَرْتِ	you blushed.
	إِحْمَرَّ	he blushed.
	إِحْمَرَّتْ	she blushed, etc.

Perfect passive		non-existent in form IX.
Imperfect active	أَحْمَرُّ	I blush.
	تَحْمَرُّ، تَحْمَرِّينَ	you blush.
	يَحْمَرُّ	he blushes.
	تَحْمَرُّ	she blushes, etc.
Imperfect passive		non-existent in form IX.
Imperative	إِحْمَرِرْ !	blush! (masc.).
	إِحْمَرِّي !	blush! (fem.).
	إِحْمَرُّوا !	blush! (masc. pl.), etc.
Active participle	مُحْمَرٌّ	blushing.
Verbal noun	إِحْمِرَارٌ	blushing, reddening.

In form IX all radicals are treated as sound even though one of them may be a weak consonant so no difficulties arise for the student, e.g.

إِعْوَجَّ	it became twisted.
يَعْوَجُّ	it becomes twisted.
مُعْوَجٌّ	(becoming) twisted.
إِعْوِجَاجٌ	bending, twisting (intrans.).

Similar to form IX is the second derived form of four-radical verbs in which the last radical is doubled and the first made vowelless as above, e.g.

طَمْأَنَ	he reassured, set at ease.
إِطْمَأَنَّ	he became at ease.
يَطْمَئِنُّ	he becomes at ease.
مُطْمَئِنٌّ	at ease, reassured.

اِطْمِئْنَانٌ (mental) ease, reassurance.

اِقْشَعَرَّ جِلْدُهُ his skin crept.

يَقْشَعِرُّ جِلْدُهُ his skin creeps.

76. Verbal Form X اِسْتَفْعَلَ

Form X is made by making the first radical of the root verb vowelless and prefixing سْتَ. Like the three preceding forms this must be prefixed by *hamzat-al-waṣl*. Form X is the reflexive of the IVth form or denotes asking, taking or using for oneself the idea contained in the root verb. It is also occasionally considerative, e.g.

أَرْسَلَ	he let loose, sent.
اِسْتَرْسَلَ شَعْرُهَا	her hair hung loose.
أَعَدَّ	he prepared, got ready (trans.).
اِسْتَعَدَّ	he prepared (intrans.), got himself ready.
أَذِنَ	he permitted.
اِسْتَأْذَنَ	he asked permission.
خَرَجَ	he came out.
اِسْتَخْرَجَ	he drew out, extracted.
حَسُنَ	it was good, fine.
اِسْتَحْسَنَ	he considered good, approved.

Taking اِسْتَعْمَلَ, he used, (from عَمِلَ he did, worked) as our example we have the following conjugation of form X:

Perfect active	اِسْتَعْمَلْتُ	I used.
	اِسْتَعْمَلْتَ، اِسْتَعْمَلْتِ	you used.
	اِسْتَعْمَلَ	he used.
	اِسْتَعْمَلَتْ	she used, etc.

Perfect passive	*ustuعmila*	أُسْتُعْمِلَ	he, it was used.
Imperfect active		أَسْتَعْمِلُ	I use.
		تَسْتَعْمِلُ، تَسْتَعْمِلِينَ	you use.
		يَسْتَعْمِلُ	he uses.
		تَسْتَعْمِلُ	she uses, etc.
Imperfect passive	*yustaعmalu*	يُسْتَعْمَلُ	he, it is used.
Imperative		! إِسْتَعْمِلْ	use! (masc.).
		! إِسْتَعْمِلِي	use! (fem.).
		! إِسْتَعْمِلُوا	use! (masc. pl.).
Active participle		مُسْتَعْمِلٌ	using.
Passive participle		مُسْتَعْمَلٌ	used.
Verbal noun		إِسْتِعْمَالٌ	using, use.

If the root verb is doubled form X conforms with the rules for doubled verbs, e.g.

	عَدَّ	he counted.
	أَعَدَّ	he prepared (trans.).
	إِسْتَعَدَّ	he prepared (intrans.).
	إِسْتَعْدَدْتُ	I prepared (intrans.).
	يَسْتَعِدُّ	he prepares.
Active participle	مُسْتَعِدٌّ	preparing, prepared, ready.
Verbal noun	إِسْتِعْدَادٌ	preparation, readiness.

If any of the radicals is *hamza* or if و or ي is the 1st or 3rd radical the conjugation of the Xth form is perfectly regular in accordance with the rules already given, e.g.

	اِسْتَأْذَنَ	he asked permission.
	يَسْتَأْذِنُ	he asks permission.
Verbal noun	اِسْتِئْذَانٌ	asking.
	اِسْتَقْرَأَ	he asked s.o. to read.
	يَسْتَقْرِئُ	he asks s.o. to read.
Verbal noun	اِسْتِقْرَاءٌ	asking s.o. to read.
	اِسْتَوْطَنَ	he settled in a place, took it as his home.
	يَسْتَوْطِنُ	he settles.
Verbal noun	اِسْتِيطَانٌ (for اِسْتِوْطَانٌ)	settling.
	أَيْقَظَ	he awoke (trans.).
	اِسْتَيْقَظَ	he awoke (intrans.).
	يَسْتَيْقِظُ	he awakes.
Verbal noun	اِسْتِيقَاظٌ	awakening.
	اِسْتَوْفَى	he demanded (his right) in full.
	يَسْتَوْفِي	he demands in full.
Active participle	مُسْتَوْفٍ	demanding fulfilment.
Passive participle	مُسْتَوْفًى	demanded in full.
Verbal noun	اِسْتِيفَاءٌ (for اِسْتِوْفَايٌ)	demanding fulfilment.

If the middle radical is و or ى the conjugation of the imperfect of form X is as in Group III of hollow verbs, e.g.

(root قوم)	اِسْتَقَامَ	he was straight, upright.
	اِسْتَقَمْتُ	I was straight, upright.

	yastaqīmu	يَسْتَقِيمُ	he is straight.
Active participle		مُسْتَقِيمٌ	straight.
Verbal noun	*istiqāmatun*	إِسْتِقَامَةٌ	straightness.
(root فيد)		إِسْتَفَادَ	he benefited (intrans.).
		إِسْتَفَدْتُ	I benefited.
		يَسْتَفِيدُ	he benefits.
Active participle		مُسْتَفِيدٌ	benefiting.
Passive participle		مُسْتَفَادٌ	acquired as a benefit.
Verbal noun	*istifādatun*	إِسْتِفَادَةٌ	benefiting.

Note that the verbal noun of the Xth form of hollow verbs, like that of their IVth form, receives an extra '*tā' marbūṭa*'.

Note also that the common verb إِسْتَطَاعَ, he was able, (imperfect يَسْتَطِيعُ), very often loses its تَ in classical Arabic, viz.

	إِسْطَاعَ	he was able.
	إِسْطَعْتُ	I was able.
	يَسْطِيعُ	he is able.
but always	إِسْتِطَاعَةٌ	ability, power.

A very few verbs of the Xth form of hollow roots (generally nouns) maintain the middle radical as strong, in which case the verbal noun does not receive the extra '*tā' marbūṭa*', e.g.

	إِسْتَصْوَبَ	he considered right (صَوَابٌ).
	يَسْتَصْوِبُ	he considers right.
Verbal noun	إِسْتِصْوَابٌ	approval.

77. Nouns of Place and Instrument of Derived Verbs

Having concluded the derived verbs the student's attention is here drawn to the fact that nouns of place and time and nouns of instrument according to the patterns given in Lesson XI *cannot be made from derived verbs.*

The noun of place is often simply the passive participle even of forms VII and IX which do not generally have a passive participle owing to their intransitive meaning, e.g.

صَلَّى يُصَلِّي he prayed.

مُصَلًّى a place of prayer, prayer-room.

إِنْعَرَجَ it turned (the road).

مُنْعَرَجٌ a turning of a road.

إِسْتَنْقَعَ ٱلْمَاءُ the water collected and became stagnant.

مُسْتَنْقَعٌ a marsh.

Such nouns of place make their plurals with the sound feminine plural ending.

The noun of instrument of derived verbs, if it occurs, is usually the active participle with plural as above, e.g.

حَرَّكَ he moved (trans.).

(pl. مُحَرِّكَاتٌ) مُحَرِّكٌ a motor, engine.

Examples:

لَمَّا سَمِعَتْ ذٰلِكَ ٱحْمَرَّ وَجْهُهَا ٱحْمِرَارًا

When she heard that she blushed violently (lit. her face became red a reddening).

تَخْضَرُّ ٱلْمُرُوجُ (sing. مَرْجٌ) فِي ٱلرَّبِيعِ

The meadows become green in Spring.

حَالَمَا يَسْتَيْقِظُونَ (سَوْفَ) أَسْتَحْضِرُهُمْ لِسَمَاعِ ٱلْمُوسِيقَى

As soon as they wake up I shall bring them to hear the music.

لَقَدِ ٱسْتَعْدَدْنَا لِسَفَرِنَا ٱلطَّوِيلِ ٱلَّذِي نَسْتَعْمِلُ أَثْنَاءَهُ جَمِيعَ وَسَائِلِ ٱلنَّقْلِ (sing. وَسِيلَةٌ)

We have prepared for our long journey during which we shall use all means of transport.

هَلِ ٱسْتَوْفَوْا جَمِيعَ شُرُوطِ ٱلْعَقْدِ؟ لَمْ يَسْتَوْفُوا شَرْطًا وَاحِدًا

Have they demanded fulfilment of all the conditions of the contract? They have not demanded fulfilment of one condition.

يَظْهَرُ أَنَّهُمْ لَنْ يَسْتَحْسِنُوا مَشْرُوعَهُ، وَلِذٰلِكَ يَنْوِي ٱلِٱسْتِقَالَةَ مِنْ مَنْصِبِهِ

It appears that they will never approve his project and so he intends to resign (lit. the resignation from) his post.

كَيْفَ تُسْتَعْمَلُ هٰذِهِ ٱلْآلَةُ ٱلْمُعَقَّدَةُ؟ إِنِّي أَخَافُ أَنْ أَسْتَعْمِلَهَا

How is this complicated instrument used? I am afraid to use it.

يَجِبُ عَلَيْكُمْ أَنْ تَسْتَفِيدُوا مِنْ تَجَارِبِ أُولٰئِكَ ٱلَّذِينَ سَبَقُوكُمْ فِي هٰذَا ٱلْمَيْدَانِ

You should (it is incumbent on you to) benefit by the experiences of those who have preceded you in this field.

أَنَا مُسْتَعِدٌّ لِإِنْكَارِ كُلِّ مَا يَتَّهِمُونَنِي بِهِ، فَإِنِّي لَمْ أَرْتَكِبْ تِلْكَ ٱلْجَرِيمَةَ

I am ready to deny (lit. for the denial of) everything of which they accuse me for I did not commit that crime.

هَلْ فِي ٱسْتِطَاعَتِكَ أَنْ تُعِيرَنِي مَبْلَغًا صَغِيرًا حَتَّى ٱلْأُسْبُوعِ ٱلْآتِي؟ لَا أَسْتَطِيعُ أَنْ أُعْطِيَكَ أَكْثَرَ مِنْ جُنَيْهٍ وَاحِدٍ

Can you (lit. is it within your power to) lend me a small sum until next week? I cannot give you more than £1.

Exercise XXII

١—يَصْفَرُّ وَرَقُ الشَّجَرِ في الخَرِيفِ وعندما تَهُبُّ الرِّيحُ يَسْقُطُ على الأَرْضِ.

٢—جَاءَ لِيُطَمْئِنَنَا على صِحَّةِ أَبِينَا وَبَعْدَمَا ٱطْمَأْنَنَّا سَأَلْنَاهُ مَتَى يَخْرُجُ أَبُونَا مِنَ ٱلْمُسْتَشْفَى.

٣—يا أيُّها المُوَاطِنُونَ، يَجِبُ عليكم أنْ تَسْتَعِدُّوا لِلْحَرْبِ لأنَّه قد أُشِيعَ أنَّ أعْدَاءَكُمْ عَازِمُونَ على مُحَارَبَتِكُمْ.

٤—لا نُبَالِي بالإشَاعَاتِ وسوف نَسْتَعْمِلُ كُلَّ ما لَدَيْنَا لِمَنْعِ المُعْتَدِينَ من الاسْتِيلَاءِ عَلَى بِلَادِنا. (لَدَى، اِعْتَدَى، اِسْتَوْلَى)

٥—يا أوْلادُ، أتَسْتَطِيعُونَ أن تُسَاعِدُونِي على رَفْعِ هذا الصُّنْدُوقِ قليلًا لأرْبُطَهُ بهذا الحَبْلِ؟ (رَفَعَ ...، رَبَطَ)

٦—قالَتِ ٱلسَّيِّدات إنَّهُنَّ قدِ ٱسْتَفَدْنَ كثيرًا من مُحَاضَرَةِ الطَّبِيبِ وطلبْنَ إليه أن يُعِيدَها عليهِنَّ في نِهَايَةِ الأُسْبُوعِ التَّالِي. (أعَادَ، تَلَا)

٧—لَنْ تَسْتَقِيلَ من مَنْصِبِها لأنَّها تَرَى أنَّ بَقاءَها أنْفَعُ لِلمُجْتَمَعِ.

٨—يا بِنْتِي، هل تَسْتَحْسِنِينَ مِثْلَ هذا التَّصَرُّفِ في شَخْصٍ يَزْعَمُ أنّه يُحِبُّكِ؟

٩—يَسْتَيْقِظُ المُسْلِمُ قُبَيْلَ شُرُوقِ الشَّمْسِ لِيُصَلِّيَ صَلَاةَ الفَجْرِ وهي إحْدَى ٱلصَّلَوَاتِ ٱلتي يَفْرِضُها عليه ٱلدِّينُ الإسْلَامِيُّ.

١٠—عندما يَحُلُّ الشِّتاءُ تُسَافِرُ أُولٰئِكَ الأوَانِسُ المَحْظُوظاتُ إلى سِوِيسَرا لِلتَّزَحْلُقِ على الجَلِيدِ واللَّعِبِ في الثَّلْجِ. (آنِسَةٌ)

Translation

1. The leaves (coll.) of the trees (coll.) become yellow in autumn and when the wind blows they fall on the ground.

2. He came to reassure us about our father's health and after we were set at ease we asked him when our father would come out of hospital.

3. Compatriots, you must prepare for war because it has been rumoured that your enemies are determined to make war on you.

4. We do not care about rumours and shall use everything we have to prevent the aggressors from taking possession of our country.

5. Boys, can you help me to raise this box a little so that I may tie it with this rope?

6. The ladies said they had benefited greatly from the doctor's lecture and asked him to repeat it to them at the end of the following week.

7. She will never resign from her post because she considers that her remaining is more beneficial to society.

8. My girl, do you approve of such behaviour in a person who says that he loves you?

9. A (the) Muslim awakens a little before sun-rise in order to pray the dawn prayer which is one of the prayers imposed upon him by the Islamic religion.

10. When winter comes (lit. alights) those fortunate young ladies travel to Switzerland to skate on the ice and play in the snow.

LESSON XXIII

78. The Optative

The optative is expressed by the perfect of the verb although in modern Arabic the imperfect is more commonly used, e.g.

رَحِمَهُ ٱللّٰهُ !	May God have mercy on him! (said on hearing of a person's death).
بَارَكَ ٱللّٰهُ فِيكَ !	May God bless you!
صَلَّى ٱللّٰهُ عَلَيْهِ وَسَلَّمَ !	May God bless him and give (him) peace! (said after the name of the Prophet Muḥammad).
رَضِيَ ٱللّٰهُ عَنْهُ !	May God be pleased with him! (said after the name of one of the Prophet's companions).

The negative of the optative is introduced by لَا *not* مَا, e.g.

لَا شَرِبْتَ مَاءً نَقِيًّا طُولَ حَيَاتِكَ !	May you not drink pure water all (lit. the length of) your life!

The verbal particle ...لَيْتَ (يَا) '(O) would that...' has the same construction as إِنَّ, the subject being in the accusative, e.g.

لَيْتَ ٱلشَّبَابَ يَعُودُ يَوْمًا !	Would that youth were to return one day!
يَا لَيْتَنَا لَمْ نَسْمَعْ ذٰلِكَ ٱلْخَبَرَ !	Would that we had never heard that piece of news!

79. Verbs of Surprise or Admiration

Surprise at or admiration of a quality *expressed by the* 1*st form of the verb* is rendered by the patterns مَا أَفْعَلَهُ or أَفْعِلْ بِهِ, e.g.

	كَذَبَ	he lied
	مَا أَكْذَبَهُ !	what a liar he *is*! (lit. what has made him lie?).
(N.B.	مَا كَانَ أَكْذَبَهُ !	what a liar he *was*!).
or	أَكْذِبْ بِهِ !	what a liar he *is*! (lit. make a liar out of him!).
	جَمُلَتْ	she was beautiful.
	مَا أَجْمَلَهَا !	how beautiful she *is*!
or	أَجْمِلْ بِهَا !	how beautiful she *is*!

Surprise and admiration are, however, more commonly expressed by the phrase ... يَا لِـ ... مِنْ, e.g.

يَا لَهُ مِنْ بَطَلٍ !	what a hero he is!
يَا لَكِ مِنْ مُمَثِّلَةٍ !	what an actress you are!
يَا لَهُمْ مِنْ طُغَاةٍ ! (sing. طَاغِيَةٌ)	what tyrants they are!

Note the two verbs نِعْمَ (fem. نِعْمَتْ) it *is* good and بِئْسَ (fem. بِئْسَتْ) it *is* bad, which are only used in the above persons and generally only in certain stock phrases from the Qur'ān, e.g.

نِعْمَ مَا فَعَلْتَ !	how well you have done!
بِئْسَ ٱلْمَصِيرُ !	what an evil fate it is!

80. 'The Sisters' of كَانَ *kāna*

The following verbs take their predicates in the accusative like كَانَ and so are known as أَخَوَاتُ كَانَ or 'the sisters of كَانَ':

لَيْسَ he *is* not (see Lesson XVIII).

مَا زَالَ (لَمْ يَزَلْ) he has not ceased to be, still is.

e.g. أَلَمْ تَزَلْ عَطْشَانَ؟ are you still thirsty?

مَا زِلْتُ (لَمْ أَزَلْ) أَذْكُرُهَا I still remember her.

(Note زَالَ يَزُولُ it died out, faded away, but مَا زَالَ لَا يَزَالُ it has not ceased to be, still is always used negatively as above.)

مَا عَادَ (لَمْ يَعُدْ) it no longer is (lit. it has not returned).

e.g. لَمْ يَعُدْ يَخْطُرُ بِبَالِي it no longer occurs to me (lit. to my mind).

كَادَ يَكَادُ he was on the point of (always followed by the imperfect indicative).

e.g. كَادَ يَقَعُ he almost fell.

أَكَادُ أَعْتَقِدُ ذٰلِكَ I (can) almost believe that.

Note especially the two following sentences:

لَمْ يَكَدْ يَسْمَعُ كَلَامَهُمْ حَتَّى... he had hardly heard their words (no sooner had he heard their words) when....

لَا نَكَادُ نَسْمَعُ ٱلْغِنَاءَ we (can) hardly hear the singing.

بَقِيَ يَبْقَى he remained, stayed.

ظَلَّ (ظَلِلْتُ) يَظَلُّ he remained, stayed.

دَامَ يَدُومُ he remained, continued to be.

e.g. بَقِينَا حَيَارَى we remained perplexed.

سَوْفَ يَظَلُّونَ يُفَكِّرُونَ فِي ٱلْأَمْرِ they will continue to think about the matter.

دُمْتَ مَسْرُورًا ! may you remain happy!

N.B. سَوْفَ أُقَاوِمُهُ مَا دُمْتُ حَيًّا I shall oppose him as long as I remain alive.

The following verbs *which all mean 'he became'* are followed by the same construction as that after كَانَ:

صَارَ يَصِيرُ	
أَصْبَحَ يُصْبِحُ	(lit. he did, (be)came in the morning صَبَاحٌ).
أَضْحَى يُضْحِي	(lit. he did, (be)came in the forenoon ضُحًى).
أَمْسَى يُمْسِي	(lit. he did, (be)came in the evening مَسَاءٌ).
بَاتَ يَبَاتُ or يَبِيتُ	(lit. he spent the night).
e.g. صَارَ غَنِيًّا	he became rich.
أَصْبَحْتَ عَالِمًا	you have become learned.
أَضْحَى تَعْبَانَ	he became tired.
أَمْسَيْتُ جَزِعًا	I have become desperate.
بَاتَ مُقَرَّرًا (مِنَ ٱلْمُقَرَّرِ)	it was (became) decided.

N.B. أَصْبَحَ, أَضْحَى and أَمْسَى have almost lost their respective ideas of morning, forenoon and evening. بَاتَ is only used in the 3rd person of the perfect with the meaning 'to become', otherwise it means 'he spent the night', e.g.

إِحْذَرُوا أَنْ تَبِيتُوا فِي ٱلْهَوَاءِ ٱلطَّلْقِ !	take care *not* to spend the night in the open air!

81. 'To begin'

The perfect active only of the three verbs جَعَلَ, he placed, put, made, أَخَذَ, he took and صَارَ, he became, are used followed by the imperfect of another verb as equivalent to the verb بَدَأَ or إِبْتَدَأَ, he began, e.g.

جَعَلْتُ أَقْرَأُ ٱلْكِتَابَ	I began to read the book.
صِرْنَا نَنْفُخُ عَلَى أَصَابِعِنَا مِنَ ٱلْبَرْدِ	we began to blow on our fingers from the cold.
أَخَذُوا يَضْرِبُونَ ٱلْأَسْرَى	they began to beat the captives.

Examples:

كَانَ أُسْتَاذِي ٱلْمَرْحُومُ رَجُلًا فَاضِلًا

My late (lit. on whom God has had mercy) professor was an excellent man.

لَيْتَكُمْ لَمْ تَحْضُرُوا فِي هٰذَا ٱلْوَقْتِ لِأَنِّي مَشْغُولٌ جِدًّا !

Would that you had not come at this time because I am very busy!

يَا لَيْتَنِي قَادِرٌ عَلَى ٱلسَّفَرِ مَعَكَ !

Would that I were able to travel with you!

لَمَّا سَمِعُوا زَئِيرَ ٱلْأَسَدِ كَادُوا يَمُوتُونَ مِنَ ٱلْخَوْفِ (or خَوْفًا)

When they heard the roar of the lion they almost died of fright.

مَا أَحْلَى أُخْتَكَ ! كَمْ عُمْرُهَا ؟

How pretty (lit. sweet) your sister is! How old is she (lit. how much is her age)?

يَا لَهُ مِنْ رَجُلٍ قَبِيحٍ ! أَكَادُ أَنْفِرُ مِنْهُ كُلَّمَا يَقْتَرِبُ مِنِّي

What a wicked (ugly) fellow he is! I almost run away from him every time he comes near me.

بَقِيتُ أَنْتَظِرُهُ حَتَّى غَابَتِ ٱلشَّمْسُ

I remained waiting for him until the sun set.

يَجِبُ عَلَيْكَ أَنْ تَجْتَهِدَ فِي ٱلْجَامِعَةِ لِكَيْ تُصْبِحَ يَوْمًا مَا عَالِمًا كَبِيرًا

You must be diligent at the University in order to become a great scholar one day. (Note مَا after يَوْمًا to indicate the indefiniteness of the time.)

بَعْدَمَا صَارُوا أَغْنِيَاءَ لَمْ يَعُودُوا يَنْظُرُونَ إِلَى أَصْدِقَائِهِمُ ٱلسَّابِقِينَ

After they became rich they no longer looked at their former friends.

إِبْقَ هُنَا حَتَّى أَعُودَ إِلَيْكَ مِنَ ٱلْقَرْيَةِ بِشَيْءٍ مِنَ ٱلطَّعَامِ

Remain here until I bring back some food for you from the village (lit. until I return to you from the village with something of food).

EXERCISE XXIII

١ــلقد وَلَدَتْ زَوْجةُ صديقي عَلِيٍّ تَوْأَمَيْنِ أَقَرَّ اللّٰهُ بِهِما أَعْيُنَ والِدَيْهِما !

٢ــيا لَيْتَنا لم نَتَّكِلْ عليهم في الضِّيقِ فإنّهم قد خَانُوا ثِقَتَنا بِهِم !
(وَثِقَ يَثِقُ)

٣ــسمِعْتُ أنّ أخاكَ قد تَطَوَّعَ لِلْخِدْمةِ في سِلاحِ الطَّيَرانِ. مَا أَشْجَعَهُ !

٤ــمَا تَزالِينَ عَطْشَى مَعَ أنّكِ شَرِبْتِ كُوبَيْنِ مِنَ الحليبِ.

٥ــمَا زَالَ الأَوْلادُ يَذْهَبُونَ إلى المَدْرَسةِ لأنّ أَباهُمْ يُرِيدُ أن يُتِمُّوا تَعْلِيمَهُمْ الثَّانَوِيَّ لِيَنتقِلُوا بَعْدَهُ إلى الجامعةِ.

٦ــلَمْ تَكَدْ تَفْتَحُ بابَ الدُولابِ حَتَّى جَرَى فَأْرٌ بَيْنَ ساقَيْها.

٧ــعندما تُصْبِحُ غنيًّا فَلا تَنْسَ أنّه ساعَدَكَ على التَّغَلُّبِ على صُعُوبَاتِكَ.

٨ــوَعَدَتْني بأن تَحْذَرَ أن تَفْتَحَ البابَ في غِيابي.

٩ــخَرَجَ جارِيًا إلى الشّارِعِ وجَعَلَ يَصِيحُ بِأَعْلَى صَوْتِهِ قَائِلًا : «اِلْحَقُوني ! ». (لَحِقَ)

١٠ــيَدْخُلُ التَّلامِذةُ الفَصْلَ في الصّباحِ ويأْخُذُونَ في قِراءةِ دَرْسِهِم على المُدَرِّسةِ.

TRANSLATION

1. The wife of my friend 'Ali has given birth to twins. May God make them the delight of their parents' eyes! (lit. may God cool with them their parents' eyes).

2. Would that we had not relied on them in distress for they betrayed our trust in them.

3. I have heard that your brother has volunteered for service in the Air Force (lit. the flight arm). How brave he is!

4. You (fem.) are still thirsty although you have drunk two glasses of milk.

5. The boys still go to school because their father wants them to complete their secondary education in order to go on (lit. transfer) to the University.

6. She had hardly opened the door of the cupboard when a mouse ran between her legs.

7. When you become rich do not forget that he helped you to overcome your difficulties.

8. She promised me that she would take care *not* to open the door in my absence.

9. He went out to the street running and began to shout at the top of his voice: 'Help!' (lit. catch up with me, come to me).

10. The pupils enter the class in the morning and begin to read their lesson to their teacher.

LESSON XXIV

82. The Cardinal Numbers

The numerals are somewhat complicated in written Arabic. The cardinal numbers are as follows:

	Arabic sign		masc.	fem.	
1	١		أَحَدٌ	إِحْدَى	(pronouns)
			وَاحِدٌ	وَاحِدَةٌ	(adjectives)
2	٢	(handwritten ٢)	اِثْنَانِ	اِثْنَتَانِ	(pronouns)
3	٣	(handwritten ٣)	ثَلَاثَةٌ	ثَلَاثٌ	
4	٤		أَرْبَعَةٌ	أَرْبَعٌ	
5	٥		خَمْسَةٌ	خَمْسٌ	
6	٦		سِتَّةٌ	سِتٌّ	
7	٧		سَبْعَةٌ	سَبْعٌ	
8	٨		ثَمَانِيَةٌ	ثَمَانٍ	
9	٩		تِسْعَةٌ	تِسْعٌ	
10	١٠		عَشَرَةٌ	عَشْرٌ	

The cardinal numbers from 3 to 10 are followed by the nouns they define in the *indefinite plural genitive*, e.g.

ثَلَاثَةُ رِجَالٍ 3 men.

خَمْسَةُ كُتُبٍ 5 books.

سِتُّ بَنَاتٍ 6 girls.

ثَمَانِي مُدُنٍ 8 cities.

They are all of the 1st declension except ثَمَانٍ 8 (fem.) which is declined like the plural of مَعْنًى (see Lesson XI, 4), viz.

nom. and gen. ثَمَانٍ (ثَمَانِي مُدُنٍ),

acc. ثَمَانِيَ (ثَمَانِيَ مُدُنٍ),

and إِحْدَى 1 (fem.) which is indeclinable.

Note the following:

هَلْ قَابَلْتَ أَحَدًا مِنْ مَعَارِفِي فِي ٱلْحَفْلَةِ؟ قَدْ قَابَلْتُ إِحْدَى صَاحِبَاتِكَ وَلٰكِنِّي نَسِيتُ ٱسْمَهَا

Did you meet any of my acquaintances at the party? I met one of your lady friends but I have forgotten her name.

Note the anomaly that the masc. of the cardinal numbers from 3 to 10 ends in *tā' marbūṭa* whereas the fem. drops it.

To continue:

	Arabic sign		masc.	fem.
11	١١		أَحَدَ عَشَرَ	إِحْدَى عَشْرَةَ
12	١٢	nom.	إِثْنَا عَشَرَ	إِثْنَتَا عَشْرَةَ
		(acc. and gen.	إِثْنَيْ عَشَرَ	(إِثْنَتَيْ عَشْرَةَ
13	١٣		ثَلَاثَةَ عَشَرَ	ثَلَاثَ عَشْرَةَ
14	١٤		أَرْبَعَةَ عَشَرَ	أَرْبَعَ عَشْرَةَ
15	١٥		خَمْسَةَ عَشَرَ	خَمْسَ عَشْرَةَ

	Arabic sign	masc.	fem.
16	١٦	سِتَّةَ عَشَرَ	سِتَّ عَشْرَةَ
17	١٧	سَبْعَةَ عَشَرَ	سَبْعَ عَشْرَةَ
18	١٨	ثَمَانِيَةَ عَشَرَ	ثَمَانِيَ عَشْرَةَ
19	١٩	تِسْعَةَ عَشَرَ	تِسْعَ عَشْرَةَ

The cardinal numbers from 11 to 19 are indeclinable (with the exception of 12) and are followed by the nouns they define in the *indefinite singular accusative*, e.g.

أَحَدَ عَشَرَ رَجُلًا 11 men.

أَرْبَعَةَ عَشَرَ كِتَابًا 14 books.

سِتَّ عَشْرَةَ بِنْتًا 16 girls.

ثَمَانِيَ عَشْرَةَ مَدِينَةً 18 cities.

To continue:

	Arabic sign	masc.	fem.
20	٢٠	عِشْرُونَ	—
21	٢١	أَحَدٌ وَعِشْرُونَ	إِحْدَى وَعِشْرُونَ
22	٢٢	إِثْنَانِ وَعِشْرُونَ	إِثْنَتَانِ وَعِشْرُونَ
23	٢٣	ثَلَاثَةٌ وَعِشْرُونَ	ثَلَاثٌ وَعِشْرُونَ
30	٣٠	ثَلَاثُونَ	—
40	٤٠	أَرْبَعُونَ	—
50	٥٠	خَمْسُونَ	—
60	٦٠	سِتُّونَ	—
70	٧٠	سَبْعُونَ	—
80	٨٠	ثَمَانُونَ	—
90	٩٠	تِسْعُونَ	—

As can be seen from the above table the multiples of 10 from 20 to 90 are of common gender. The ending ...ونَ is the masc. sound plural nominative ending. The accusative and genitive will therefore be عِشْرِينَ, ثَلَاثِينَ, etc. These cardinal numbers are followed by the nouns they define in the *indefinite singular accusative*, e.g.

ثَلَاثُونَ جُنَيْهًا (لِيرَةً، دِينَارًا)   £30.

خَمْسُونَ ٱمْرَأَةً   50 women.

In compound numbers such as 23, 45 or 96 it will be seen that the units come first and are fully declined, but it is the number nearest the noun which governs it. Thus all numbers from 11 to 99 are followed by their nouns in the *indefinite singular accusative*, e.g.

ثَلَاثَةٌ وَعِشْرُونَ كِتَابًا   23 books (nom.).

أَرْبَعًا وَأَرْبَعِينَ بِنْتًا   44 girls (acc.).

تِسْعَةٍ وَثَمَانِينَ حِصَانًا   89 horses (gen.).

Other cardinal numbers are:

100	١٠٠	مِئَةٌ	or مِائَةٌ (note that the *'alif* has no force) pl. مِئَاتٌ and مِئُونَ.
200	٢٠٠	مِئَتَانِ	
300	٣٠٠	ثَلَاثُمِئَةٍ	or ثَلَاثُ مِئَةٍ (N.B. nom.).
400	٤٠٠	أَرْبَعُمِئَةٍ	
500	٥٠٠	خَمْسُمِئَةٍ	
600	٦٠٠	سِتُّمِئَةٍ	
700	٧٠٠	سَبْعُمِئَةٍ	
800	٨٠٠	ثَمَانِمِئَةٍ	(often ثَمَانِي مِئَةٍ)
900	٩٠٠	تِسْعُمِئَةٍ	

1,000	١٠٠٠	أَلْفٌ
2000,	٢٠٠٠	أَلْفَانِ
3,000	٣٠٠٠	ثَلَاثَةُ آلَافٍ
1,000,000	١٠٠٠٠٠٠	مِلْيُونٌ (أَلْفُ أَلْفٍ) pl. مَلَايِينُ

These cardinal numbers are followed by the nouns they define in the *indefinite singular genitive*, e.g.

مِئَةُ رَجُلٍ	100 men.
مِئَتَا بَيْتٍ	200 houses (nom.).
مِئَتَيْ بَيْتٍ	200 houses (acc. and gen.).
أَرْبَعُمِئَةِ صَفْحَةٍ	400 pages.
أَلْفُ فَارِسٍ	1,000 horsemen.
ثَلَاثَةُ آلَافِ عَرَبَةٍ (عَرَبِيَّةٍ) (سَيَّارَةٍ)	3,000 motor cars.

N.B. أَلْفٌ has an indefinite plural أُلُوفٌ 'thousands'.

In classical Arabic a compound number such as 1,953 was read from right to left, viz.

١٩٥٣، ثَلَاثَةٌ وَخَمْسُونَ وَتِسْعُمِئَةٍ وَأَلْفٌ

but in modern Arabic we read the thousands, then the hundreds, then the units and lastly the tens, viz.

١٩٥٣، أَلْفٌ وَتِسْعُمِئَةٍ وَثَلَاثَةٌ وَخَمْسُونَ

83. The Ordinal Numbers

	masc.	fem.
1st	اَلْأَوَّلُ (أَوَّلُ) pl. اَلْأَوَائِلُ	اَلْأُولَى pl. اَلْأُوَلُ
2nd	اَلثَّانِي (ثَانٍ)	اَلثَّانِيَةُ
3rd	اَلثَّالِثُ	اَلثَّالِثَةُ

	masc.	fem.
4th	اَلرَّابِعُ	اَلرَّابِعَةُ
5th	اَلْخَامِسُ	اَلْخَامِسَةُ
6th	N.B. اَلسَّادِسُ	اَلسَّادِسَةُ
7th	اَلسَّابِعُ	اَلسَّابِعَةُ
8th	اَلثَّامِنُ	اَلثَّامِنَةُ
9th	اَلتَّاسِعُ	اَلتَّاسِعَةُ
10th	اَلْعَاشِرُ	اَلْعَاشِرَةُ

These are all declined regularly like adjectives of the form فَاعِلٌ.

	masc.	fem.
11th	N.B. اَلْحَادِيَ عَشَرَ	اَلْحَادِيَةَ عَشْرَةَ
12th	اَلثَّانِيَ عَشَرَ	اَلثَّانِيَةَ عَشْرَةَ
13th, etc.	اَلثَّالِثَ عَشَرَ	اَلثَّالِثَةَ عَشْرَةَ

N.B. The ordinal numbers from the 11th to the 19th are *indeclinable*.

	masc.	fem.
20th	اَلْعِشْرُونَ	—
21st	N.B. اَلْحَادِي وَٱلْعِشْرُونَ	اَلْحَادِيَةُ وَٱلْعِشْرُونَ
22nd	اَلثَّانِي وَٱلْعِشْرُونَ	اَلثَّانِيَةُ وَٱلْعِشْرُونَ
23rd, etc.	اَلثَّالِثُ وَٱلْعِشْرُونَ	اَلثَّالِثَةُ وَٱلْعِشْرُونَ
30th, etc.	اَلثَّلَاثُونَ	—
100th	اَلْمِئَةُ	—
1,000th	اَلْأَلْفُ	—

Modern Arabic forms such ordinal numbers as اَلْعِشْرِينِيُّ 20th, اَلْمِئَوِيُّ 100th, اَلْأَلْفِيُّ 1,000th.

84. Fractions

These are formed according to the pattern فُعْلٌ (pl. أَفْعَالٌ) from the radicals of the ordinals, viz.

a half	نِصْفٌ	(exception)
a third	ثُلْثٌ	pl. أَثْلَاثٌ
a quarter	رُبْعٌ	
a fifth	خُمْسٌ	
a sixth	سُدْسٌ	
a seventh	سُبْعٌ	
an eighth	ثُمْنٌ	
a ninth	تُسْعٌ	
a tenth	عُشْرٌ	

85. Days of the Week

The days of the week (أَيَّامُ ٱلْأُسْبُوعِ) are:

Sunday	ٱلْأَحَدُ	or	يَوْمُ ٱلْأَحَدِ
Monday	(ٱلِٱثْنَانِ)		يَوْمُ ٱلِٱثْنَيْنِ
Tuesday	ٱلثُّلَاثَاءُ		etc.
Wednesday	ٱلْأَرْبِعَاءُ		
Thursday	ٱلْخَمِيسُ		
Friday	ٱلْجُمْعَةُ		
Saturday	ٱلسَّبْتُ		

86. Months

The months of the Christian year (اَلسَّنَةُ ٱلْمِيلَادِيَّةُ contracted م) are:

	Egypt and Sudan	Eastern Arab World	
January	يَنَايِرُ	كَانُونُ ٱلثَّانِي	
February	فَبْرَايِرُ	شُبَاطُ	
March	مَارِسُ	أَذَارُ	(مَارْتُ)
April	إِبْرِيلُ	نَيْسَانُ	
May	مَايُو	أَيَّارُ	(مَايِسُ)
June	يُونِيُو (يُونِيَةُ)	حَزِيرَانُ	
July	يُولِيُو (يُولِيَةُ)	تَمُّوزُ	
August	أُغُسْطُسُ	آبُ	
September	سِبْتَمْبَرُ	أَيْلُولُ	
October	أُكْتُوبَرُ	تِشْرِينُ ٱلْأَوَّلُ	
November	نُوفَمْبَرُ	تِشْرِينُ ٱلثَّانِي	
December	دِيسَمْبَرُ	كَانُونُ ٱلْأَوَّلُ	

The months of the Muslim (lunar) year (اَلسَّنَةُ ٱلْهِجْرِيَّةُ contracted ھ) are:

اَلْمُحَرَّمُ	Muḥarram.
صَفَرُ	Ṣafar.
رَبِيعُ ٱلْأَوَّلُ	Rabīع al-'Awwal,
رَبِيعُ ٱلثَّانِي	Rabīع al-Thānī.
جُمَادَى ٱلْأُولَى	Jumādā ⁀l-'Ūlā.
جُمَادَى ٱلْآخِرَةُ	Jumādā ⁀l-'Ākhira.
رَجَبُ	Rajab.

شَعْبَانُ Shaعbān.

رَمَضَانُ Ramaḍān (the month of fasting).

شَوَّالُ Shawwāl.

ذُو ٱلْقَعْدَةِ Dhū ◠l-Qaعda.

ذُو ٱلْحِجَّةِ Dhū ◠l-Ḥijja (pilgrimage month).

87. Festivals

The principal festivals (أَعْيَادٌ) are:

Christmas عِيدُ ٱلْمِيلَادِ

Easter عِيدُ ٱلْقِيَامَةِ or عِيدُ ٱلْفِصْحِ

The Festival of the Sacrifice عِيدُ ٱلْأَضْحَى or ٱلْعِيدُ ٱلْكَبِيرُ (the Greater Festival) on the 10th of Dhū ◠l-Ḥijja, the culminating day of the pilgrimage to Mecca when the pilgrims sacrifice animals at nearby *Minā*.

The Festival of the Breaking of the Fast عِيدُ ٱلْفِطْرِ or ٱلْعِيدُ ٱلصَّغِيرُ (the Lesser Festival) on the 1st of Shawwāl after the fasting month of Ramaḍān.

The Birthday of the Prophet Muḥammad مَوْلِدُ ٱلنَّبِيِّ on the 12th of Rabīع al-'Awwal.

88. Dates

The date, Christian or Muslim, is written as follows, e.g.

Sunday, 23rd April 1950:

فِي يَوْمِ ٱلْأَحَدِ ٢٣ إِبْرِيلَ سَنَةَ ١٩٥٠م ٱلْمُوَافِقِ ٦ رَجَبٍ سَنَةَ ١٣٦٩هـ

read in full:

ـــ ٱلثَّالِثِ وَٱلْعِشْرِينَ مِنْ (شَهْرِ) إِبْرِيلَ سَنَةَ أَلْفٍ وَتِسْعِمِئَةٍ وَخَمْسِينَ مِيلَادِيَّةً، ٱلْمُوَافِقِ لِلسَّادِسِ مِنْ (شَهْرِ) رَجَبٍ سَنَةَ أَلْفٍ وَثَلَاثِمِئَةٍ وَتِسْعٍ وَسِتِّينَ هِجْرِيَّةً.

EXERCISE XXIV

١—أُعْلِنَ الدُّسْتُورُ المِصْرِيُّ في يَوْمِ ٱلِٱثْنَيْنِ السادِسَ عَشَرَ من شَهْرِ فَبْرَايِرَ سَنَةَ أَلْفٍ وتِسْعِمِائَةٍ وسِتٍّ وخَمْسِينَ المُوافِقِ للثّالِثِ من شَهْرِ جُمادَى الآخِرةِ سَنَةَ أَلْفٍ وثَلاثِمائَةٍ وخَمْسٍ وسَبْعِينَ.

٢—أَمَرَ الضّابِطُ خَمْسَةَ رِجالٍ بأن يَسْتَعِدُّوا لِلتَّقَدُّمِ إلى خُطُوطِ الأَعْداء لِيَقْطَعُوا الأَسْلَاكَ الشّائِكَةَ. (خَطٌّ، سِلْكٌ)

٣—تَدْرُسُ ثَمانِي بناتٍ عِلْمَ الكِيمِيَاء في هذا الفَصْلِ ويَأْمُلْنَ أن يَجِدْنَ وَظَائِفَ في شَرِكَةٍ كيماوِيّةٍ بَعْدَ إتْمامِ دِراسَتِهِنّ. (وَظِيفَةٌ)

٤—بَعْدَ مُضِيِّ أَحَدَ عَشَرَ يَوْمًا كادَ المَلّاحُونَ يَمُوتُونَ عَطَشًا ولٰكن في اليومِ الثّانِيَ عَشَرَ شاهَدُوا سَفِينَةً تَتَقَدَّمُ نَحْوَهُمْ.

٥—لهذا الجَمّالِ خَمْسَةٌ وعِشْرُونَ جَمَلًا ومِائَتانِ وخَمْسٌ وثَلاثُونَ ناقَةً يَنْوِي بَيْعَها بَعْدَ أن يَسُوقَها إلى الخُرْطُومِ.

٦—في السَّنةِ الهِجْرِيّةِ ٱثْنا عَشَرَ شَهْرًا مِثْلَ السَّنةِ المِيلادِيّةِ ولٰكنّها أَقْصَرُ بِعَشَرَةِ أَيّامٍ.

٧—نَرْجُو أن تُعْطِيَهُ هَدِيّةً في عِيدِ ميلادِهِ ٱلأَمْرُ الذي سَيَمْلَأُ قَلْبَهُ بَهْجةً وسُرورًا.

٨—يَصُومُ المُسْلِمُونَ طُولَ شَهْرِ رَمَضانَ ويُفْطِرُونَ في بَقِيّةِ الشُّهُورِ.

٩—وُلِدَ سيِّدُنا المَسِيحُ في بَيْتَ لَحْمَ وعِيدُ ميلادِهِ أَكْبَرُ عِيدٍ عِنْدَ المسيحِيِّينَ.

١٠—تُوُفِّيَ سيِّدُنا مُحَمَّدٌ نَبِيُّ الإِسْلامِ في المدينةِ المُنَوَّرةِ في الثّالِثَ عَشَرَ من رَبِيعٍ الأَوَّلِ في السَّنةِ الحادِيَةَ عَشْرَةَ بعد الهِجْرةِ.

TRANSLATION

1. The Egyptian Constitution was proclaimed on Monday, 16th February 1956 (3rd Jumādā II 1375).

2. The officer ordered five men to be ready to advance to the enemy lines in order to cut the barbed wire.

3. Eight girls study chemistry in this class and they hope to find employment in a chemical company after completion of their study.

4. After (the passing of) eleven days the sailors almost died of thirst but on the twelfth day they saw a ship advancing towards them.

5. This camelherd has 25 camels and 235 she-camels which he intends to sell after driving them to Khartoum.

6. The Moslem year has twelve months like the Christian year but it is ten days shorter.

7. We hope you will give him a present on his birthday which (lit. the matter which) will fill his heart with joy and happiness.

8. The Muslims fast throughout the month of Ramaḍān but they do not fast (lit. they break their fast) in the other months (lit. the remainder of the months).

9. Our Lord Christ was born in Bethlehem and his birthday is the greatest festival with the Christians.

10. Our Lord Muḥammad, the Prophet of Islām, died in Medina (the Enlightened City) on 13th Rabī‘ I in the eleventh year of the Hijra (after the emigration).

LESSON XXV

89. Notes on Syntax

The syntax of any language is best learned by intensive reading which enables the student to acquire a natural feeling for the correct construction without overloading his memory with a host of rules and exceptions. The Arabic language, unlike English, is surprisingly free from idiom although both metaphor and simile play important parts, especially in Arabic literature of the Middle Ages. So if an Arabic sentence is translated literally, word for word, the student can almost always make passable sense of it and so can turn it into more idiomatic English.

The most important points of Arabic syntax have been dealt with in the preceding lessons but it might be useful to underline here a few of these:

(i) The usual order of words in a simple sentence is verb+subject +object+complementary words, e.g.

أَخَذَ مُحَمَّدٌ كِتَابَ أَخِيهِ مِنَ ٱلدُّرْجِ

Mohammed took his brother's book from the drawer.

If the subject is placed first it is considered more elegant to introduce the sentence with إِنَّ, e.g.

إِنَّ مُحَمَّدًا أَخَذَ كِتَابَ أَخِيهِ مِنَ ٱلدُّرْجِ

Interrogative subjects always precede the verb, e.g.

مَنْ يُرِيدُ أَنْ يَذْهَبَ مَعَنَا ؟

Who wishes to go with us?

كَمْ تِلْمِيذًا يَدْرُسُونَ فِي تِلْكَ ٱلْمَدْرَسَةِ ؟

How many pupils study in that school?

(ii) If the verb comes before its subject it must always be in the singular, but if it follows its subject it must agree in gender and number, e.g.

شَرِبَ ٱلْأَوْلَادُ قَلِيلًا مِنَ ٱلْمَاءِ

The boys drank a little (of) water.

إِنَّ ٱلْأَوْلَادَ أَكَلُوا قَلِيلًا مِنَ ٱلْأَرُزِّ

The boys ate a little (of) rice.

اِشْتَرَى ٱلرَّجُلَانِ فَرَسًا عَرَبِيَّةً

The (two) men bought an Arabian mare.

إِنَّ ٱلْحَارِسَيْنِ قَتَلَا لِصًّا بِٱللَّيْلِ

The (two) guards killed a thief in the night.

بَكَتِ ٱلنِّسَاءُ وَقَطَّعْنَ ثِيَابَهُنَّ

The women wept and tore their garments.

If the *preceding* verb of a feminine plural subject is separated from this by any word the verb may be in the *masculine* singular, e.g.

نَزَلَ عَلَى ٱلسَّطْحِ ثَلَاثُ حَمَامَاتٍ

Three pigeons alighted on the roof.

(iii) A broken plural which does not refer to a rational being is grammatically feminine singular, e.g.

جُلِّدَتِ ٱلْكُتُبُ بِأَمْرِ أَمِينِ ٱلْمَكْتَبَةِ

The books were bound by order of the librarian (lit. trustee of the library).

اِشْتَرَيْتُ أَشْيَاءَ تَنْفَعُنِي أَثْنَاءَ سَفَرِي

I bought things which would be useful to me during my journey.

لَا تُوجَدُ هٰذِهِ ٱلتَّعَابِيرُ ٱلْغَرِيبَةُ فِي قَامُوسِي

These strange ways of expression are not (to be) found in my dictionary.

(iv) An adjective in the accusative or a verbal noun plus adjective in the accusative is the most common way of rendering an adverb, e.g.

مَشَى سَرِيعًا

He walked quickly.

دَرَسَتِ ٱلْمَوْضُوعَ دِرَاسَةً وَاسِعَةً

She studied the subject widely.

(v) An adjective or verbal noun in the accusative or the imperfect indicative of a verb is used to express the manner in which something is done or the purpose for which it is done, e.g.

دَخَلَ بَاكِيًا (يَبْكِي) فَقَصَّ عَلَيَّ قِصَّتَهُ

He came in weeping and told me his story.

قَامُوا إِكْرَامًا لَنَا

They stood up in our honour.

رَمَى ٱللُّصُوصُ أَنْفُسَهُمْ فِي ٱلنَّهْرِ هَارِبِينَ (يَهْرُبُونَ) (لِيَهْرُبُوا) مِنْ مُتَّبِعِيهِمْ

The thieves threw themselves into the river fleeing from their pursuers.

بَدَأَتِ ٱلْمُدَرِّسَةُ ٱلدَّرْسَ مُشِيرَةً إِلَى ٱلسَّبُّورَةِ

The teacher began the lesson pointing to the blackboard.

قَامَتِ ٱلنِّسَاءُ طَالِبَاتٍ (يَطْلُبْنَ) حُقُوقَهُنَّ

The women arose demanding their rights.

(Note that an active participle used as a verb may take a direct object as above.)

90. Conditional Sentences

Conditional sentences present the student with some difficulty. Roughly speaking they can be divided into two groups, (i) in which the condition is fulfillable and (ii) in which the condition is not or no longer fulfillable or in which it is hardly probable that it will be fulfilled.

In the first case the conditional clause is introduced by إِنْ or more commonly by إِذَا 'if'. In the second case it is introduced by لَوْ 'if'.

After إِنْ the conditional and finite clauses may be either in the perfect or jussive (!) mood, e.g.

إِنْ ضَرَبْتَ ضُرِبْتَ
or إِنْ تَضْرِبْ تُضْرَبْ
or إِنْ ضَرَبْتَ تُضْرَبْ
or إِنْ تَضْرِبْ ضُرِبْتَ

} If you strike you will be struck.

N.B. The last of these constructions is very rare.

Note especially the omission of the finite clause in classical Arabic in phrases such as:

إِنْ قُلْتَ لِي ٱلْحَقَّ وَإِلَّا غَضِبْتُ عَلَيْكَ

If you tell me the truth (it will be all right) otherwise I shall become angry with you, i.e. tell me the truth or else, etc.

After إِذَا we have the perfect in the conditional clause and either the perfect or the jussive mood in the finite clause, e.g.

إِذَا ذَهَبْتَ ذَهَبْتُ (أَذْهَبْ) مَعَكَ

If (when) you go I go with you.

إِذَا ٱجْتَهَدتَّ نَجَحْتَ (تَنْجَحْ)

If you are industrious you will succeed.

إِذَا تَكَلَّمَ بِصَرَاحَةٍ صَدَّقْتُهُ (أُصَدِّقْهُ)

If he speaks openly I shall believe him.

After إِذَا it is not unusual to find the imperfect indicative in the finite clause, e.g.

إِذَا سَافَرْتُمْ بِٱلْبَحْرِ تَرَوْنَ (تَرَوْا) (رَأَيْتُمْ) جَبَلَ طَارِقٍ

If you travel by sea you will see Gibraltar.

If the finite clause after a condition introduced by إِذَا is a nominal clause or begins with an imperative or prohibition it must be introduced by فَ, e.g.

إِذَا حَضَرْتَ ٱلْحَفْلَةَ فَلَا تَنْسَ أَنْ تُسَلِّمَ عَلَى صَاحِبَةِ ٱلدَّعْوَةِ

If you go to (are present at) the party do not forget to greet the hostess (lit. the mistress of the invitation).

إِذَا لَمْ تُرِدْ أَنْ تُكَلِّمَهُ فَوَلِّ لَهُ ظَهْرَكَ

If you do not want to speak to him turn your back on him.

N.B. A negative verb in a conditional is generally rendered by لَمْ plus the jussive mood, as in the above sentence.

إِذَا دَفَعَ لِي حَقِّي فَلَكَ مِنِّي جُنَيْهَانِ

If he pays me my due I shall give you £2.

Conditional sentences are also very often expressed by an imperative plus the jussive mood in the finite clause, e.g.

تَعَالَ مَعِي تَرَ مَا يَسُرُّكَ

Come with me and you will see what will please you (i.e. if you come with me, etc.).

عِشْ قَنِعًا تَكُنْ مَلِكًا

Live satisfied and you will be a king (i.e. if you live satisfied, etc.).

When لَوْ ('if' in an unfulfilled or doubtful condition) is used the finite clause is introduced by لَ, e.g.

لَوْ جَاءَ لَأَكْرَمْتُهُ
If he were to come (but he will not) I would honour him.

لَوْ كُنْتُ غَنِيًّا لَسَاعَدْتُكَ
If I were rich I would help you.

لَوْ كُنْتَ رَجُلًا لَأَبَيْتَ ٱلضَّيْمَ
If you were a man you would refuse to be oppressed.

لَوْ لَمْ أَكُنْ عِنْدَكُمْ لَاتَّهَمُونِي
If I had not been with you they would have accused me.

The plu. perfect is common after لَوْ, e.g.

لَوْ كَانُوا خَانُوا لَبَانَ عَلَى وُجُوهِهِمْ
If they had betrayed it would have been apparent on their faces.

لَوْ كُنَّا سَمِعْنَا ذٰلِكَ لَأَخْبَرْنَاكُمْ
If we had heard that we should have informed you.

Note the sense of لَوْ in the following cases:

(i) After وَدَّ 'he *would have* wished' it is equivalent to أَنْ but, but does *not* take the following verb in the subjunctive, e.g.

يَوَدُّ أَحَدُهُمْ لَوْ يُعَمَّرُ أَلْفَ سَنَةٍ
Any one of them would like to be given life for 1,000 years.

وَدِدْتُمْ لَوْ تُصْبِحُونَ أَغْنِيَاءَ
You would have liked to become rich.

(ii) It is used plus the imperfect indicative to express a wish, e.g.

لَوْ تَنْزِلُ عِنْدَنَا فَتُحَدِّثُنَا عَنْ سَفَرِكَ
Why do you not (please) stop with us to tell us about your journey?

Note the subjunctive after فَ meaning 'so that' following a finite clause expressing a wish, command or prohibition.

The same construction as that after إِذَا is often found after the following pronouns:

مَا	what.	مَهْمَا	whatever.
مَنْ	who.	كُلُّمَنْ	whoever.
أَيْنَ	where.	أَيْنَمَا	wherever.
حَيْثُ	where.	حَيْثُمَا	wherever.
كُلَّمَا	whenever.	كَيْفَمَا	however.
مَتَامَا	whenever, e.g.		

مَا شَاءَ ٱللّٰهُ كَانَ وَمَا لَمْ يَشَأْ لَمْ يَكُنْ

What God wills will be and what He does not will will not be.

وَمَنْ طَلَبَ ٱلْعُلَى مِنْ غَيْرِ كَدٍّ   أَضَاعَ ٱلْعُمْرَ فِي طَلَبِ ٱلْمُحَالِ

He who seeks the heights (i.e. eminence) without effort wastes his life in seeking the impossible.

مَنْ (كُلُّمَنْ) أَكْرَمَنِي أَكْرَمْتُهُ

Whoever honours me I honour him, i.e. I honour whoever honours me.

مَهْمَا قُلْتَ (تَقُلْ) لَا أُصَدِّقُكَ

Whatever you say I shall not believe you.

Exercise XXV

١—إِذَا لم تَجْلِبْ معنا كُلَّ شَيْءٍ نَحْتَاجُ إليهِ تَعَذَّرَ علَيْنا أن نَعِيشَ هُناكَ.

٢—إِنْ أَنْكَرَ ذٰلك أَثْبَتْنَا انّه كاذِبٌ.

٣—إِذَا أَعْطَيْتَنِي ثَلَاثَةَ جُنَيْهاتٍ فَإِنّي مُسْتَعِدٌّ أن أُعْطِيَكَ الكُتُبَ التي تُعْجِبُكَ كثيرًا.

٤—لَوْ أَمْسَكَ يَدَهَا أَثْنَاءَ سَيْرِهِما على ضَفَّةِ النَّهْرِ لَمَا وَقَعَتْ في الماء.

٥—سَاعِدْ والِدَتَكَ تَرْضَ عَنْكَ وتَضْحَكْ لَكَ دائمًا.

٦—أَيْنَمَا ذَهَبْتَ ذَهَبْتُ مَعَكَ ومَهْما قُلْتَ لي قَبِلْتُهُ.

٧—إذا زُرْنَا فَرَنْسا فسوف نَشْتَرِي أَشْيَاءَ كثيرةً وَنَرْجِعُ بِها إلى لَنْدَنَ.

٨—لَوْ لم يَكُنْ خائفًا أن يُعْرَفَ لَقَبِلَ الدَّعْوَةَ إلى حَفْلَةِ الوزيرِ.

٩—إذا قَرَأْتَ لي قليلًا بَعْدَ العَشاء ٱسْتَطَعْتُ أن أَنَامَ بِسُهُولةٍ.

١٠—إذا وَقَفَ القِطارُ خارِجَ المَحَطّةِ فَلا تُحاوِلْ أن تَرْكَبَ وإلّا فَمِنَ المُمْكِنِ أن تُغَرَّمَ غَرامةً كبيرةً.

Translation

1. If we do not bring with us everything we need it will be impossible for us to live there.

2. If he denies that we shall prove that he is lying.

3. If you give me three pounds I am ready to give you the books you admire (lit. which fill you with admiration) so much.

4. If he had held her hand while they were walking along the river-bank she would not have fallen into the water.

5. Help your mother and she will be pleased with you and will always smile on you.

6. Wherever you go I shall go with you and whatever you say to me I shall accept it.

7. If we visit France we shall buy many things and bring them back (lit. return with them) to London.

8. If he had not been afraid that he would be recognized he would have accepted the invitation to the Minister's party.

9. If you read to me a little after supper I shall be able to go to sleep easily (with ease).

10. If the train stops outside the station do not try to get in, otherwise it is possible that you may be fined heavily.

APPENDIX I

The Patterns of the Broken Plural

1.		أَفْعَالٌ	See Lesson IV.		
2.		فُعُولٌ			
3.		فُعُلٌ			
4.		فِعَالٌ			
5.		أَفْعُلٌ			
6.		فُعَلَاءُ			
7.		أَفْعِلَاءُ			
8.		فُعْلَانٌ			
9.		فَعَالِلُ			
10.		فَعَالِيلُ			
11.		فَعْلٌ (rare)	e.g.	صَاحِبٌ	a companion, pl. صَحْبٌ
				تَاجِرٌ	a merchant, pl. تَجْرٌ
12.		فُعْلٌ	e.g.	أَحْمَرُ	red, pl. حُمْرٌ
				خَضْرَاءُ	green (fem.), pl. خُضْرٌ
13.		فِعَلٌ	e.g.	قِطْعَةٌ	a piece, slice, pl. قِطَعٌ
	pl. of	فِعْلَةٌ		خِرْقَةٌ	a rag, pl. خِرَقٌ
14.		فُعَلٌ	e.g.	عُلْبَةٌ	a box, pl. عُلَبٌ
	pl. of	فُعْلَةٌ		أُمَّةٌ	a nation, pl. أُمَمٌ
15.		فَعِيلٌ	e.g.	حِمَارٌ	a donkey, pl. حَمِيرٌ
				عَبْدٌ	a slave, pl. عَبِيدٌ

16.	فُعَّلٌ	e.g.	نَائِمٌ	asleep, pl. نُوَّمٌ
	pl. of فَاعِلٌ		رَاكِعٌ	bowing, pl. رُكَّعٌ
17.	فُعَّالٌ	e.g.	نَائِبٌ	a deputy, M.P., pl. نُوَّابٌ
	pl. of فَاعِلٌ		تَاجِرٌ	a merchant, pl. تُجَّارٌ
18.	فَعَلَةٌ	e.g.	مَاهِرٌ	clever, expert, pl. مَهَرَةٌ
	pl. of فَاعِلٌ		سَاحِرٌ	a magician, pl. سَحَرَةٌ
19.	فُعَلَةٌ	e.g.	دَاعٍ	calling, pl. دُعَاةٌ
	pl. of فَاعِلٌ of a weak root		قَاضٍ	a judge, pl. قُضَاةٌ
20.	فِعَلَةٌ (rare)	e.g.	قِرْدٌ	a monkey, pl. قِرَدَةٌ
			دِيكٌ	a cock, pl. دِيَكَةٌ
21.	فِعْلَةٌ	e.g.	أَخٌ (أخو)	a brother, pl. إِخْوَةٌ (see note, p. 27)
			صَبِيٌّ	a boy, pl. صِبْيَةٌ
22.	فِعَالَةٌ (rare)	e.g.	حَجَرٌ	a stone, pl. حِجَارَةٌ
			صَاحِبٌ	a companion, pl. صِحَابَةٌ and صَحَابَةٌ
23.	فُعُولَةٌ (rare)	e.g.	عَمٌّ	a (paternal) uncle, pl. عُمُومَةٌ
			خَالٌ	a (maternal) uncle, pl. خُؤُولَةٌ
24.	أَفْعِلَةٌ	e.g.	سُؤَالٌ	a question, pl. أَسْئِلَةٌ
	generally pl. of فَعَالٌ		جَوَابٌ	an answer, pl. أَجْوِبَةٌ
25.	فَعْلَى	e.g.	أَسِيرٌ	a captive, pl. أَسْرَى
	generally pl. of فَعِيلٌ equivalent to مَفْعُولٌ		قَتِيلٌ	killed, pl. قَتْلَى

26.	فُعْلَان	e.g.	أَخ	a brother, pl. إِخْوَان (see note p. 27)	
	generally co-existent with and synonymous to 21		صَبِيّ	a boy, pl. صِبْيَان	
27.	فَوَاعِل	e.g.	نَادِرَة	an anecdote, pl. نَوَادِر	cognate to 9
	pl. of فَاعِلَة and occasionally فَاعِل		سَاحِل	a coast, pl. سَوَاحِل	
28.	فَعَائِل	e.g.	جَزِيرَة	an island, pl. جَزَائِر	
	pl. of فَعِيلَة and فَعَالَة		رِسَالَة	a message, pl. رَسَائِل	
29.	فَعَالِ	e.g.	صَحْرَاء	a desert, pl. صَحَارِ	
	co-existent with 30 or pl. of فَاعِلَة of a weak root		دَعْوَى	a claim, pl. دَعَاوِ	
			جَارِيَة	a girl, pl. جَوَارِ	
30.	فَعَالَى	e.g.	صَحْرَاء	a desert, pl. صَحَارَى	
	co-existent with 29 or pl. of فَعْلَان		كَسْلَان	lazy, pl. كَسَالَى	

(Items 27–29 are bracketed together as "cognate to 9".)

N.B. As noted in Lesson IV many words have more than one broken plural form.

APPENDIX II

Phonetic Changes in Arabic

The following is a summary of the principal phonetic changes which occur in Arabic words in which one of the radicals is و or ي:

Verbs

If و is the middle radical:

َوُ... *awu*, َوَ... *awa* and َوِ... *awi* become َا... *ā*, e.g.

طَالَ (for طَوُلَ) it was long.

قَالَ (for قَوَلَ) he said.

نَامَ (for نَوِمَ) he slept.

If ي is the middle radical:

ـَيَـ... *aya* and ـَيِـ... *ayi* become ـَا... *ā*, e.g.

بَاعَ	(for بَيَعَ)	he sold.
هَابَ	(for هَيِبَ)	he feared.

(N.B. ـَيُـ... *ayu* does not occur in the middle of a word.)

If و or ي is the middle radical and the first radical is vowelless, then the vowel of the weak radical is thrown forward to the first radical and becomes long, e.g.

يَطُولُ	(for يَطْوُلُ)	it is long.
يَقُولُ	(for يَقْوُلُ)	he says.
يَنَامُ	(for يَنْوَمُ)	he sleeps.
يَبِيعُ	(for يَبْيِعُ)	he sells.
يَهَابُ	(for يَهْيَبُ)	he fears.

If و is the last radical:

ـَوَ... *awa* becomes ـَا... *ā*, e.g.	دَعَا	(for دَعَوَ)	he called.
ـَوُو... *awū* becomes ـَوْ... *aw*, e.g.	دَعَوْا	(for دَعَوُوا)	they called.
ـُوُ... *uwu* becomes ـُو... *ū*, e.g.	يَدْعُو	(for يَدْعُوُ)	he calls.
ـُوُو... *uwū* becomes ـُو... *ū*, e.g.	يَدْعُونَ	(for يَدْعُوُونَ)	they call.
ـُوِي... *uwī* becomes ـِي... *ī*, e.g.	تَدْعِينَ	(for تَدْعُوِينَ)	you (fem.) call.
ـِوَ... *iwa* becomes ـِيَ... *iya*, e.g.	رَضِيَ	(for رَضِوَ)	he was pleased.
ـِوُو... *iwū* becomes ـُو... *ū*, e.g.	رَضُوا	(for رَضِوُوا)	they were pleased.

If ي is the last radical:

ـَيَ... *aya* becomes ـَى... *ā* (ـَا... before pronominal suffixes), e.g.

رَمَى (رَمَاهُ) (for رَمَيَ) he threw.

يَ... *ayu* becomes ى... *ā*, e.g. يَسْعَى (for يَسْعَيُ) he runs.

يُو... *ayū* becomes وْ... *aw*, e.g. يَسْعَوْنَ (for يَسْعَيُونَ) they run.

يِي... *ayī* becomes يْ... *ay*, e.g. تَسْعَيْنَ (for تَسْعَيِينَ) you (fem.) run.

يُ... *iyu* becomes ي... *ī*, e.g. يَرْمِي (for يَرْمِيُ) he throws.

يُو... *iyū* becomes و... *ū*, e.g. يَرْمُونَ (for يَرْمِيُونَ) they throw.

يِي... *iyī* becomes ي... *ī*, e.g. تَرْمِينَ (for تَرْمِيِينَ) you (fem.) throw.

Nouns

Most of the phonetic changes which take place in the verbs take place in the nouns with weak radicals, e.g.

دُعَاةٌ (for دُعَوَةٌ) callers. مَقَامٌ (for مَقْوَمٌ) a place.

بَاعَةٌ (for بَيَعَةٌ) sellers. وَفَاةٌ (for وَفَيَةٌ) death.

N.B. Exceptions sometimes occur, e.g. خَوَنَةٌ pl. of خَائِنٌ a traitor.

Final وُ... *awu*, وَ... *awa* and وِ... *awi* become ا... *ā*, e.g.

اَلْعَصَا (for اَلْعَصَوُ) the stick.

With nūnation وٌ... *awun*, وًا... *awan* and وٍ... *awin* become اً... *an*,

e.g. عَصًا a stick.

Final يُ... *ayu*, يَ... *aya* and يِ... *ayi* become ى... *ā*, e.g.

اَلْهُدَى (for اَلْهُدَيُ) the guidance.

With nūnation يٌ... *ayun*, يًا... *ayan* and يٍ... *ayin* become ىً... *an*,

e.g. هُدًى guidance.

Final وٌ... *iwun* and وٍ... *iwin* become ٍ... *in*, e.g.

رَاضٍ (for رَاضِوٌ) pleased.

ـِوًا ... *iwan* becomes ـِيًا ... *iyan*, e.g.

رَاضِيًا (for رَاضِوًا) pleased (acc.).

Final ـِيٌ ... *iyun* and ـِيٍ ... *iyin* become ... *in*, e.g.

رَامٍ (for رَامِيٌ) a thrower, archer.

Final ـِوُ ... *iwu*, ـِوِ ... *iwi*, ـِيُ ... *iyu* and ـِيِ ... *iyi* become ـِي ... *ī*, e.g.

اَلرَّاضِي for اَلرَّاضِوُ

اَلرَّامِي for اَلرَّامِيُ

Printed in the United States
22159LVS00001B/157-162